WID

Tort Law

Tort Law
Third edition

Sue Hodge

WILLAN
PUBLISHING

Published by
Willan Publishing
Culmcott House
Mill Street, Uffculme
Cullompton, Devon
EX15 3AT, UK
Tel: +44(0)1884 840337
Fax: +44(0)1884 840251
E-mail: info@willan.co.uk
website: wwww.willanpublishing.co.uk

Published simultaneously in the USA and Canada by

Willan Publishing
c/o ISBS, 5804 N.E. Hassalo St,
Portland, Oregon 97213-3644, USA
Tel: +001(0)503 287 3093
Fax: +001(0)503 280 8832
E-mail: orders@isbs.com
website: www.isbs.com150

First edition published 2002
Third edition 2004

ISBN 1-84392-098-0 (paper)

British Library Cataloguing-in-Publication Data
A catalogue record for this book is available from the British Library

Project management by Deer Park Productions, Tavistock, Devon
Set in the UK by GCS, Leighton Buzzard, Beds.
Printed in the UK by T.J. International Ltd, Padstow, Cornwall

Contents

Preface to third edition

I had hoped that the third edition would need little in the way of amendments and rewriting – I was very mistaken. The law of torts continues to change and develop rapidly. In this edition you will find that most chapters have been extensively revised to take account of important decisions made since 2001. For example, *Fairchild v Glenhaven Funeral Services Ltd* (2001) has made considerable difference to the rules relating to proof of damage in negligence and *Transco plc v Stockport Metropolitan Borough Council* (2003) has clarified the rules relating to *Rylands v Fletcher*. All this activity means that the book has again increased somewhat in length but I have done my best to keep the changes to the minimum required for accurate and up-to-date understanding of the A-level syllabus which is its prime purpose.

The specimen questions have been updated to include questions from the A2 examinations in 2003 and January 2004. The material for the Special Study Paper for OCR Module 3 for the examinations from June 2005 to January 2007 is included so that, with careful use of the book, students and teachers should be able to become really familiar with the material upon which OCR will base questions for that period.

I must again thank Brian Willan and his colleagues for their help in preparation of this text. My own students continue to make frank but constructive comments which have been useful in preparing this edition.

The law is, I hope and believe, accurate as at the end of March 2004.

Acknowledgements

I am indebted to the A-level examination boards, AQA and OCR, for permission to reproduce past examination questions and the specimen materials relating to the new examination.

There are many people to whom I owe thanks for help in writing this book. Brian Willan and his long-suffering colleagues have guided me through the process of producing a book for publication; my family and friends have supported me with their help and understanding throughout; my mother, who, despite not being in the least bit interested in law, read the entire manuscript to list all the cases and statutes referred to.

Any errors or omissions are of course my responsibility.

Publisher's acknowledgements

We are indebted to OCR (Oxford, Cambridge and RSA Examinations) and AQA (Assessment and Qualifications Alliance) for permission to reproduce questions and other material from past examination papers and specimen papers.

Advice on possible answers to questions reproduced in this book are provided by the author, and have not been provided or approved by the boards.

Crown copyright material is reproduced with the permission of the Comptroller of Her Majesty's Stationery Office.

Table of legislation

Table of cases

Introduction

What is tort?

Academic writers have found difficulty in explaining the answer to this question in a way which conveys the essence of this branch of the civil law. All seem to agree that the word itself is a surviving relic of the Norman French used in the English courts after 1066 and simply means 'a wrong'. The definition which is quoted most frequently is that given by Winfield:

> Tortious liability arises from the breach of a duty primarily fixed by law; such duty is towards persons generally and its breach is redressible by an action for unliquidated damages.
>
> (Winfield, p.4)

A simpler definition is as follows:

> a wrong which entitles the injured party to claim compensation from the wrongdoer.
>
> (Martin and Gibbins, p.235)

It seems that one thing the definitions have in common is to tell us that the law of torts is concerned with breach of a duty which the law recognises, and compensation of those who suffer as a result of the breach. We will return to this question at the end of the book and see whether it is possible reach a better answer to the original question – 'What is tort?'

The development of the law

The origins of this branch of the law can be traced back to the fourteenth century when the word trespass was used to describe any direct and forcible injury to person, land or chattels, a much wider meaning than the word has today. From the original law of trespass, many of the modern torts have gradually developed. The other medieval law known as 'action on the case' led to the development of law relating to injuries which were consequential to the wrong but where the wrong was either not forcible or not direct.

The existence of law reports dating back over the centuries, as well as old textbooks, enables anyone who is interested to trace the development of the modern individual torts back to the original actions for trespass. It is not appropriate to look at this in detail in this book, although until 1964 it was not clear that the old division would be irrelevant in a modern case. In *Letang v Cooper* (1964) the claimant argued that the old rules were still relevant in deciding whether or not a claim was outside the appropriate time limit imposed by the Limitation Act 1939. If she was right, she could make a successful claim; if she was wrong, her claim was made too late and she could not succeed. When the matter came before the Court of Appeal, the judges decided that where personal injury is inflicted intentionally, the cause of action lies in trespass. If it is inflicted unintentionally, the cause of action lies in negligence.

> These forms of action have served their day. They did at one time form a guide to substantive rights; but they do so no longer. Lord Atkin told us what to do about them: 'When these ghosts of the past stand in the path of justice, clanking their medieval chains, the proper course for the judge is to pass through them undeterred.'
> (See *United Australia Ltd v Barclays Bank Ltd* [1941] *per* Lord Denning MR in *Letang v Cooper.*)

Letang v Cooper (1964)
Mrs L was on holiday when she decided to sunbathe on the grass area which was also used to park cars. While she was lying there, Mr C drove in and, not seeing Mrs L, ran over her legs. The claim was brought more than three years after the accident. Mrs L's argument was that based on the old law of trespass, her action could be brought within six years of the accident whereas the time limit for an action on the case was only three years. As her injuries were caused by the direct action of Mr C, trespass should apply. *Held*: The old rules no longer apply. Intentional injury will give a claim based in trespass, but unintentional injury will give a claim based in negligence. Mrs L's claim was unsuccessful.

Sources of the modern law

Much of the law relating to torts comes from the common law and is found in precedent. The doctrine of precedent is governed by the principle of *stare decisis* (stand by the decision), which means that once a point of law has been decided by the courts, the law must be applied in a similar way in any subsequent case involving the same law and similar facts. A judge explains the law relevant to the case before the court to support the decision. The explanation of the law is known as the *ratio decidendi* and it is this which is binding in later cases before other courts.

A judge will sometimes give additional explanation saying, 'had the facts been so and so, then the relevant law would have been …' In the appeal courts, the judges will not always agree with one other. The minority judgments are not ignored, although they do not affect the decision. Additional explanation and minority judgments are referred to as *obiter dicta* (things said by the way) and have been used to further the development of the law. Examples of the way in which *obiter dicta* have contributed to the development of the law of tort can be seen in relation to the rules of negligent misstatement which stem from *obiter* in the case of *Hedley Byrne & Co Ltd* v *Heller & Partners Ltd* (1964), and in the rules relating to compensation for nervous shock which stem from *obiter* in the case of *McLoughlin v O'Brian* (1981). (For fuller details of these issues, see Chapter 2, pp. 41–51.)

The doctrine of precedent can be inflexible as the hierarchy of the courts means that decisions by courts higher in the system bind all courts below them, and in the case of the Court of Appeal generally bind the court itself in similar cases in the future. Until 1966 the House of Lords was also always bound by its own earlier decisions. An example of the injustice which this sometimes caused is to be found in the rules governing the liability of an occupier for injuries caused to trespassers while on the occupier's land. In *Addie (Robert) & Sons (Collieries) Ltd v Dumbreck* (1929) the House of Lords ruled that no compensation would be paid to a person who was injured while trespassing on another's land. Despite the injustice this caused to trespassers, particularly children, when there was an obvious danger and also a likelihood that a trespasser might come onto the land, the law remained as the House of Lords had declared it to be. However, in 1966 the Lord Chancellor issued a Practice Statement which said,

> Their Lordships recognise that too rigid an adherence to precedent may lead to injustice in a particular case and also unduly restrict the proper development of the law. They propose, therefore, while treating former decisions of this House as normally binding, to depart from a previous decision when it appears right to do so.
> (Practice Direction : Judicial Precedent [1966])

When the case of *British Railways Board v Herrington* (1972) came before the House of Lords, the Practice Statement was used and the precedent set by *Addie v Dumbreck* was overruled, the court recognising that a limited duty of common humanity should be owed to trespassers enabling compensation to be awarded where it was just to do so.

While some modern judges will admit to a degree of 'law making', not all the problems of the common law can be dealt with in this way; and in any case only a very few cases actually reach the House of Lords each year. This means that Parliament has to act to create new law by means of legislation. Once Parliament is convinced of a need, the necessary Act will be passed. In 1957, the Occupiers' Liability Act was passed, followed by the Occupiers' Liability Act 1984. Both Acts were designed to deal with specific problems resulting from unsatisfactory common law rules relating to actions for compensation for injuries caused by dangers on someone else's land.

As society becomes more complex and, in some ways, more dangerous, legislation is introduced to regulate and administer matters of general concern and to give additional protection to those at risk. Examples of such legislation include the Animals Act 1971 and the Consumer Protection Act 1987, both of which introduce new statutory rights of action.

British membership of the European Union has provided another source of remedies for wrongs. The Consumer Protection Act 1987 was passed to fulfil obligations imposed on all Member States by the Directive on Liability for Defective Products (Directive 87/374) to ensure that persons injured by a defective product had an effective remedy available to them.

International law may also have an effect on national law. In 1951 the United Kingdom became a signatory to the European Convention on Human Rights and Individual Freedoms. As an international treaty, the Convention could not have any enforceable legal effect until it had been incorporated into British law. This was done by the Human Rights Act 1998 which came into effect in October 2000. The Convention sets out various rights which each person has and the Act provides a mechanism for the enforcement of such rights by individuals. The Convention is having a far-reaching effect in many parts of English law, and the law of torts is no exception. As we shall see in relevant parts of the book, the courts have used the Convention to make some extensive changes, sometimes giving a remedy where none existed under common law and more often making changes to make existing law compatible with Convention rights. In torts, the influence of the Convention is most clearly seen in relation to:

- trespass to the person (Chapter 1)

- nuisance (Chapter 6)

- defamation (Chapter 9)

- breach of statutory duty (Chapter 10).

Law, ethics and morality

If a system of law is to work in a democratic society such as ours, it is essential that it should reflect the moral beliefs of the majority of the members of that society while protecting the views of the minority. Public opinion is very relevant. No legislature can afford to ignore it as law which does not have general public support is unlikely to be effective.

Morality comes from cultural, religious and ethical principles. Our cultural views are formed by the society in which we live and by our family heritage. Over the centuries, religious beliefs have played a large part in forming society. Each religion has its own moral values but all provide, to the believer, a code for behaviour distinguishing between actions which are regarded as right and those which are wrong. Although some believe that if national law conflicts with a religious law, the religious law should be followed, in most societies this is not the case. Actions which are lawful may not be permitted by religious law, and something which is forbidden by religious law is not necessarily unlawful.

Most people would claim that their lives are governed by a moral code. In some cases the reasons for certain beliefs are clearly dictated by religion, but many would find it difficult to say why an action is right or wrong; our instinct simply tells us that this is so. For example, it is commonly accepted that it is wrong to tell a lie but most of us would find it difficult to say why – it's just wrong. We would find it easier to explain why we use the socially acceptable 'white' lie – usually to avoid causing unhappiness to someone else – but we would be unable to explain why even a white lie is morally acceptable.

From time to time we need to try to find reasons for our beliefs and it is in this connection that the branch of philosophy known as ethics comes to our aid. There are two major ethical theories, both of which can be seen to have an influence on the law:

- the theory of consequentialism (utilitarianism). This states that the moral rightness of an action must be decided by its consequences and the 'happiness', such as pleasure or friendship, which it creates. The theory is sometimes paraphrased as 'The end justifies the means', or 'We ought to promote the greatest good for the greatest number.' According to this theory the white lie is an acceptable action as it is designed to promote the happiness of the person to whom we are lying.

- the theory of non-consequentialism (deontology). This states that actions are right or wrong regardless of the consequences. Thus it is right according to this theory always to tell the truth because telling the truth is itself right. No regard need to be taken of the potential consequences of truth-telling and a white lie is wrong.

Each theory can be applied to most of our actions. Our choice to follow one theory or the other is one which we make on the basis of our personal moral values.

There are four ethical principles which have particular relevance to the law:

- autonomy (personal freedom to make choices)
- non-maleficence (to do no harm)
- beneficence (an obligation to do good)
- justice (fairness).

The principle of *autonomy* ensures that an individual's choice will be respected by others even if they believe the choice to be wrong. We are free to act in accordance with our self-chosen plan.

Non-maleficence and *beneficence* are in some ways the two sides of a single coin. Non-maleficence says that we ought not to inflict evil or harm (a negative duty) while beneficence imposes positive duties to prevent or remove evil or harm and to do or promote good. 'Harm' can include injury to reputation, property, privacy or liberty while 'good' can be explained as any action which benefits another. Many actions in reality require us to balance the risks of harm against the potential benefit. Often the final decision is based on proportionality, 'Is the benefit worth the cost of any harm which might be caused?' – a consequentialist approach which states that the action is justified because it causes the greatest good for the greatest number.

The principle of *justice* is linked to the concept of fairness – one acts justly towards a person when that person has been given what they deserve whether by way of reward or punishment. Injustice involves denial of something to which a person is entitled. Aristotle summarised the principle as, 'Equals must be treated equally, and unequals must be treated unequally.' A more modern explanation is that each person should receive their worth.

Law reflects the moral beliefs of society and can change as the beliefs change, always echoing the beliefs of the majority but also protecting the minority. In the United Kingdom freedom of speech is regarded as a fundamental right, but the freedom is limited by laws designed to protect others. Examples include:

- race relations legislation
- obscenity laws
- laws relating to public order
- the common law tort of defamation.

It can be argued that this approach is based in the ethical theory of consequentialism – law should have as its goal the greatest happiness of the greatest number – but individual freedoms must be compatible with the freedom of the majority.

The law reflects and reinforces the right to autonomy by giving a remedy if the right is infringed. In the law of torts this protection is provided by the common law rules of trespass to the person. The right is also protected by the criminal laws relating to assault.

In seeking to balance individual freedom with the freedom of the majority, both the common law and legislation demonstrate the influence of the principles of non-maleficence and beneficence. Examples include the Environmental Protection Act 1990 and the Environment Act 1995 and the common law relating to the tort of private nuisance.

Law must also reflect the ethical principle of justice. Legal rules must be applied fairly; among other things, this requires the system to allow equal access to the courts by means of schemes which ensure availability of legal advice and help. The doctrine of precedent supports the principle of justice in that like cases lead to like results. Justice is also achieved by legislation, for example against discrimination. The law can be used to make society a fairer place in which to live.

Law may reinforce ethical or moral beliefs. The law of contract is concerned with enforcing promises, the criminal law of perjury reinforces a duty to tell the truth. In the law of torts, the tort of negligence, in particular, gives a remedy for breach of a duty and, through the concept of fault, acknowledges that certain actions are morally blameworthy so that each person is dealt with 'according to his deserts'.

As you read this book, your attention will be drawn to moral, ethical and social issues which have influenced the development of the particular torts.

1   Trespass to the person

Trespass is one of the oldest parts of the law and also one of the most important. Trespass to the person gives an individual an enforceable right to bodily integrity and has been a major source of protection of some basic human rights. In effect the tort provides that no person may be threatened with the use of force or touched or imprisoned by someone who does not have either lawful authority or the consent of the victim.

The tort is actionable *per se*, in other words the victim does not have to prove actual damage or injury, merely the facts which constitute the tortious act. In modern times, the tort has enabled the courts to ensure that police officers and store detectives are liable to pay compensation for unlawful actions. The tort does not always give adequate protection, as will be seen, and Parliament has acted to deal with specific problems. Reference will be made to relevant legislation at appropriate times in the course of this part of the book.

The tort divides itself neatly into three parts – assault, battery and false imprisonment – but some issues, such as consent, are relevant to all three parts. This text will define and explain the individual parts and then deal with the issues which the parts have in common.

The constituent parts

Assault

Definition

The Shorter Oxford Dictionary defines assault as 'an onset with hostile intent; an attack with blows or weapons'. In the criminal law the word 'assault' is used as a general term to cover various crimes against the person. In the law of tort, however, the word has a specific meaning which can be summarised as a threat that force will be used against the victim. A more formal definition is 'some conduct by the defendant which causes the victim reasonably to fear that force is about to be used upon their person'.

Figure 1.1

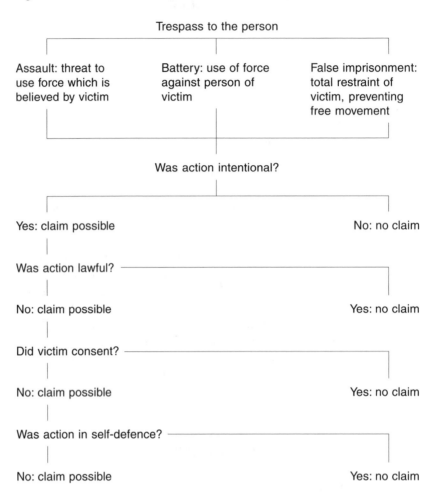

Threatening conduct

In many cases the conduct is obviously threatening, for example shaking one's fist in someone's face will usually cause that person to fear that a punch is about to be thrown at them. Other factors may be relevant and in some cases have the effect of preventing the action from amounting to an assault.

The physical action may be accompanied by words. These can have the effect of enhancing the threat; for example, 'I'll get you for that' may well make the threat more credible. On the other hand, words can have the effect of negating the threat by making it clear that the threatened use of force will not occur.

> ### *Tuberville v Savage* (1669)
> In this case there was an assault when the perpetrator put his hand on his sword and said, 'T'were not assize time, I'd not take such language from you'. The victim alleged that he had been in fear that he was about to be attacked with the sword. It was decided that the words used meant that had the judges not been in town on assize, this would indeed have occurred but that as the judges were there, nothing further would happen. There was no assault.

Opinion has been divided as to whether or not words alone can amount to an assault. One old case, *Meade's Case* (1823), held that words alone cannot be an assault; more recently, in 1955, a criminal case, *R v Wilson*, held that they could. The position now appears to be that certainly in relation to criminal law, and therefore almost certainly in relation to the law of tort, threatening words alone can be enough. In *R v Ireland* (1997) it was held by the House of Lords that a threat made by telephone could be a criminal assault if the victim had reason to believe that the threat would be carried out in the near future – 'in a minute or two'.

It must be possible for the threatened action to be carried out immediately (*Thomas v National Union of Mineworkers* [1986]) and, if this is so, it may not matter that others intervene to prevent the threatened action (*Stephens v Myers* [1830]).

> ### *Thomas v NUM* (1986)
> Mr T was a miner who continued to go to work during a miners' strike. Mr T and other working miners were 'bussed' into work each day through an aggressive crowd of pickets who made violent gestures and shouted threats at those on the bus. The pickets were held back by the police, and in any case Mr T and the others were on the bus. The threats could not be immediately carried out and thus there was no assault against Mr T.

> ### *Stephens v Myers* (1830)
> Mr S was the chair at a meeting which became heated. Mr M became very angry and so disruptive that the people at the meeting voted to turn him out. He said that he would

pull Mr S out of the chair rather than be expelled and went towards Mr S with his fist clenched. Others intervened to stop him before he could reach Mr S. The lawyer acting for Mr M said that there could be no assault as Mr M had been unable to carry out the threat, but the witnesses said that he clearly intended to do so had he not been restrained. Mr M was found liable for assault on the basis that he was advancing towards the chairman with the intent of hitting him.

The victim must believe that force will be used

The assailant's behaviour must lead the victim to believe that force is about to be used against him. This belief must be genuine. This means that, even though there is no requirement that the belief be reasonable in the circumstances, an unreasonable belief is less likely to be thought to be genuine. It is not necessary for the victim to suffer fear or be scared. The point was made in the following case:

R v St George (1840)
An unloaded gun was pointed at the victim. As the victim did not know that the gun was not loaded, the apprehension that he was about to be shot was reasonable – the defendant was found guilty of assault.

Do you think that the law does enough to protect us from threats of violence?

Battery

Definition

'Battery' is defined by the Shorter Oxford Dictionary as 'the action of battering or assailing with blows; ... an unlawful attack upon another by beating, etc., including technically the least touching of another's person or clothes in a menacing manner'. As will be seen, the definition of the tort is in fact very similar. Battery is the direct and intentional application of force to another person.

Touching

The least touch may amount to a battery. There is no requirement that the victim should be injured in any way, so that an unwanted kiss may be enough. Case law gives examples of activities which have been held to amount to a battery. In *Pursell v Horn* (1838) throwing water over someone's clothes amounted to a battery; in *Nash v Sheen* (1953) applying a 'tone rinse' to a customer's hair without permission was a battery.

It must be remembered that the tort is actionable *per se* so that it is unnecessary to prove that any injury whatsoever has resulted from the touching.

Is hostility necessary?

Everyone is frequently touched in the course of going about daily life, for example when travelling on public transport during the rush-hour. In an old case, *Cole v Turner* (1704), Holt CJ said that 'the least touching in anger is a battery'. Where, however, does this leave the unwanted kiss? For some time it was thought that touching is not a battery if it is generally acceptable in the ordinary course of life. This approach was partially rejected by the Court of Appeal in *Wilson v Pringle* (1987) when it said that battery involves a 'hostile' touching, in other words interference to which the victim is known to object.

> **Wilson v Pringle (1987)**
> A schoolboy was carrying his bag over his shoulder when it was pulled by the defendant, another schoolboy. The victim fell over and was injured. The judge said that the touching must be hostile and that hostility, which he did not define, could be inferred from the particular circumstances of the case. The pulling in this case was probably only a prank.

It would, however, be impossible for a health care professional to be liable for battery were the element of hostility always required as the usual reason for treatment is to benefit the patient! In such cases, the important issue is whether or not the patient consented to the treatment; if this was not the case then a battery has occurred despite the lack of hostility. *F v West Berkshire Health Authority* is the leading case on this point.

> ### *F v West Berkshire Health Authority* (1989)
> A mentally impaired woman in her thirties, but with a mental age of four or five, had a sexual relationship and was therefore likely to become pregnant. She was believed to be incapable of coping with childbirth and would be unable to raise a child. She was unable to consent to her sterilisation so the doctors asked the court for help. *Held*: it was in her best interests to be sterilised.

> Make a list of the ways in which you have been touched while going about your daily business and decide which of the touchings could be a battery as defined by the law.

False imprisonment

Definition

The dictionary does not help with this definition. The essence of the tort is that a person has been restrained, whether by arrest, confinement or otherwise, or prevented from leaving any place, by the defendant acting intentionally, without any lawful authority and without the consent of the victim.

Restraint

The restraint must be total. In other words, if there is a reasonable and safe means of escape, the restraint cannot be false imprisonment. *Bird v Jones* (1845) is the key case here.

> ### *Bird v Jones* (1845)
> The defendants closed off part of Hammersmith Bridge in London so that paying spectators could watch a regatta. The claimant insisted he wanted to go along that part of the bridge and climbed into the enclosure without paying. He was stopped from going forward but told he could go back onto the other part of the bridge where he would be able to cross it on the side away from the enclosure. He refused and remained in the enclosure for half-an-hour. He had an escape route, therefore the defendants were not liable for false imprisonment.

The restraint need not be supported by physical actions or barriers. A police officer who unlawfully tells someone that he is under arrest may be liable for false imprisonment even if the officer does not touch the victim. The victim does not have to take the risk of being forcibly prevented from trying to escape.

False imprisonment can also occur when the victim does not know about the detention! In *Meering v Grahame-White Aviation Co. Ltd* (1920) Lord Atkin explained this by giving examples of circumstances when it might happen – if the victim is drunk or unconscious. The judge also said that the amount of any damages payable might be less if the victim did not know about the imprisonment.

> ### *Meering v Grahame-White Aviation Co Ltd* (1920)
> Mr M's employers, the defendants, suspected him of theft. They sent two works policemen to bring him in for questioning. He was taken to a waiting-room where he said that if he was not told why he was there he would leave. He agreed to stay once he was told that enquiries were being made into the disappearance of certain items. Unknown to him, the works police, who had been told not to let him leave the room until the Metropolitan Police arrived, remained outside the room to make sure that he did not leave. *Held*: restraint within defined bounds which is a restraint in fact, even though the victim does not know about it, may be an imprisonment. Mr M was entitled to damages.

False imprisonment does not happen when the alleged imprisoner imposes a reasonable condition for allowing the victim to leave. Case law examples show that this defence is likely to arise from some agreement between the victim and the wrongdoer. *Robinson v Balmain Ferry Co Ltd* (1910) and *Herd v Weardale etc Co Ltd* (1915) are cases in point.

> ### *Robinson v Balmain Ferry Co Ltd* (1910)
> The victim had paid to go into the defendant's premises in order to take a ferry across the river. He knew he would have to pay again to get out on the other side. As he had just missed a ferry, the victim wanted to leave by the way he had gone in. He was not allowed to do so until he had paid the second fee. As the victim had known about the

payments before he entered the premises, the court decided that the requirement of payment was a reasonable condition and that false imprisonment had not happened.

Herd v Weardale etc Co Ltd **(1915)**

In this case a miner had gone down into the pit and then refused to do the work he was asked to do. He demanded to be taken back to the surface five hours before his shift was due to end. He had to wait for twenty minutes. As the miner was in the wrong, because he was in breach of his contract of employment, no false imprisonment occurred.

You have been 'larking around' in your garden with some friends, one of whom locks you in the shed for a joke and then refuses to let you out. There is a window in the shed, about half a metre above your head. The window does not open but is just about wide enough for you to be able to get through it. Do you have a claim against your friend for false imprisonment?

Defences

Lawful authority – arrest

A person who has lawful authority to make an arrest or to detain a person cannot be liable for trespass to the person.

The actions of police officers are lawful provided the requirements of the Police and Criminal Evidence Act 1984 (commonly referred to as PACE) are obeyed. The rules vary according to whether the offence is 'an arrestable offence', i.e. one for which sentence is fixed by law, such as murder; any offence for which a person could be jailed for at least five years for a first offence, such as theft; or an offence which is specifically named as an arrestable offence, such as taking a vehicle without authority.

Anyone, a police officer or a private person, may arrest someone who is in the act of committing an arrestable offence or who is reasonably suspected to be doing so (s.24(4) PACE). A person guilty of an arrestable offence may be arrested by anyone as may any person reasonably suspected of being guilty (s.24(5) PACE). A police officer has additional powers under s.24(6) PACE which allows an arrest to be made without a warrant if the officer has 'reasonable grounds for suspecting that an arrestable offence has been committed' and reasonable grounds for suspecting the person arrested. A police officer can also arrest anyone who is about to commit an arrestable offence or who is reasonably suspected of being about to do so (s.24(7) PACE).

A private citizen does have power to make a 'citizen's arrest' but may be risking an action for false imprisonment if an arrestable offence has not in fact been committed. This is a risk which is regularly taken by store detectives detaining alleged thieves (shoplifters).

A police officer also has power to arrest without a warrant where a non-arrestable offence is reasonably suspected and the officer reasonably believes that a summons will not be able to be served (perhaps because the alleged wrongdoer refuses to give a name and address).

Reasonable force may be used by any person making an arrest. If the amount of force used is not reasonable, the victim may successfully claim compensation for assault and/or battery.

> Young people in particular sometimes believe that they are unfairly targeted by the police when exercising powers to stop and search. Look back to the section of the Introduction on 'Law, ethics and morality'. Which ethical principles apply in this situation? Look at this both from the point of view of the young person and from the point of view of the police.

Lawful authority – the Mental Health Act 1983

A person suffering from mental disorder may be detained and in some cases treated even though that person has not agreed to go into hospital, nor agreed to the treatment. It is not appropriate to set out full details of the Act's provisions in a general book such as this, but the Act does set out stringent conditions which must be satisfied before a person loses the right to make their own decision.

Consent

A person who has consented to being touched or detained cannot claim compensation for trespass to the person. There are two areas where the concept of consent causes some difficulty – sporting activities and medical treatment.

A person who takes part in sport consents to the risks that are an essential part of the sport when it is played within the rules. No consent is given to actions which are outside the rules. In *Condon v Basi* (1985) the victim suffered a broken leg as a result of a tackle which the referee held to be a foul. The court held that the defendant was liable for battery. A footballer who deliberately cuts down an opponent may well find that a claim for compensation against him is successful. In *McNamara v Duncan* (1979) the defendant deliberately came into contact with the claimant who at the time was not in possession of the ball. The court held that this amounted to a battery.

Consent to medical treatment is needed for all forms of health care. If treatment is given without consent, the health care worker may be liable for trespass to the person. The patient's decision or right to autonomy must always be respected, even if the health care worker believes the decision to be wrong. This was shown in the sad case of Ms B.

> ### *Ms B v An NHS Hospital Trust [2002] EWHC 429 (Fam)*
> In February 2001 Ms B became completely paralysed and needed to be kept alive on a ventilator. She could just move her head and was able to speak with difficulty. In April 2001 she told the doctors that she wanted the ventilator turned off. Although it was at first accepted that she had capacity to make such a decision, those caring for her found it very difficult. It was decided that she did not have capacity. Her treatment on the ventilator continued. Eventually she started proceedings for a declaration that she had capacity to make the decision and for damages for trespass to the person. The court held that Ms B was in fact competent to make her own decisions about treatment and awarded a small sum by way of damages for trespass to the person. (She was moved to another hospital where, some time later, the ventilator was turned off and Ms B died.)

In order to give consent, the patient must have sufficient understanding to make the decision, must be free of any pressure (duress) and understand in broad terms why the treatment is being suggested and what it involves. The fact that a person suffers from mental illness does not of itself mean that the necessary understanding is lacking. The following case made this point.

> ### *Re C (Adult: Refusal of Treatment)* (1994)
> Mr C was an elderly man who suffered from paranoid schizophrenia and had been a patient in Broadmoor special hospital for 30 years. In 1993 he was found to have gangrene and doctors told him that unless he had his foot amputated, he would very probably die. Mr C did not consent and

asked the court to rule that the health authorities could not amputate then or at any time in the future. It was decided that in spite of his illness Mr C did understand the nature, purpose and effects of the treatment and the consequences of refusal. He won the ruling he had asked for.

Problems arise where the person to be treated is unable to consent, for example because they are unconscious or suffering from some mental problems which means that they do not understand. In such cases, a health care worker may do anything which is essential to save life or prevent serious deterioration, or which is in the best interests of the patient.

The Court of Appeal has recently stated that the doctrine of necessity may assist when a difficult decision needs to be made about the future of an adult person with serious learning disabilities. In *Re F (Adult: Court's Jurisdiction)* (2000) it was held that a court has jurisdiction to make lifestyle decisions as to the future care of an adult in circumstances where statutory powers under the Mental Health Act 1983 did not cover the situation. The Court of Appeal held that the doctrine of necessity existed in such circumstances. (For further discussion of the doctrine see Chapter 11, p. 223.)

Re F (Adult: Court's Jurisdiction) (2000)

T, a young woman with a mental age of 5–8 years, had reached 18 and could no longer be cared for under powers contained in the Mental Health Act 1983. There was a need for her to remain in local authority accommodation having supervised contact with her family. The local authority, having no power to carry out this action under statute, applied to the court for a declaration that the action would not be unlawful. *Held*: using the doctrine of necessity, the court had power to grant the order sought so that the court could consider what was best for T.

The problem of decision-making for people who lack capacity may shortly be made a little easier. The Mental Incapacity Bill was published in June 2004 and is likely to become law. Under its provisions, it will be presumed that everyone has capacity to make their own decisions. The bill sets out a list of things which must be taken into account where a person is in fact unable to do so. It will also allow people to use a formal procedure to make known their wishes about what should happen to them before they become incapacitated or to appoint a person to make decisions on their behalf.

> Daisy is aged 80. She sometimes gets a bit confused but generally she is mentally very capable. She has decided that she does not want to change her dress and has been wearing the same clothes for over six weeks, day and night. Other people have noticed that she is dirty and smelly. You are working in the home where Daisy lives and have been told to strip her and wash her as this is for her own good. Would you do as you have been told? What are the ethical and legal reasons for your decision?

In the case of treatment for a child, the issue is complicated. The basic rule is that a child of 16 can usually make his or her own decision (Family Law Reform Act 1969 s.8(1)). Parents, guardians or the court make decisions for younger children. But it is not as simple as it appears. Children have the right to have their views taken into account (Children Act 1989 s.3) and, if of 'sufficient age and understanding', are capable of giving their own consent. A child is said to be of sufficient understanding when able to appreciate fully the issues involved. A child's refusal can be overridden, however, if it is in the child's best interests that treatment should be given, even if the child is 16 or 17 years old. This rule was stated in *Re W (A Minor) (Medical Treatment)* (1992).

Re W (A Minor) (Medical Treatment) (1992)
A 16-year-old girl suffered from anorexia nervosa. She refused to go into a specialist unit for treatment and the court was asked to decide whether she could be treated without her consent. *Held*: the Family Law Reform Act 1969 s.8 did not mean that a child's refusal could not be overridden if it were in her best interests to do so. Miss W could be given the necessary treatment.

Self-defence

A person who uses reasonable force to defend himself or others will not be liable for trespass to the person. The force used must be proportionate to the perceived danger as was held in *Cockcroft v Smith* in 1705.

> *Cockcroft v Smith* (1705)
> A lawyer bit off the finger of a clerk during a scuffle in court. This was not a reasonable response to the threat posed by the clerk who had thrust his fingers towards the lawyer's eyes.

Children

A parent has the right to use reasonable force to correct a child. The purpose of the punishment must be understood by the child and it must be in proportion to the wrongdoing. The issue of corporal punishment, even by parents, is controversial. As rights of children are seen as being of greater importance, it is possible that the Human Rights Act may be used to deal with the problem. The Act incorporates Article 3 of the European Convention on Human Rights which bans 'inhuman or degrading treatment'. The European Court of Human Rights has found that the caning of a child by their step-parent is a violation of Article 3. (*A v United Kingdom* [1998], *The Times,* 1 October 1998.) It is possible that Article 3 will have a similar effect on parents' rights.

Other protection

The criminal law

Assault and battery are crimes as well as torts. A person may be prosecuted and punished if found guilty of a wide range of activities which would also amount to one of the torts. By the provisions of the Offences Against the Person Act 1861, once someone has been prosecuted in the magistrates' court and been acquitted or has served a prison sentence and/or paid compensation ordered by the court, no action can then be taken in the civil courts for compensation for the torts.

Wrongful interference or intentional harm

Trespass to the person is only committed when the action is direct. This left a gap when harm was caused by the defendant but only indirectly. In *Wilkinson v Downton* (1897) it was held that when a defendant had done something which was calculated to cause harm to the victim, this amounted to an infringement of a legal right to safety if there was no justification for the act.

> ***Wilkinson v Downton*** (1897)
> D, who had a peculiar sense of humour, told Mrs W that
> her husband had been smashed up in an accident in which
> he had broken both legs and that Mrs W was to fetch Mr
> W home. This gave Mrs W a violent shock, causing her to
> vomit and suffer serious and permanent physical damage
> as well as threatening her sanity.

There is no need to prove that the defendant actually intended to
cause the harm. It may be calculated to do so when the behaviour was
capable of terrifying a normal person and the defendant knew or ought
to have known that this could be the effect.

In order to bring an action, the claimant must suffer actual damage,
whether this is physical harm or psychiatric illness. This is illustrated
by *Janvier v Sweeney* (1919) when a private detective pretended to be a
police officer to get some papers from the claimant, telling her that
she was in danger of being arrested as a spy. As a result the claimant
suffered psychiatric trauma.

Protection from Harassment Act 1997

The Act creates a statutory tort of harassment. By s.3 where a person
'has pursued a course of conduct which amounts to harassment and
which he knows or ought to know amounts to harassment' contrary
to s.1(1), the victim can seek damages and/or an injunction in the civil
courts. 'Harassment' can be anything – text messages, telephone calls,
verbal threats and abuse or anything else – which occurs more than
once. The conduct must cause the victim to fear that violence will be
used against them (s.4(1)) or cause them alarm or distress (s.7(2)).
Examples of such conduct include threats made to a dog (*R (a child) v
DPP* [2001]).

In deciding whether the conduct amounts to harassment, the court
will take into account whether a reasonable person 'in possession of
the same information [as the defendant] would think [it] amounted to
harassment ...' It is a defence under s.1(3) for the defendant to show
that the conduct was

(a) pursued for the purposes of crime prevention or detection;

(b) required by law; or

(c) was reasonable in the particular circumstances.

Is there a common law tort of harassment?

Until the Protection from Harassment Act 1997 was passed, the only protection for a victim of indirect harm was found in *Wilkinson v Downton*. This left a person who had been the victim of harassing behaviour, but who had not suffered actual damage, without a remedy. The courts seemed to make moves towards the development of a common law tort of harassment to cover this situation but this has changed. In *Wong v Parkside Health NHS Trust* [2001] the Court of Appeal discussed the position.

> ### *Wong v Parkside Health NHS Trust* (2001)
> Ms W was the victim of serious harassment by three fellow employees. Her employers failed to deal with the situation properly and eventually Ms W left the employment on the grounds of ill-health. In addition to a claim against the employers for negligence, a claim against a fellow employee was based on 'the tort of intentional harassment'. The court held:
>
> * *Wilkinson v Downton* gave a remedy for actual damage caused by an indirect but calculated act
>
> * there is no tort of intentional harassment going beyond *Wilkinson v Downton*
>
> * Parliament has dealt with the problem by creating a civil remedy for harassment (Protection from Harassment Act 1997) which allows a remedy where the claimant has suffered anxiety rather than actual physical or psychiatric damage.

Human Rights Act 1998

As we have seen, the incorporation of Convention rights will have an effect in relation to trespass to the person. Article 3 prohibiting 'inhuman or degrading treatment' was used in *A v UK* (1998). There is no remedy in trespass to the person for lawful but unpleasant behaviour. In such circumstances Article 3 and/or Article 8 (the right to respect for private and family life) may provide a remedy.

There must be behaviour which is inhuman or degrading. This was shown in *Pretty v United Kingdom* (2002).

> ### *Pretty v United Kingdom* (2002)
> Mrs Pretty was dying from motor-neurone disease and wanted her husband to help her to commit suicide. Had he done so, he would have committed a criminal offence under the Suicide Act 1961. She asked the European Court of Human Rights to declare that the Act meant that she was being subjected to inhuman treatment. The court did not agree. It was the illness which caused the problem, not the Act, which went no further than was necessary to protect vulnerable people.

In the case of *Keenan v United Kingdom* (2001) a prisoner committed suicide after he received an extra 28 days in prison only nine days before he was due to be released. It was held that this, together with poor medical care, did amount to inhuman treatment.

Once a breach of the Convention is found, the victim is usually entitled to compensation. In the future, cases will only need to go to the European Court of Human Rights as a very last court of appeal. British courts are now required in all cases to give effect to the Convention and the case law of the European Court.

Ethical issues

The ethical principle of autonomy gives individuals the right to make their own decisions and to have those decisions respected. The tort of trespass to the person underlines this right. As we have seen, it is possible for the principle of autonomy to be overridden in some circumstances where the law makes specific provision for this to happen.

In relation to the issue of consent to treatment, the principle of paternalism may justify treatment despite lack of consent – it is in the patient's best interests even if the patient does not think so. While this would not usually be a defence to the tort, in those cases where the victim's ability to make their own decision is impaired, it may protect the alleged abuser.

The ethical principle which underlies the Police and Criminal Evidence Act 1984 can be said to be the principle of utilitarianism – an action is justified if it is taken for the greatest good of the greatest number. It can be argued that it is everyone's interest that criminals should be arrested and brought to trial but it is acknowledged that the principle can be abused. Abuse of police powers has been the subject of much discussion over recent years and there have been a number of successful civil actions for damages for trespass to the person.

The principle of justice is also relevant. Aristotle states that equals must be treated equally and unequals must be treated unequally. Retributive justice is concerned to ensure that persons bear responsibility for their own behaviour and be treated in proportion to the alleged wrong which they have committed. Although this is more properly dealt with in a book dealing with the principles of sentencing, the principle of retributive justice is relevant to trespass to the person. The court, when deciding the amount of any damages to be awarded against the abuser, will take into account any provocation on the part of the victim. The defence of contributory negligence may also be relevant.

SUMMARY

Assault

- threat to use force against the person of someone else

- person threatened must believe in the threat – *R v St George* (1840)

- must be possible to carry out threatened action – *Thomas v NUM* (1986)

- words can negate a threat – *Tuberville v Savage* (1669)

- words alone may be capable of being an assault – *R v Ireland* (1997)

Battery

- direct and intentional application of force to someone else

- is there a need for hostility? – *Wilson v Pringle* (1987); *F v West Berks. H. A.* (1989)

False imprisonment

- total restraint of someone preventing them from leaving any place

- restraint not total if there is a safe means of escape – *Bird v Jones* (1845)

- restraint not total if reasonable condition for escape imposed – *Robinson v Balmain Ferry Co Ltd* (1910)

Defences

- lawful authority – Police and Criminal Evidence Act 1984; Mental Health Act 1983

- consent – problems can arise in context of sport (*Condon v Basi* 1985) and in context of health treatment (*Re C [Adult: Refusal of Treatment]* 1994)

- self-defence: force must be proportionate to threat – *Cockcroft v Smith* (1705)

- parental discipline of child – child must understand why, force used must not be excessive

Other protection

- criminal prosecution

- wrongful interference or intentional harm

- Protection from Harassment Act 1997

- Human Rights Act 1998

QUESTIONS

1. Albert and Brenda have lived next door to Cedric and Doris for many years. Following a serious argument last year between Brenda and Doris the relationship between the neighbours has deteriorated.

   Recently Cedric, while pretending to throw a stone at Albert, shouted at him saying 'Why don't you move? I'll get you if you stay here.' Albert is now afraid of going into his garden as he believes that it was only because he ran away that Cedric did not throw the stone.

   In revenge, Brenda bolted the door to Doris's shed one day while Doris was inside. There is a window at head height on one side of the shed. However, Doris did not get out until Cedric heard her shouts about two hours later.

   Matters reached a head last weekend when Albert and Cedric met in the same public house. They argued and Albert threw his beer over Cedric, who retaliated by punching Albert, knocking him down.

   Advise both couples what legal action they might take against each other. (OCR 1999)

2. Helen has come into hospital for the birth of her fifth baby. Unfortunately the birth is difficult and Helen is advised that she needs to have a caesarean section. Helen consents to the operation. During the operation the surgeon, Keith, taking the view that it would be better for her not to have any more babies, sterilises her.

   When Helen recovers, Keith tells her what he has done. Helen is very angry as she and her husband had always intended to have more children and this will now be impossible.

Advise Helen whether or not she can bring an action against Keith. (Do not discuss the issue of vicarious liability on the part of Keith's employers.) (OCR January 2004)

3. 'Tort has a significant role to play in the protection of civil liberties' (Stanton, *The Modern Law of Tort*).

   In the light of the defences available, does the tort of trespass to the person play such a role? (Oxford 1996)

4. 'It is the duty of the courts to be ever zealous to protect personal freedom, privacy and dignity of all who live in these islands' (Donaldson LJ in *Lindley v Rutter* 1981).

   To what extent do the rules relating to trespass to the person used by the courts provide such protection? (OCR January 2002)

2   Negligence – the duty of care

Definitions

The tort of negligence is probably one of the most difficut to understand and yet it is in many ways the most important tort. While the topic is dealt with in several shorter chapters, to make it more digestible, it should be remembered that each chapter relates to the others and this section of the book needs to be regarded as a whole.

The word 'negligence' is defined by the Shorter Oxford Dictionary as 'want of attention to what ought to be done or looked after; lack of proper care in doing something'. According to the Dictionary, people are negligent if they are 'inattentive to what ought to be done'. An ordinary person, if asked to explain the term, might well say that it means carelessness. A lawyer, if asked the same question, would not find it so easy to answer and is likely to start talking about ideas of duty, breach and damage. As will be seen, the lawyer's explanation reflects the purpose of the tort, which is primarily to ensure that a person who suffers loss as a result of another person's act, or failure to act when there is a duty to do so, should be entitled to compensation.

Life would, however, be impossible if every time something went wrong it led to a bill to cover loss. How would individuals ensure they had the means to meet such a bill, how would business anticipate likely costs and, most importantly, how would insurance companies fix a premium which reflected the risk?

The tort of negligence, which has developed over the centuries as part of the common law, attempts to answer these questions by acknowledging principles which help to decide what duty is owed and to whom and to set a standard of acceptable behaviour. Principles have also evolved to limit the amount of compensation which may be payable.

Judges have attempted to give a definition. Baron Alderson said,

> Negligence is the omission to do something which a reasonable man, guided upon those considerations which ordinarily regulate the conduct of human affairs, would do or doing something which a prudent and reasonable man would not do.
>
> (*Blyth v Birmingham Waterworks Co* [1856])

In 1934 Lord Wright said,

In strict legal analysis, negligence means more than heedless or careless conduct, whether in omission or commission: it properly connotes the complex concept of duty, breach and damage thereby suffered by the person to whom the duty was owing.
(*Lochgelly Iron and Coal Co Ltd v M'Mullan* [1934])

Although the tort of negligence seems to divide itself into the separate issues of duty, breach and damage mentioned by Lord Wright – and this book will follow tradition in looking at the tort in this way – it is important to remember that the separate issues must in fact be read together to make a complex whole.

General principles

It is essential that there should be some mechanism for deciding when a legal duty of care should be owed. For many years, the tort developed case by case, the courts deciding in each particular set of circumstances the nature and extent of the duty. In 1932 the case of *Donoghue v Stevenson* reached the House of Lords. The judgment is important for two reasons:

1 It was decided that a manufacturer of a defective product owed a duty of care to the ultimate consumer.

2 It attempted to formulate a basic principle which could be applied in appropriate cases to decide whether or not a duty of care was owed.

> *Donoghue v Stevenson* (1932)
> Mrs D went to a café with a friend who bought her a bottle of ginger beer. The bottle was opaque so that the contents could not be seen and it was sealed as it had been when it came from the manufacturer. Mrs D drank half the ginger beer but when the rest was poured into her glass, out floated the remains of a decomposing snail. Mrs D was made ill by the experience and wanted compensation.

The basic principle, the neighbour principle, which came from the judgment, is so important that 'the case of the snail in the bottle of ginger beer' is known to all law students in common law-based jurisdictions throughout the world.

The neighbour principle

The basic principle to emerge from the case was explained by Lord Atkin who, while acknowledging that the tort was 'based upon a general public sentiment of moral wrongdoing for which the offender must pay', stated that 'acts or omissions which any moral code would censure cannot in a practical world be treated so as to give a right to every person injured by them to demand relief'. His solution has become known as the 'neighbour principle'.

> The rule that you are to love your neighbour becomes in law, you must not injure your neighbour; and the lawyer's question, 'Who is my neighbour?', receives a restricted reply. You must take reasonable care to avoid acts or omissions which you can reasonably foresee would be likely to injure your neighbour. Who, then, in law is my neighbour? The answer seems to be – persons who are so closely and directly affected by my act that I ought reasonably to have them in contemplation as being so affected when I am directing my mind to the acts or omissions which are called in question.

From this statement, it can be seen that in order for a duty of care to be owed there must be reasonable foresight of harm to persons whom, it is reasonable to foresee, may be harmed by one's acts or omissions. It should be remembered that the establishment of a duty of care does not necessarily mean that compensation will be available for breach; it is merely the first step for a 'victim' seeking a remedy.

The 'two-stage' test

Since 1932, the neighbour principle has led to the recognition of a duty of care in a number of diverse situations, in some ways making it easier for a victim to establish a case. The courts have, however, been forced to acknowledge that there needs to be some limit on the scope of the principle.

Lord Wilberforce enunciated his 'two-stage' test in *Anns v Merton London Borough Council* in 1978.

1   Is there a 'sufficient relationship of proximity' between the wrongdoer and the victim so that the wrongdoer ought to contemplate that the wrongdoing might cause injury to the victim?

2   If the answer to the first question is 'yes,' are there any factors which ought to negate or limit the scope of the

duty, the class of persons to whom it is owed or the extent of damages for any breach?

> **Anns v Merton London Borough Council (1978)**
> The lessees of a building discovered in 1970 that there were structural movements causing the walls to crack. The movements were caused by inadequate foundations. The defendants, as local authority, had had the responsibility to see that the building conformed to the plans originally approved. In fact the foundations were shallower than the plans required. It was alleged that the inspection had either not been carried out or had been carried out inadequately; either way the claimants alleged that the defendant had been negligent. This case is also important in relation to the concept of pure economic loss dealt with later in this section. The claimant won the case.

On the basis of Lord Wilberforce's views, the issue is fairly simple and it led some people to believe that a duty of care would be owed in all circumstances unless there was some good reason, in a particular case, why this should not be so. The implications of such a wide interpretation were immense, especially from the economic point of view, and it was not long before 'the retreat from Anns' began.

The retreat from Anns

As some judges began to take the view that the two-stage test was leading to the 'opening of the floodgates' (a concept which is not acceptable), refinements were introduced leading to an approach which was restricted but still flexible and true to the neighbour principle. Today the court will ask:

1   Was damage foreseeable?

2   Is there a sufficiently close relationship (sufficient proximity) between the wrongdoer and the victim?

3   Is it just and reasonable to impose a duty of care?

In *Caparo Industries plc v Dickman* (1990) Lord Bridge summarised the position, asking whether 'the situation should be one in which the court considers it fair, just and reasonable that the law should impose a duty of a given scope on the one party for the benefit of the other'.

> ### *Caparo Industries plc v Dickman* (1990)
> The claimants were shareholders in Fidelity plc. After reading the annual accounts audited by the defendants, they bought additional shares and ultimately made a successful take-over bid. Once the bid had been accepted they discovered that the accounts showed a profit of £1.3 million when they should have shown a loss of £465,000. The claimants alleged that the defendants had been negligent. Although the case is more important for the points it settles in relation to negligent misstatement dealt with later in this chapter, the decision in fact turned on whether or not the defendants owed a duty of care to the claimants. The court decided that no such duty was owed.

None of the questions asked by the courts is conclusive, the weight given to each depending on the particular facts. Thus it is possible in some cases for the risk of damage to be so obvious that reasonable proximity can be deduced.

Can there be a general principle to decide the existence of a duty of care?

It may be that Lord Atkin, in attempting to create a general principle, was attempting the impossible. Over the years since 1932, the courts have struggled with the proposition and have formulated principles. It is not easy for an ordinary person to deduce from these principles exactly when a legal duty of care is owed, and the non-lawyer may still depend on 'the general public sentiment of moral wrongdoing' as a guide for action.

The unforeseen victim

While it is often easy to establish from previous cases that a duty is owed in particular circumstances (for example, all road users owe a duty of care to all other road users), the victim has to establish a sufficient relationship with the wrongdoer to lead to a conclusion that in the particular circumstances the particular wrongdoer owes a particular duty to this particular victim.

It is not usually enough for the victim to establish the existence of a duty to people generally. The first hurdle is to establish that in all

Figure 2.1: Historical development of duty of care

Donoghue v Stevenson 1932:	Duty of care is owed to those who may foreseeably be injured by failure to take reasonable care
Anns v Merton LBC 1978:	Duty owed if there is a sufficient relationship of proximity between claimant and defendant *unless* there is any reason why it should not exist
Caparo Industries plc v Dickman 1990 (the modern test):	The court will ask: (a) Was damage reasonably foreseeable? (b) Was there sufficient proximity between claimant and defendant? (c) Is it just and reasonable to impose a duty of care? If answer to each question is 'yes', duty of care has been established

the circumstances the victim was owed a legal duty of care by the alleged wrongdoer. In *Bourhill v Young* (1943) Lord Russell said that 'such a duty [of care] only arises towards those individuals of whom it may reasonably be anticipated that they will be affected by the act which constitutes the alleged breach'.

> ### *Bourhill v Young* (1943)
> Mrs B was a fishwife who was travelling on a tram. As she got off the tram and picked up her basket, a motorcyclist passed the tram and some 45 metres away crashed into a car and was killed. The rider was negligent, but did he owe a duty to Mrs B who went to the site of the crash where she saw blood on the road? She alleged that as a result she suffered shock and she gave birth to a still-born child about a month later. It was held that the rider owed no duty to Mrs B – she was standing behind a solid barrier and not within his field of vision and she was in no way at risk from his speed.

'The Case of the Pregnant Fishwife' also has important implications in relation to the development of the law relating to 'nervous shock' and will be referred to again later.

It is perhaps true to say that generally sins of omission are regarded as being less 'wrong' in the moral sense than intended/positive acts.

In law there is generally no duty to act to prevent harm, whatever the moral outrage that failure to act may cause. Certain relationships will, however, give rise to liability for an omission. Case law gives rise to some principles which are generally accepted as forming a basis for such liability.

A person who undertakes a task has a duty to perform it carefully.

Thus in *Barnett v Chelsea & Kensington Hospital Management Committee* (1969) it was held that an accident and emergency department of a hospital owed a duty of care to those who sought help and could be liable for the negligent omission of its staff to treat such persons properly. In *Mercer v South Eastern & Chatham Railway Companies' Management Committee* (1922) a practice of locking a gate to a railway crossing when a train was coming led those who used the path to believe that if the gate was unlocked it was safe to cross. In the circumstances the court held that there was liability for failure to lock the gate – an omission.

Personal relationships can lead to liability for omissions.

Or, to put it another way, they impose a positive duty to prevent harm; for example, an employer owes such a duty to employees, a parent owes such a duty to a child. The essence of the relationship is that the victim has relied, expressly or impliedly, on the alleged wrongdoer to keep the victim free from harm. Case law shows that medical staff owe a duty of care to patients who are suicidal to take precautions against a suicide attempt (*Self v Ilford & District Hospital Management Committee* [1970]); prison authorities owe a similar duty to prisoners in their care (*Knight v Home Office* [1990], as do the police (*Reeves v Commissioner of Police for the Metropolis* [1997]).

In some circumstances, there may be liability for failure to control the actions of a third party.

The obligation to act may arise where it is clear that the third party is a threat to others and there is a sufficiently close relationship between that person and the person allegedly 'in control', i.e. in a position to do something to prevent the potential damage.

In *Smith v Littlewoods Organisation Ltd* (1987) the claimant had suffered loss when his premises were damaged as a result of an arson attack on next door premises which had been bought as a derelict cinema by the defendants and left empty pending redevelopment.

Did the defendant owe a duty of care to the claimant to prevent the risk of arson or other activities causing damage to the defendant's premises?

The judges took different approaches. One judge, Lord Goff, took the view that 'it is not possible to invoke a general duty of care; for it is well recognised that there is no general duty to prevent third parties from causing ... damage'. Other judges took the view that there was a more positive duty on the defendant 'to take reasonable care that the condition of the premises they occupied was not a source of danger to neighbouring property'. (Lord Griffiths)

---

1   To what extent does the modern test for a duty of care, set out in *Caparo Industries plc v Dickman* (1990), reflect Lord Atkin's view that the tort was 'based upon a general public sentiment of moral wrongdoing'?
2   Should a sober passenger being driven by a driver who is known to be drunk owe a duty of care to someone else who is injured by the driver's negligence?

The issue of public policy and public authorities

In *Caparo Industries plc v Dickman* (1990) the third question to be asked when deciding if there is a duty of care is

'Is it just and reasonable to impose a duty of care?'

One of the issues to be considered in connection with this question is that of public policy. The courts are reluctant to impose an unreasonable burden on police officers, social workers and other public servants who carry out very difficult jobs by making them constantly worried that any mistake could lead to an allegation that they had been negligent.

In *Home Office v Dorset Yacht Co Ltd* (1970) the court held that where damage caused was the natural and probable outcome, as opposed to a merely foreseeable and possible outcome, of an act by a public servant, a duty of care could exist.

Home Office v Dorset Yacht Co Ltd (1970)
A group of young criminals were working under supervision in Poole Harbour. The officers supervising them went to bed and to sleep although they knew that some of the

youngsters had convictions and had previously escaped from Borstal (a young offenders prison). Seven did escape and went aboard a nearby yacht which they moved and in doing so collided with another yacht which was damaged by the collision and by the youngsters when they went on board. The Yacht Co alleged that the Borstal officers owed a duty of care to the company and therefore the Home Office had vicarious liability for their torts. *Held*: the escape should have been anticipated and guarded against by the officers. The taking of the yacht and the damage caused was an easily foreseeable consequence of the officers' failure to carry out their duties properly and the Home Office was liable.

In a later case, *Hill v Chief Constable of West Yorkshire* (1988), the judgment indicated that a 'blanket immunity' was available, at least to a police force, on the ground of public policy and that generally the police do not owe a general duty of care.

Hill v Chief Constable of West Yorkshire **(1988)**
The mother of one of the victims of Peter Sutcliffe (the Yorkshire Ripper) alleged that her daughter had been killed because the police had negligently failed to follow their own procedures. Had they done their job properly, Sutcliffe would have been caught before her daughter was murdered. *Held*: her claim must fail on the ground of public policy and also because there was insufficient proximity between the police and her daughter, the victim.

The consequences of a blanket immunity could mean that a person who had suffered serious damage would be unable to claim any compensation. Matters became more difficult following *X (Minors) v Bedfordshire County Council* (1995) when the House of Lords appeared to decide that a local authority which had a duty imposed on it by statute, did not therefore owe a common law duty of care to victims if the duty was performed negligently. This reinforced the idea that public authorities had immunity from an action for negligence.

> **X (Minors) v Bedfordshire County Council (1995)**
> Four children were referred to the Council in 1987 as being
> seriously neglected. The allegations continued but the
> Council did not take the children into care until 1992 by
> which time it was clear that they had suffered very serious
> neglect which might have long-standing consequences for
> their health. The children sued for damages arising from
> the Council's negligence and breach of statutory duty. *Held:*
> There was no legal basis for the action.

Later cases showed that the decision in *X (Minors) v Bedfordshire County Council* was not as far-reaching as it seemed at first. In *W and Others v Essex County Council* (1998), another case about the statutory duty to protect children, it was held that there was no blanket immunity if the decision reached by the Council was so unreasonable that it fell outside the scope of the statute. The matter was considered again, by the House of Lords, in *Barrett v Enfield London Borough Council* (1999). Lord Browne-Wilkinson said that whether or not a common law duty of care was owed by a public authority depends on:

> Weighing in the balance the total detriment to the public interest
> in all cases from holding [public authorities] liable in negligence
> as against the total loss to all would-be plaintiffs [claimants] if
> they are not to have a cause of action in respect of the loss they
> have individually suffered.

X (Minors) v Bedfordshire County Council (1995) was taken to the European Court of Human Rights where it became known as *Z v The United Kingdom* (ECHR) (Application no. 29392/95 10th May 2001). The European Court held that the rights of the children had been infringed under Article 3 (prohibition of torture, inhuman and degrading treatment) and under Article 13 (guarantee of the right to a fair trial). The children were awarded compensation. In the course of the judgment the European Court approved the development of the law in *W and Others v Essex County Council* (1998) and *Barrett v Enfield LBC* (1999).

It seems that at the end of the day a duty of care can be owed by a public authority to anyone who can be foreseen as likely to suffer if the authority performs its duty negligently. (For further discussion of potential remedies in similar situations, see Chapter 10, 'Breach of Statutory Duty.')

Special duty situations

Pure economic loss

The courts have long been cautious about the concept of 'pure economic loss'. It is accepted that financial loss which results from physical damage to a person or to property is recoverable, but financial loss can arise in a number of ways which are not necessarily the consequence of the negligent act. In one sense the arguments are artificial: the person who has to spend money to repair a defective item is as much out of pocket as the person who has to spend money to repair damage caused by someone else. The courts have taken the view that it is necessary to impose some limitation on the extent of the duty so far as economic loss is concerned in order to avoid what Cardozo CJ described, in an American case, as

> liability in an indeterminate amount for an indeterminate time to an indeterminate class.
>
> (*Ultramares Corporation v Touche* [1931])

The basic principle was explained by Blackburn J in *Cattle v Stockton Waterworks* (1875), when he acknowledged that the law was imperfect in that it did not provide a remedy for all wrongdoing, but stated that it was a wise decision to provide a remedy only for the 'proximate and direct consequences of wrongful acts'.

The problem is clearly illustrated by *Spartan Steel v Martin & Co* (1973) in which Lord Denning MR openly acknowledged that the decision was based in policy. 'Whenever the courts set bounds to the damages recoverable ... they do it as a matter of policy so as to limit the liability of the defendant.' He went on to consider the nature of the claim – damages for loss caused by a power failure – stating that 'if claims for economic loss were permitted for this particular hazard, there would be no end of claims ... it is better to disallow economic loss altogether, at any rate when it stands alone, independent of any physical damage'. The court was also influenced by the fact that normally such losses are shared among everyone affected; to impose liability on the defendant would be to impose a very heavy financial burden.

> ### *Spartan Steel v Martin & Co* (1973)
> The defendants negligently cut through a power cable which supplied electricity to the claimant's factory. As a result, a melt in progress had to be wasted in order to prevent serious

> damage, costing the claimant £400 in lost profit. The
> claimant also lost £1,767 profit which it would have made
> on further melts carried out during the period when power
> was cut off. It was held that the profit of £400 was
> recoverable but the other sum was not.

The issue frequently arises where a person has acquired a defective
item of property and needs to spend money to repair it and/or make
it safe. In *Dutton v Bognor Regis Urban District Council* (1972) the council
was held liable for the negligent failure of its building inspector to
discover inadequate foundations which later led to damage to the
building. It was held that although the claimant had only suffered the
cost of the necessary repairs, nonetheless this could be recovered. In
Anns v Merton London Borough Council (1978) the facts were similar and
the claimant recovered the cost of repair. In both cases the judges
argued that the building was a complex structure and that the
foundations were a separate whole which had caused damage to the
rest of the building.

Anns was followed by *Junior Books Ltd v Veitchi Co Ltd* (1983) in
which a subcontractor, who was a specialist in laying floors, was held
to have entered into a relationship of reliance with the claimants.
Although there was no actual contractual relationship between the
parties, the court held that the relationship was in fact akin to a
contractual relationship in which the claimant clearly relied on the
skill and expertise of the defendants, and that in such circumstances
there could be a claim for pure economic loss.

It was almost immediately obvious that the concept of reliance in
Junior Books was flawed and the retreat began. In *Muirhead v Industrial
Tank Specialities Ltd* (1986) it was suggested that *Junior Books* was decided
on its own very particular facts and did not give rise to any general
principle.

Eventually, *Murphy v Brentwood District Council* (1991) came before the
courts. The case was concerned with defective foundations of a house
which led to further structural problems. The House of Lords took the
view that the house was not a complex structure but a whole. The reasons
for the decision in *Anns* were rejected, that case being overruled, and the
reasoning in *Junior Books* was distinguished on the basis that it was confined
to the very particular facts of that case.

Professional liability

Certain categories of professional advisers will have liability for
pure economic loss where they have been negligent. This

39

particularly applies to surveyors and solicitors and, probably, other professionals.

The question of a solicitor's liability to persons other than his client was considered in *White and Another v Jones and Another* (1995) when the House of Lords held that 'there would be no injustice in imposing liability upon a negligent solicitor ... where, in the absence of a remedy in this form, neither the testator's estate nor the disappointed beneficiary will have a claim for the loss caused by his negligence'.

> ### *White v Jones* (1995)
> A father made a will cutting out his daughters from any inheritance. They were later reconciled and the father instructed his solicitors to make a new will reinstating the daughters to their inheritance. Because of delay in the solicitors' office, the solicitors had an appointment to see the father some two months later. The father died before that date and his will was never changed. The issue to be decided by the court was whether or not the solicitors owed a duty of care to the daughters. *Held:* a duty was owed to particular beneficiaries and the solicitors were liable.

Until recently barristers and solicitors acting as advocates in court could not be sued in negligence for the way in which they conducted the case. This principle was confirmed in *Rondel v Worsley* (1967), one of the reasons for the decision being that it would be against public policy to abolish the traditional immunity. The matter has been reconsidered by the House of Lords in *Arthur J S Hall v Simons* (2000) when it was held that the immunity should be abolished. The main reason given by the judges was that other professionals can be sued for negligence and 'It tends to erode confidence in the legal system if advocates, alone among professional men, are immune from liability for negligence' (per Lord Steyn). The judge went on to say that 'in today's world the decision [in *Rondel v Worsley*] no longer correctly reflects public policy.'

Liability of surveyors was considered in *Smith v Eric Bush* (1989) and *Harris & Anor v Wye Forest District Council & Anor* (1989). The case was about the liability of a surveyor who had done a survey on behalf of a lender to make sure that the premises provided adequate security for the loan. After the buyer moved in, it became apparent that the surveyor had been negligent and that the premises suffered from a serious structural defect. The surveyor had been acting for and paid by the building society. It was held that

> The essence of the case against [the surveyor] is that he as a professional man realised that the purchaser was relying on him to exercise proper skill and judgment in his profession and that it was reasonable and fair that the purchaser should do so.
>
> (*per* Kerr LJ)

In *Caparo Industries plc v Dickman* (1990) Lord Bridge suggested that the important features of cases such as *White v Jones* and *Smith v Bush* was that the

> defendant giving advice or information was fully aware of the nature of the transaction which the [claimant] had in contemplation, knew that the advice or information would be communicated to him directly or indirectly and knew that it was very likely that the [claimant] would rely on that advice or information in deciding whether or not to engage in the transaction in contemplation.

Case law would seem to have left certain categories of professional advisers at more risk than others for consequences of bad advice. It is perhaps reasonable that this should be the case, based on the argument put forward by Lord Bridge in *Caparo Industries plc v Dickman.*

The law seems to say that unless a negligent act causes physical damage to something or someone other than the negligent thing itself, no compensation can be recovered. Is this fair to an 'innocent' victim?

Negligent misstatement

A negligently made statement may have far-reaching effects. As there is generally no clearly defined barrier to the spread of such a statement, the courts have developed careful rules to limit the scope of liability. Yet again we see that the courts are concerned that there should not be 'liability for an indeterminate amount for an indeterminate time to an indeterminate class' (Cardoza CJ in *Ultramares Corporation v Touche* [1931]). Despite limitations, a person who relies on a negligent misstatement may find that there is a remedy if as a result of the reliance loss is suffered.

A person owes a duty to be careful in making a statement only if there is a special relationship between that person and the person relying on the statement. The basis of the rules is found in *Hedley Byrne & Co Ltd v Heller & Partners Ltd* (1964), in which it was stated that where there is a special relationship between the parties, a party relying on a negligent misstatement and thereby suffering loss can establish that a duty of care was owed and is therefore enabled to recover consequential loss. Lord Devlin defined the required relationship as,

> a responsibility that is voluntarily accepted or undertaken, either generally where a general relationship, such as that of solicitor and client or banker and customer, is created, or specifically in relation to a particular transaction.

Lord Pearce made it clear that if the facts disclose 'a social approach to the enquiry no such special relationship or duty of care would be assumed'. Lord Pearce's views were a relief to many professionals, for example doctors, accountants and lawyers who are frequently asked for advice when at parties or other social functions. It is clear that a special relationship may exist where,

> the party seeking information ... was trusting the other to exercise such a degree of care as the circumstances required, where it was reasonable for him to do that, and where the other gave the information or advice when he knew or ought to have known that the inquirer was relying on him.
>
> (*per* Reid LJ in *Hedley Byrne & Co Ltd v Heller & Partners Ltd*)

Hedley Byrne & Co Ltd v Heller & Partners Ltd **(1964)**
The claimants were advertising agents who were about to incur financial liability on behalf of a client. They asked their own bankers for a reference about the client which was provided by the defendants. The letter said that the client was respectable and 'good for its ordinary business engagements. Your figures are larger than we are accustomed to see.' The letter also contained a disclaimer. A short time later, the client went into liquidation, costing the claimants £17,000. The disclaimer meant that the defendants were not liable, although a duty of care existed.

From the judgments in *Hedley Byrne* it appeared that victims needed to establish three things if they were to establish that a duty of care was owed in respect of a statement:

1   that there was reliance by the victim on the other party's
     skill and judgment or ability to make careful enquiry;

2   that the other party knew, or ought reasonably to have
     known, that the victim was relying on the statement;

3   that it was reasonable in the circumstances for the victim
     to have such reliance on the other party.

In *Caparo Industries plc v Dickman* (1990) annual accounts audited
by the defendants were relied on by the claimant as the basis for a
takeover bid which, although successful, actually caused a large loss.
In considering whether the accountants, the defendants, were liable
for negligent misstatement the court stated that if a duty of care was to
be established it was necessary for the claimant to show that

> the defendant giving advice was fully aware of the nature of the
> transaction which the plaintiff had in contemplation, knew that
> the advice would be communicated to him directly or indirectly
> and knew that it was very likely that the plaintiff would rely on
> that advice in deciding whether or not to engage in the transaction
> in contemplation.
>
> (*per* Lord Bridge)

In the circumstances, the defendants were held to have owed a
duty of care to the shareholders of the company concerned in relation
to the end of year accounts but that to impose a wider duty would be
to open the possibility of indeterminate liability to which the courts
are consistently opposed. This case appears to add a fourth requirement
to the rules set out in *Hedley Byrne*:

4   that the other party knew, or ought to have known, the
     purpose for which the defendant required the advice or
     information.

More recently, the courts have, additionally to the requirement of
reliance, emphasised the notion of assumption of responsibility by
the defendant. In *Henderson v Merrett Syndicates Ltd* (1994) the House
of Lords held that the doctrine of assumption of responsibility could
apply to anyone rendering a professional or quasi-professional service,
and there could be liability for negligent misstatement regardless of
whether or not there was a contractual relationship between the parties,
provided the victim could also show reliance on the advice.

Another case from the same year has given rise to concern in relation
to employment references. It had long been understood that a reference
given by an employer which was untrue or defamatory of the

employee, was actionable only in defamation and that the employer was protected by the defence of qualified privilege unless malice could be proved. (See the section on defamation in Chapter 9 for more detail on this.) In *Spring v Guardian Assurance plc* (1994) the House of Lords held that an employer owes a duty of care to an employee to take reasonable care in compiling a reference. Lord Goff said

> where the plaintiff entrusts the defendant with the conduct of his affairs, in general or in particular, the defendant may be held to have assumed responsibility to the plaintiff, and the plaintiff to have relied on the defendant to exercise due skill and care, in respect of such conduct.

Spring v Guardian Assurance plc (1994)
Mr S was employed by the company but was dismissed and looked for a job with one of the company's competitors. Under LAUTRO rules the potential new employer had to obtain a reference from the company. The reference was so bad that Mr S was not offered the job. Mr S sued in negligence, alleging that he was owed a duty of care, that the company had not exercised due care and that Mr S was therefore entitled to damages. The House of Lords agreed.

Figure 2.2: Development of liability for negligence misstatement

Hedley Byrne & Co v Heller & Partners Ltd (1964):	Claimant can succeed if a special relationship exists between claimant and defendant *and* claimant relies on defendant's advice or information

To decide if 'special relationship' exists, the court will ask:

(a) Did claimant trust defendant to take care?

(b) Did defendant know claimant was relying on the defendant?   *Hedley Byrne v Heller* (1964)

(c) Was claimant's reliance reasonable in the circumstances?

(d) Did defendant know or ought defendant to have known why claimant required advice or information?   *Caparo Industries plc v Dickman* (1990)

(e) Did defendant assume responsibility to give advice or information?   *Henderson v Merrett Syndicates* (1994)

While the courts have generally declined to impose liability for a statement made on a social occasion, liability may be imposed where the victim has no means of checking the information, and where it is clear that the answer is important and will be relied on. For example, in *Chaudhry v Prabhaker* (1988), a knowledgeable friend was held to owe a duty of care in relation to negligent advice about a car given to the claimant who knew nothing about cars.

> You are very excited as you have just started a job in a legal office. You have exaggerated the amount of responsibility which you have been given and have led your friends to believe that you are now an expert on legal questions. One of your friends has a problem arising out of a road traffic accident and asks your advice while you are having a cup of coffee together. You actually know very little about the relevant law but tell your friend what should be done. In fact the advice is wrong and as a result your friend loses a lot of money. Is your friend likely to be able to make you pay compensation?

Nervous shock

General issues

It is only comparatively recently that the nature of psychiatric illness has been better understood and that it has been accepted that there can be a proper diagnosis in the same way as for physical illness or injury. Even today, however, there is some suspicion of psychiatric illness and something of an attitude of distrust on the part of the general public, a belief that the victim is making it up.

The courts, however, now accept that psychiatric illness, including neurosis and personality change, once it is properly diagnosed and identified, is a genuine form of injury that can result from breach of a duty of care. Where the victim's illness is caused directly by the incident, in other words where the claimant is a primary victim, the normal rules apply. All such a claimant need prove is that injury, whether physical or mental, was foreseeable. Where, however, the victim's nervous shock has been caused indirectly by the defendant, as a result of trauma caused to another person, the rules differ and progress in clarifying the law has been slow.

In *Dulieu v White* (1901) it was held that a person could claim but only if they were within the range of potential physical injury. This approach was further developed in *Hambrook v Stokes* (1925) when it was held that a person who saw or heard the incident for themselves, with their unaided senses, could recover compensation for nervous shock resulting from fear that others had been injured. *Bourhill v Young* (1943) ('the case of the pregnant fishwife') held that, additionally, nervous shock must be foreseeable.

The modern approach stems from *McLoughlin v O'Brian* (1983).

> ### *McLoughlin v O'Brian* (1983)
> Mrs M was at home when her husband and three children were involved in a car accident caused by the defendant's negligence. She was told about the accident and was taken to the hospital. There she was told that her youngest daughter was dead. She saw her other daughter through a window, crying with her face cut and covered with dirt and oil. Her son could be heard shouting and screaming and she later saw him with his face and side covered with bandages. Her husband was covered in mud and oil and sobbing. As a result of this horrific experience, Mrs M suffered severe shock, organic depression and a change of personality.

The judges in the House of Lords were divided as to the approach to be taken. The majority decision was that the simple test of foresight would suffice, Lord Bridge stating,

> I can see no grounds whatever for suggesting that to make the defendant liable for reasonably foreseeable psychiatric illness caused by his negligence would be to impose a crushing burden on him out of proportion to his moral responsibility.

Lord Wilberforce, giving a minority judgment, held that the usual test of reasonable foresight of injury needed to be subject to some limitation. On policy grounds, he suggested that the class of persons who could claim, their proximity to the incident and the means by which the shock was caused were all relevant in deciding whether or not to admit a claim.

Following the 1989 Hillsborough disaster in which 95 spectators were killed and some 400 injured at the start of a football match which was being televised, relatives and friends of the victims suffered nervous shock and sought a remedy from the South Yorkshire Police, alleging that the incident had been caused by police negligence. In the course of the judgment, in which most of the claims by the relatives and friends were dismissed, the House of Lords set out criteria which apply only to such claims, i.e. to claims by those who, while not the direct victims of an incident, are nonetheless so affected by the trauma caused to another person by the defendant's negligence that they suffer nervous shock. Such people are known as the secondary victims. In order to succeed in such a claim, the **secondary victims** must prove the following:

1   **They are within the relevant class of persons, i.e. that there are or were close ties of love and affection with the primary victim**. Such ties will be presumed where the relationship is one of marriage or that of parent and child but other claimants will need to prove that such a relationship exists.

> Try to make a list of the kinds of things which the courts could use to decide whether or not you have 'close ties of love and affection' with (i) your brothers and sisters; (ii) your best friend.

2   **The injury was caused through their own sight or hearing of the incident or the immediate aftermath**. What is meant by the phrase 'the immediate aftermath' is not clear. The judges acknowledged that this need not be sight or hearing of the actual event but must be sufficiently close to be classed as 'the immediate aftermath'.

> The courts seem to have taken the view that being forewarned that you are about to see the dead body of a loved one, perhaps to confirm the identity of the deceased, is enough to diminish the shock suffered by you. Do you agree?

3   **The means by which the claimant received the shock are relevant**. Usually, provided the proper rules of broadcasting are followed, it will not be possible to identify individual victims from televised pictures. A person who is made ill simply by watching a broadcast, knowing that a loved one is at the actual scene, will be unable to recover. It was, however, acknowledged by the judges that in some circumstances, such as a live transmission of pictures from an event involving identifiable persons, the issue might need to be viewed differently. (*Alcock v Chief Constable of South Yorkshire* [1991])

It might be thought that with *Alcock v Chief Constable of South Yorkshire* the problem had been solved, at least for the time being. This was not, however, to prove to be the case.

The question of whether a victim is a primary or secondary victim is very important. In *Page v Smith* (1995) it was held that a primary victim is one who is within the range of foreseeable injury, i.e. someone who is directly involved in the accident. In *White and Others v Chief Constable of South Yorkshire* (1999) it was clearly stated that all other victims are secondary victims who must satisfy the criteria laid down in *Alcock*. Where a primary victim suffers nervous shock, compensation is recoverable regardless of whether or not such shock was foreseeable provided that a duty to avoid causing personal injury can be established; in other words, if the possibility of injury is foreseeable, it does not matter whether the actual injury is physical or psychological. Where the case involves a secondary victim, that person has to prove that it was reasonably foreseeable that nervous shock could be caused to a person of reasonable fortitude and phlegm. This means that someone who is in some way already suffering from a psychiatric condition has no claim if the condition is made worse unless it can be shown that a person of reasonable fortitude and phlegm could also have been made ill in the circumstances.

 The phrase 'immediate aftermath' has caused problems. How long does it last? In *McLoughlin v O'Brian* (1983) the aftermath extended to a mother's arrival at the hospital where she saw her family in a dreadful state. In an Australian case, *Jaensch v Coffey* (1984), it was held that the aftermath extended to the hospital to which the primary victim was taken and lasted until the state produced by the accident had been improved, for example the blood and gore had been dealt with. In *Alcock*, the House of Lords refused to extend the aftermath to the identification of a body at the mortuary some eight hours after the death. In *Taylor v Somerset Health Authority* (1993) the judge decided that a visit to a mortuary to identify the body soon after the claimant had been told of her husband's death could not be the immediate aftermath.

The courts have also found it difficult to decide whether the incident itself which causes the shock must be a single traumatic event or if it can be a longer drawn-out process. In *Sion v Hampstead Health Authority* (1994) the 14 days during which a father watched his son, who had been injured in a motor cycle accident, deteriorate and die did not give the father a claim. There had been no sudden and unexpected shock as the son's death was anticipated. In *Tredget and Tredget v Bexley Health Authority* (1994) the court held that events over two days effectively amounted to one event. The claimant gave birth in circumstances described as 'chaotic' or 'pandemonium' and her baby died after two days in intensive care. The judge held that it would be unrealistic to separate out the events. The problem caused by these cases has perhaps been resolved by the Court of Appeal in a recent case.

> ### North Glamorgan NHS Trust v Walters (2002)
> Mrs Walters' 10-month-old son was suffering what was wrongly diagnosed as a relatively mild form of hepatitis. In fact he was suffering a much more serious strain and needed a liver transplant. Had he been properly diagnosed and treated he would probably have lived. As it was, he was taken into hospital where Mrs Walters stayed with him. She woke to find her son making choking noises and bleeding from the mouth. He had had a fit but Mrs Walters was later told that he would be unlikely to suffer any permanent serious brain damage. In fact he had suffered irreparable brain damage. The baby was transferred to another hospital for a liver transplant. When Mrs Walters arrived at the second hospital she was told that the baby had suffered severe brain damage and was on a life support machine. A liver transplant could not be performed. The next day, after being told that her son would have no quality of life, Mrs Walters agreed that the life support should be withdrawn and the baby died.

Mrs Walters suffered pathological grief reaction, a recognised psychiatric illness, caused by exposure to distressing events over a period of two days. The defendants, the first hospital, admitted negligence but argued that the claimant's nervous shock had not been caused by a single traumatic event. Holding that Mrs Walters was entitled to damages for nervous shock, Lord Justice Ward said: 'It is a seamless tale with an obvious beginning and an equally obvious end. It was … undoubtedly one drawn-out experience.'

Lord Justice Clarke said:

> '… the sudden and unexpected shock or series of shocks over a short period … leading to the death of Eliot in her arms, which together had the devastating effect on her … lead to the conclusion that … she is entitled to recover damages for the pathological grief reaction which she suffered as a result of the defendant's negligence.'

It appears that whether or not nervous shock has been caused is simply a question of fact and common sense. There is no hard-and-fast rule which prevents the shock being caused by a series of interconnected events which it would be unrealistic to separate from one another.

Rescuers and bystanders

Rescuers give rise to particular problems as the consequences for such persons are often identifiable as nervous shock. While a rescuer probably comes within the category of a secondary victim, the courts have shown reluctance to prevent such persons from recovering compensation, partly on the basis that a rescuer is in many ways an unwilling participant in the event. 'Professional rescuers' from services such as the police or fire brigade may suffer from nervous shock but can they obtain compensation or are they expected to be better able than other people to endure horrific scenes?

The position has been clarified to some extent by *White and Others v Chief Constable of South Yorkshire* (1999). The case concerned police officers who had been involved with the victims of the Hillsborough disaster and who had suffered nervous shock as a result of their experiences. The House of Lords held that there is no authority for the idea that a rescuer is in any different position from other secondary victims, Lord Hoffman saying

> There does not seem to me to be any logical reason why … they should be given special treatment as primary victims when they were not within the range of foreseeable physical injury and their psychiatric injury was caused by witnessing or participating in the aftermath of accidents which caused death or injury to others.

The rule for rescuers and bystanders is the same as that for other categories of claimants. A person, whether a rescuer or direct victim, will be able to claim damages on the basis that, looking objectively at the facts, that person was directly involved and well within the range of foreseeable physical injury. Others will be classified as secondary victims and must fulfil the *Alcock* criteria. The police officers' claim failed as they had not exposed themselves to danger nor had they reasonably believed that they were doing so. An example of a situation where an amateur rescuer was able to succeed is found in *Chadwick v British Transport Commission* (1967) when the claimant's case succeeded after his involvement with rescuing people from a major train crash at Lewisham in 1957 in particularly dangerous and horrific circumstances. A professional rescuer who succeeded was a fireman involved with the underground fire at King's Cross Station who had put himself in danger by going down into smoke and flame filled tunnels to try to rescue those who were trapped. (*Hale v London Underground Ltd* [1993]).

The distinction between rescuers and bystanders had been of some importance in earlier cases, for example in *McFarlane v E E Caledonia Ltd* (1994). The events witnessed by Mr McFarlane were truly horrific – he was on board a ship which was near to a burning oil rig for some hour and three-quarters and came within 100 metres of the fire which killed 164 men, some of whom were his friends and colleagues. He was not, however, viewed by the courts as a participant in the event but as a mere bystander and he was unable to recover compensation.

It is clear that, following *White and Others v Chief Constable of South Yorkshire*, there is no longer any need to make such a distinction. The test is a simple one – did the claimant come within the range of foreseeable physical injury? Only if this is the case can the claimant be viewed as a primary victim.

The rules can still lead to apparent injustice. In *Greatorex v Greatorex* (2000) the claimant was a fireman who was called to rescue a driver from a car accident. The driver was in fact the claimant's son. As a result, the claimant suffered nervous shock and sued his son, the defendant. On the basis of *White v Chief Constable of South Yorkshire* (1998) the claimant could not qualify as a primary victim but as the father of the victim it might be thought that he could succeed as a secondary victim. This was not in fact the decision of the court. It was held that he could only succeed if he could establish that the defendant owed a duty of care to himself not to inflict self-harm. To create such a duty would, in the court's view, be an infringement of the defendant's right to self-determination and individual liberty. It would be wrong to impose such a duty.

Liability to an unborn child

A health care professional clearly owes a duty of care to a patient but some problems have arisen in relation to pregnancy. In *McKay v Essex Area Health Authority* (1982) it was held that a doctor owed no duty of care to a baby who was born severely damaged as a result of her mother having come into contact with German measles during the pregnancy. The doctor had failed to warn the mother, who would have had the option to terminate the pregnancy. The child's claim against the doctor was rejected as this would recognise a right to be aborted, which is against public policy.

In other circumstances, a child injured before birth by negligence of any person other than its mother is owed a duty of care by the perpetrator (Congenital Disabilities (Civil Liability) Act 1976). The claim arises only once the child has been born alive.

Policy issues

It is clear that modern judges will generally acknowledge that issues of policy play a part in determining the decision. Traditionally judges have denied that this is so but, as has been seen, much of the reasoning behind recent decisions has been prompted by policy. In relation to both economic loss and liability for nervous shock, the judges have taken on board the difficulties which might be caused were there no rules to limit potential liability. The statement by Cardoza CJ, in *Ultramares Corporation v Touche* (1931), when he referred to 'liability in an indeterminate amount for an indeterminate time to an indeterminate class' has been quoted by English judges on many occasions as a summary of the unacceptable consequences were Lord Atkin's neighbour test to be given unfettered application.

In *Murphy v Brentwood District Council* (1991) Lord Oliver said

> It is not easy to discern the logic in holding that a sufficient relationship of proximity exists between [the supplier of electricity] and a factory owner who has suffered loss because material in the course of manufacture is rendered useless, but that none exists between [the supplier] and the owner of an adjoining restaurant who suffers the loss of profit on the meals which he is unable to prepare and sell. In both cases the real loss is pecuniary. The solution has been achieved pragmatically not by the application of logic but by the perceived necessity as a matter of policy to place some limits – perhaps arbitrary limits – to what would otherwise be an endless, cumulative causative chain bounded only by theoretical foreseeability.

In *McLoughlin v O'Brian* (1983) Lord Wilberforce summarised the policy arguments against treating nervous shock in the same way for both primary and secondary victims as follows:

(a) Such extension may lead to a proliferation of claims, and possibly fraudulent claims, to the establishment of an industry of lawyers and psychiatrists who will formulate a claim for nervous shock damages for all, or many, road accidents and industrial accidents.

(b) An extension of liability would be unfair to defendants, as imposing damages out of proportion to the negligent conduct complained of. In so far as such defendants are insured, a large additional burden will be placed on insurers, and ultimately upon the class of person insured.

(c) To extend liability beyond the most direct and plain cases would greatly increase evidentiary difficulties and tend to lengthen litigation.

(d) An extension of the scope of liability ought only to be made by the legislature, after careful research.

Figure 2.3: Nervous shock: Is a claim possible?

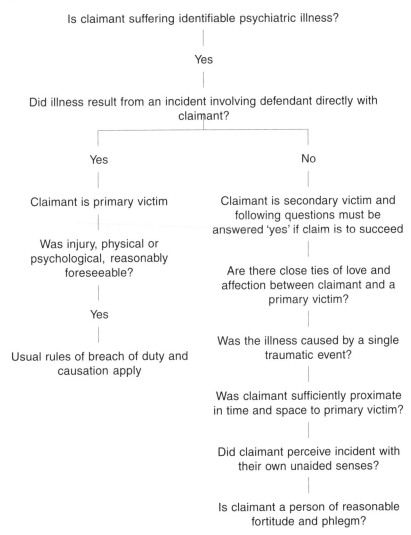

It is perhaps correct to say that the courts have taken a pragmatic view, accepting that it is better for society to know where it stands and thus be able to obtain affordable insurance which ensures that a relatively limited liability can be met. Failure to have such rules would possibly lead potential defendants to decide against taking out necessary insurance cover on the basis that liability is unlikely to be incurred and that if it ever happens, it might be less expensive simply to meet the claim rather than pay potentially unnecessary insurance premiums for years. Unfortunately such an attitude would be of little benefit to a victim who has suffered loss if a defendant was unable to meet the level of damages awarded.

Certainly a person denied compensation because of a policy decision feels a real sense of injustice and could argue that the ethical principles of justice and equality mean that all those injured should be treated in the same way. However, the ethical theory of utilitarianism seeks to justify such rules on the basis that an action, or set of rules, is justified if it produces more good than an alternative action or set of rules. The balance which the courts presently seek to impose can be argued to follow the theory of utilitarianism in that the greatest good for the greatest number is achieved by the limitations set by the judges.

> In your view, can the different rules which apply to primary and secondary victims of nervous shock be justified?

SUMMARY

Basic duty of care

* defendant owes duty of care to claimant:
    if damage is foreseeable resulting from failure to take reasonable care
    if there is sufficient proximity between the claimant and the defendant
    if it is just and reasonable to impose a duty of care

Special duty situation – pure economic loss

* generally no duty of care owed to prevent pure economic loss – *Spartan Steel v Martin* (1973)

Special duty situation – negligent misstatement

- duty of care will apply where a special relationship exists between claimant and defendant – *Hedley Byrne & Co v Heller & Partners Ltd* (1964)

- special relationship exists if following questions can be answered 'yes':
  did claimant trust defendant to take care when giving advice or information?
  did defendant know that claimant was relying on the advice or information?
  was the reliance reasonable in the circumstances?
  did defendant know or ought defendant to have known why claimant required the advice or information?
  did defendant assume responsibility?

Special duty situtation – nervous shock

- claimant must suffer identifiable psychiatric illness resulting from single traumatic incident

- illness can be caused by fear for claimant's own safety or fear for the safety of others – *Dulieu v White* (1901); *Hambrook v Stokes* (1925)

- if claimant is primary victim usual rules relating to duty of care apply

- if claimant is secondary victim, it must be proved that

  claimant was sufficiently proximate to the incident or its immediate aftermath – *McLoughlin v O'Brian* (1982), *North Glamorgan NHS Trust v Walters* (2002)

  nervous shock was reasonably foreseeable – *Page v Smith* (1995)

  the incident was perceived using the claimant's own unaided senses – *Alcock v Chief Constable of S. Yorkshire* (1991)

QUESTIONS

1. Jessica was killed during a televised, sponsored bungee jump when her harness broke. Peter, who set up the jump and provided the equipment, had negligently failed to inspect the webbing on the harness.

   Jessica's father, Steven, and her best friend, Natasha, were present and saw the fall. Both were taken to hospital suffering from shock.

   Mary, Jessica's mother, did not witness the accident but had to identify the body three hours later. The accident was also seen on live television by Jessica's grandmother, Rosemary.

Six months later Steven, Natasha and Mary have all been diagnosed as suffering from nervous shock. Steven was being treated for depression before the accident occurred. Rosemary has since become tearful and withdrawn.

Advise Steven, Natasha, Mary and Rosemary on their rights to sue Peter in negligence. (Oxford 1997)

2. Shiraz borrowed money from his bank to develop certain land into a housing estate. He did this following a survey carried out by Molly, on behalf of the bank, in which she declared the site suitable for the purpose. However, massive subsidence occurred as soon as heavy equipment was brought onto the site. A different surveyor, appointed by Shiraz at this point, found that the collapse was because the site was over a network of mining tunnels. Shiraz was forced to abandon his plans and as a result has lost a lot of money.

    To ease his resulting financial difficulties, Shiraz decided to take over a building company. He chose one having examined the audited accounts prepared by Thomas, an accountant, without making any further enquiries. The accounts, which showed the company to be in a healthy financial position, in fact turned out to have greatly exaggerated its standing, with the result that Shiraz is likely to lose a lot more money.

    Advise Shiraz as to any possible claims he may have. (Oxford 1997)

3. In *Donoghue v Stevenson* (1932) Lord Atkin attempted to create a basic principle which could be used in all cases to decide whether or not a duty of care is owed to the victim of negligence.

    Discuss the extent to which it has been successful. (OCR January 2004)

4. A person who gives information to others runs the risk of unlimited liability, as such information is likely to be spread among a large group of persons even if it was originally only given to one person.

    To what extent do the rules relating to negligent misstatement help to protect a person giving information from such liability? (OCR January 2002)

5. Critically evaluate the law applying to claims for compensation for nervous shock. In your opinion, is the law satisfactory? (OCR 1998)

6. In relation to claims in negligence for damages for nervous shock, discuss whether the different rules which apply to primary and secondary victims can be justified. (OCR 1999)

3   Negligence – breach of duty, causation and damage

Breach of the duty of care

The so-called 'reasonable man'

Once a duty of care has been established, the next hurdle faced by the victim is to show that the defendant has acted in a way which is in breach of that duty. In order to do this, it is essential that there be some mechanism to decide the standard of behaviour which can be expected from the defendant. The conduct of the claimant may also be relevant; this will be considered in the later chapter on defences.

The concept of the 'reasonable man' may offend some in the modern world where political correctness would require the use of the term the 'reasonable person'. Over the years, however, the description has stuck; he is also known as 'the man on the Clapham omnibus' and 'the ordinary man in the street'. To some people, the phrase is almost derogatory. The writer A. P. Herbert, in *Uncommon Law*, described the reasonable man as an 'excellent but odious character' who is 'devoid of any human weakness, with not one single saving vice'. Readers will form their own opinion in due course.

The reasonable man will, according to Baron Alderson, be 'guided upon those considerations which ordinarily regulate the conduct of human affairs' and will do or omit to do only those things which a 'prudent and reasonable man' would do or omit to do.

While lawyers understand the concept, the explanations given are not readily comprehensible to the non-lawyer who may well ask, 'But how do the courts decide what a reasonable man would or would not do?' The non-lawyer will, however, understand the need for a test which can be used in all cases, recognising the risks of injustice were there to be no rules.

It is not possible to compile a list of actions or omissions which will amount to a breach of the duty of care but past cases can be used to give guidance as to the matters which should be taken into account when deciding on appropriate action.

The standard is *objective*, thus the personal difficulties which might be encountered by a particular defendant are rarely relevant. The issue is looked at from the point of view of the claimant who is entitled to expect the courts to give protection from actions which do not conform to an acceptable standard. The concept decides whether or not the defendant was careless and also decides the level of safety the claimant is entitled, in the circumstances, to expect.

In *Bourhill v Young* (1943) Lord Macmillan said,

> The duty to take care is the duty to avoid doing or omitting to do anything the doing or omitting of which may have as its reasonable and probable consequence injury to others, and the duty is owed to those to whom injury may reasonably and probably be anticipated if the duty is not observed.

In *Glasgow Corporation v Muir* (1943) Lord Macmillan further explained that the test of the reasonable man

> eliminates the personal equation and is independent of the idiosyncrasies of the particular person whose conduct is in question. The reasonable man is presumed to be free both from over-apprehension and from over-confidence.

The reasonable man reaches a decision which carefully balances all the known facts, and those facts which can be anticipated, to enable him to identify any risk. This allows him to opt for a course of action or omission which minimises the risk to any person likely to be affected by it. Case law provides some useful examples but it must be remembered that each case will be decided on its own particular facts.

In *Bolton v Stone* (1951) Lord Reid said,

> the test to be applied is whether the risk of damage to a person on the road was so small that a reasonable man in the position of [the cricket club], considering the matter from the point of view of safety, would have thought it right to refrain from taking steps to prevent the danger. I think that it would be right to take into account not only how remote is the chance that a person might be struck but also how serious the consequences are likely to be if a person is struck.

In the same case, Lord Radcliffe said,

> It seems to me that a reasonable man, taking account of the chances of an accident happening, would not have felt himself called upon either to abandon the use of the ground for cricket or to increase the height of his surrounding fences.

> **Bolton v Stone** (1951)
> In this case the claimant was standing in a street when she was struck and injured by a cricket ball. The wicket was some 65 metres from a 5 metre high fence and some 90 metres from the claimant herself. The evidence was that a similar incident had occurred only six times in the previous 28 years and that on each of the previous occasions, no one had been injured and nothing had been damaged. Mrs Bolton received no compensation despite her serious injuries.

A case heard shortly after *Bolton v Stone* provides a good example of other matters which might influence a court in reaching its decision. In *Paris v Stepney Borough Council* (1951) the claimant, who was sighted in only one eye, was employed to do a job which entailed a small risk of causing eye-injury. The accident happened and as a result Mr Paris was totally blind. His original disability did not increase the risk that he, rather than another member of the workforce, would sustain injury but clearly the potential consequences for him were far worse than those for other employees who were fully sighted. A reasonable employer would have recognised this fact and would have provided Mr Paris with protective eye-wear even though this, at that time, would not have been required for other employees.

The practicability of taking precautions will also be relevant. In *Latimer v AEC Ltd* (1952), a case in which the claimant alleged a factory owner was negligent when he was injured by slipping on an oily floor, Lord Denning held that the owners' attempts to minimise the risk by putting sawdust down had fulfilled the duty of care to their employees. Although all risk could have been avoided by closing the factory, to do so would have been unreasonable:

> In every case of foreseeable risk, it is a matter of balancing the risk against the measures necessary to eliminate it. It is only negligence if, on balance, the defendant did something he ought not to have done, or omitted to do something which he ought to have done … it is quite clear the defendants did everything they could reasonably be expected to do. It would be quite unreasonable … to expect them to send all the men home.

So far one can perhaps argue that the guidance is merely that which would be provided by common sense. It is more difficult to grasp that the same rules apply to all, those expert in a particular skill or art and those who are novices. It is worth restating that the matter is always

Figure 3.1

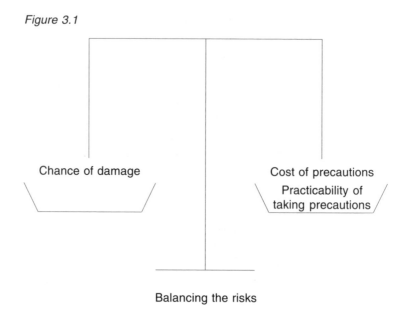

Chance of damage

Cost of precautions
Practicability of
taking precautions

Balancing the risks

looked at from the point of view of the claimant – what is the claimant reasonably entitled to expect from the defendant in relation to safeguarding the claimant?

It has long been established that the claimant is entitled to expect that the defendant will exercise a degree of care which is appropriate to the task which the defendant has undertaken. In *Nettleship v Weston* (1971), a case involving alleged negligent driving by a learner-driver, Lord Denning said that the civil law 'requires of him the same standard of care as any other driver' despite the fact that 'morally the learner-driver is not at fault'. Lord Denning admitted that his view was in part based on the fact that the learner was the one covered by insurance and to reach a different decision might mean that the claimant could not recover damages. This is an illustration of the way in which public policy can play a part in assisting the decision of a court.

The view that anyone undertaking a task which involves risk should be reasonably competent and will be liable if they fail to demonstrate that level of competence has led many professional codes of practice/ conduct to state that a professional is expected to refuse to undertake any task where such competence is lacking. This is of course a source of much difficulty in relation to those whose jobs may be at stake if the employer does not accept that the refusal is reasonable and/or refuses to provide necessary training.

The courts have not, however, changed their basic view following *Nettleship v Weston*. In *Wilsher v Essex Area Health Authority* (1987), a case concerning alleged medical negligence, Lord Mustill said that, it would be a false step to subordinate the legitimate expectation of the patient that he will receive from each person concerned with his care a degree of skill appropriate to the task which he undertakes, to an understandable wish to minimise the psychological and financial pressures on young doctors.

The court did, however, acknowledge that although the junior doctor had primary liability, his employers could also bear primary responsibility, alongside him, for failure to employ properly qualified staff to carry out the necessary treatment.

> ### *Wilsher v Essex Area Health Authority* (1987)
> A child was born prematurely, suffering from, among other problems, oxygen deficiency. A 'junior and inexperienced' doctor was a member of the team caring for the child in a paediatric intensive care unit. The junior doctor placed a catheter in the vein rather than the artery to monitor blood oxygen levels. The mistake was not noticed for several days during which the child received excess oxygen. The child was later diagnosed as suffering from severe visual impairment. This could have been caused by one of a number of problems including the excess oxygen. As will be seen, this case has important implications in deciding when damages should be payable. Suffice it to say for the moment, that the child, despite the doctor's negligence, did not receive any compensation. The issue of whether or not damages should have been payable is dealt with later in this section.

---

1   Do you think that A. P. Herbert's description of the 'reasonable man' as 'devoid of any human weakness, with not one single saving vice' is accurate?
2   Try to create your own summary of what you believe the reasonable man to be.

Professionals

As has been seen, there is only one standard of care required, that of the reasonable man. It is obvious, however, that people vary in the degree of expertise which each has and thus in reality differing standards are expected. A person rendering first aid will be expected to have the level of skill appropriate to a first aider while a doctor in an accident and emergency department will be expected to have the level of skill appropriate to such specialism.

The judges do not pretend to have all the necessary knowledge to be able to set a standard and depend on the evidence which they hear to reach a decision. Where specialist knowledge is required, it is inevitable that the judges have to rely on the opinions of those who are expert in that particular field. Most of the cases which have come before the courts concerning such issues relate to medical negligence claims, but the rules apply to all those who profess to have expert knowledge or who undertake a particular task.

This could mean that a professional is judged by others working in the same field and thus the accusation could be made that professionals are not subject to the same law as others, that the profession is judge in its own cause. The judges have tried to ensure that at the end of the day, the decision as to whether or not a proper standard has been met is made by the judges, not by other members of the same profession.

In *Lanphier v Phipos* (1838) Lord Tindale said of a professional,

> he undertakes to bring a fair, reasonable and competent degree of skill.

In *Bolam v Friern Hospital Management Committee* (1957) McNair J said,

> A man need not possess the highest expert skill; it is ... sufficient if he exercises the ordinary skill of an ordinary competent man exercising that particular art.

He went on to state what has become known as the **Bolam principle** – a doctor

> is not guilty of negligence if he has acted in accordance with a practice accepted as proper by a responsible body of medical men skilled in that particular art.

It was made clear that this did not mean that medical opinion needed to be unanimous as to the practice. There is scope for disagreement but a person who goes against virtually the whole body of professional opinion is unlikely to have exercised a sufficient standard of care.

The Bolam principle was approved in later cases and came to be seen as the only test for an appropriate standard of practice by any professional, not just doctors. It began to be suggested, particularly in medical cases, that the judges were deferring too much to the professions and failing to ensure that an appropriate standard had been set, thus allowing the professions to 'close ranks' at the expense of the victims. This argument was rejected by Hirst J in *Hills v Potter* (1984) when he said,

I do not accept the argument that by adopting the Bolam principle, the court in effect abdicates its power of decision to the doctors. In every case the court must be satisfied that the standard contended for on their behalf accords with that upheld by a substantial body of medical opinion, and that this body of medical opinion is both respectable and responsible, and experienced in this particular field of medicine.

More recently in *Bolitho v City and Hackney Health Authority* (1997) Lord Browne-Wilkinson said,

if it can be demonstrated that the professional opinion is not capable of withstanding logical analysis, the judge is entitled to hold that the body of opinion is not reasonable or responsible.

It may seem that this disposes of the problems posed by Bolam but Lord Browne-Wilkinson went on to say,

It is only where a judge can be satisfied that the body of expert opinion cannot be logically supported at all that such opinion will not provide the benchmark by reference to which the defendant's conduct falls to be assessed.

It is clear that it will continue to be a defence for a professional to show that the action was in accordance with the opinion of a reasonable and responsible body of professional opinion even where there are differing views held by groups of professionals. The judge will not be concerned to decide which of two competing opinions, both of which are reasonable and responsible, is in fact the right one. It is likely that judges will only very rarely come to the conclusion that an opinion is unreasonable.

Professionals have a duty to ensure that they keep up to date although they are not expected to read every obscure article and adjust practice in the light of that one article. In *Crawford v Board of Governors of Charing Cross Hospital* (*The Times*, 8 December 1953), a doctor was not liable for failing to adjust his practice in the light of one article published in the *Lancet* six months previously.

An error of judgment or breach of duty?

Generally the standard of the reasonable man does not ensure that an accident never happens, merely that all reasonable precautions have been taken. Although it has been argued that an error of professional judgment cannot amount to a breach of the duty of care, at the end of the day the courts have to decide what would have been an appropriate standard, and whether or not the defendant lived up to that standard. Case law has not always made this clear, as the following cases indicate.

In *Whitehouse v Jordan* (1980), Lord Denning, giving judgment in the Court of Appeal, stated his firmly held view that 'in a professional man, an error of judgment is not negligent'. Lord Denning was influenced by his view that to hold otherwise would be to make the professional wary of the 'dagger at his back'. In other words, a professional should not be made to feel afraid that each and every error may lead to liability in negligence. Lord Denning's views were rejected by the House of Lords where Lord Fraser said,

> The true position is that an error of judgement may, or may not, be negligent; it depends on the nature of the error. If it is one that would not have been made by a reasonably competent professional man professing to have the standard and type of skill that the defendant held himself out as having, and acting with ordinary care, then it is negligent. If, on the other hand, it is an error that such a man, acting with ordinary care, might have made, then it is not negligent.

Whitehouse v Jordan (1980)

The defendant was a senior doctor, due to deliver a child whose mother had been through a high-risk pregnancy. She had been in labour for 22 hours when the defendant decided to see if the child could be assisted by a forceps delivery. The defendant tried several times to pull the baby free by clamping forceps round the baby's head. It did not work and the child was later delivered by caesarian section. As a result of the birth difficulties, the child suffered cerebral palsy caused by asphyxiation, allegedly caused by the doctor pulling too long and too hard on the forceps. It was held that the doctor had made an error of judgement and was not negligent. No compensation was paid.

An error of judgement may be more excusable in circumstances where the defendant does not have time to think how to deal with an emergency. In *Wooldridge v Sumner* (1963) Lord Diplock, dealing with a claim by a spectator who had been injured at a horse show, said

> a participant in a game or competition gets into the circumstances in which he has no time or very little time to think, by his decision to take part in the game or competition at all … If in the course of the game or competition, at a moment when he really has not time to think, a participant by mistake takes a wrong measure, he is not to be held guilty of any negligence.

> ### *Wooldridge v Sumner* (1963)
> The claimant was a photographer who attended a major horse show. The edge of the arena was marked out by tubs planted with shrubs and Mr W stood just behind these. A horse called 'Work of Art' was being ridden by a very experienced and capable rider on behalf of the defendant. As the horse was attempting to take a corner it was going too fast and ran through the line of tubs, injuring Mr W. The court held that in the heat of the moment the rider had made an error of judgement and was not negligent.

Children

In theory at least there would appear to be no reason why a child should not be expected to exercise the same level of care as an adult. This view fails to take account of the very different abilities and understanding shown by children at various stages of growing up. The law has traditionally sought to protect children both from exploitation and from their own unwise actions. It is quite clear that a person may suffer damage as a result of a child's carelessness; what is not so clear is that the child should bear legal responsibility for such actions.

There are to date no English cases dealing directly with this point. In an Australian case, *McHale v Watson* (1966), the Australian High Court took the view that a child should be judged by the standard, not of the reasonable man, but of the ordinary child of the same age as the defendant. The Canadian courts have taken a similar view. It seems that this may be the view of an English court. In *Mullin v Richards* (1998) the Court of Appeal held that a trial judge had erred when he failed to take account of the fact that both parties were aged only 15 years.

> ### *Mullin v Richards* (1998)
> Two schoolgirls, Teresa and Heidi both aged 15, had a sword fight with plastic rulers. One ruler snapped and Teresa suffered eye injury when a piece of plastic flew into her eye. At first instance, the judge held that the injury was foreseeable and that Teresa was entitled to compensation. The Court of Appeal held that the judge had erred when he failed to take into account the fact of the girls' age. It held that what had happened was simply a children's game and Heidi's appeal was allowed.

> Do you agree with the judges in *Mullin v Richards* that at 15 the girls were simply playing a children's game? At what age do you think that a child is old enough to have responsibility for its own carelessness?

In some circumstances it is argued that parents should have legal responsibility for the actions of their children. In relation to the law of torts, a parent does not have such responsibility, but may have responsibility for their own failure; for example, for their own negligence in supervising the child, or for failure to ensure that a child undertaking an activity which is dangerous to others is given proper instruction.

> Should parents have liability for their child's negligent actions? At what age should such responsibility cease?

Proof of fault

The usual civil rules as to the burden of proof apply to any claim for negligence. The claimant therefore has to prove that a duty was owed by the defendant to the claimant and that, on the balance of probabilities, the defendant was in breach of that duty. (The resulting damage must also be proved – see pp. 68–71.)

In many cases, the question of proof does not raise a problem for the victim. Often the issue is one of fact; for example, was the defendant driving too fast in the circumstances or not? In some cases the victim will not find it to be so simple. How can a person who is unconscious prove what happened while they were on the operating table; how does a person struck on the head by a falling object prove that the object fell as a result of the defendant's negligence?

To assist victims in this kind of situation, the courts have shifted the burden of proof to the defendant to a limited extent. Victims must still show that they were owed a duty of care but the courts may then assume, by way of inference from proved facts, that the accident would not have happened unless the defendant had been negligent. The doctrine has been known for many years as the doctrine of *res ipsa loquitur*. Following the Woolf reforms and the abolition of the use of Latin, it is now known as 'the thing speaks for itself'. A classic example of the doctrine was given by Lord Denning in a case involving an allegation of negligence by a doctor:

> If the plaintiff had to prove that some particular doctor or nurse was negligent, he would not be able to do it. But he was not put to that impossible task: he says, 'I went into hospital to be cured of

two stiff fingers. I have come out with four stiff fingers and my hand is useless. That should not have happened if due care had been used. Explain it if you can.'

(*Cassidy v Ministry of Health* [1951])

The doctrine can only be used where there is no other explanation of the facts. The rules were stated by Lord Erle in *Scott v St Katherine Docks Co* (1865) when he said,

> where the thing is shown to be under the management of the defendant or his servants, and the accident is such as in the ordinary course of things does not happen if those who have the management use proper care, it affords reasonable evidence, in the absence of explanation by the defendant, that the accident arose from want of care.

> ### *Scott v St Katherine Docks Ltd* (1865)
> Mr S was visiting the defendants' premises, a warehouse, when a large bag of sugar fell on him. The defendants' employees had been unloading sugar nearby using a hoist but there was nothing to show what had actually happened beyond the fact that the bag had undoubtedly fallen and struck Mr S. Mr S was successful in his claim only because the courts were prepared to accept that the accident would not have happened had it not been for carelessness by someone somewhere.

Once it has been established that the doctrine applies, and this will only be possible where there is no other obvious explanation, it is open for the defendant to show that in fact there was no negligence; in other words, that the defendant throughout complied with the standard of the 'reasonable man'.

A defendant may refute the implication of breach of the duty of care by putting forward some other reasonable explanation of the facts. One example of the effect of this rule is given by *Pearson v North Western Gas Board* (1968). Mrs Pearson claimed damages for injuries which she had suffered and for the death of her husband when a gas main exploded and destroyed their home. At first sight it would seem that the doctrine must apply and that she would be able to establish her case. The defendants, however, were able to show that the leak of gas was unpredictable and was possibly caused by the passage of heavy vehicles causing the main to fracture. Mrs Pearson lost her case.

Where, however, no reasonable explanation can be given, the defendants may well find themselves liable. In *Ward v Tesco Stores Ltd*

(1976), the claimant succeeded when she slipped on some yoghurt which had been spilled and not wiped up. The floor was cleaned five or six times daily and also if a spillage was noticed. There was no evidence to show how long the yoghurt had been on the floor before the claimant fell, nor indeed to show how the yoghurt had come to be spilt in the first place. The courts took the inference that there had been negligence on the part of the supermarket and the claimant was therefore able to succeed in her claim on the basis of the doctrine.

Causation and remoteness of damage

A person can only be liable for negligence if they have actually caused the damage suffered by the victim or in some way made a less than trivial contribution to it. A victim therefore has to prove not only that a duty is owed by the defendant in the circumstances, and that the defendant was in breach of that duty, but also that as a result the victim suffered damage. The damage may be caused to either the person of the victim or to property. Special rules apply where there is more than one cause of the damage.

The 'but for' test

The test simply asks, 'Would the damage have occurred had it not been for the breach of duty?' It is a simple test and will sometimes provide the answer to the claimant's action.

The best known example of the way in which the test works is found in *Barnett v Chelsea & Kensington Hospital Management Committee* (1969). In this case the claimant was able to establish the existence of a duty and breach, but she was unable to succeed in her action because she could not prove that the breach had in any way contributed to the damage.

> ### *Barnett v Chelsea & Kensington Hospital Management Committee* (1969)
> Mr B and two colleagues were on duty as night-watchmen. At about 5 a.m. they all drank some tea and soon afterwards they all began to be sick. At about 8 a.m. they went to the local hospital's casualty unit where they were seen by a nurse. Mr B was obviously very ill and left it to his colleagues to explain to the nurse what had happened. The nurse rang through to the duty doctor but he was himself ill and told the nurse to tell the men to go away and consult their own

general practitioners. The men did as they were told and left the hospital. By 2 p.m. the same day Mr B had died. His widow sued on his behalf, alleging negligence by the nurse and the doctor for which the hospital management would have liability as employers. The widow was able to establish that a duty of care was owed to her late husband and that there had been a breach of that duty. The forensic evidence, however, showed that Mr B died as a result of arsenic poisoning and that, even if he had been admitted to the hospital, nothing could have been done to save him. Mr B's death was not caused by the actions of the hospital staff, nor did such actions contribute in any way to his death. The case remains a mystery – the inquest verdict was 'murder by person or persons unknown'.

The 'but for' test where there is more than one possible cause

Problems can sometimes arise where there is more than one possible cause of damage. It is essential that the victim proves a link between the breach of duty and the damage. An example of the operation of this rule is found in *Wilsher v Essex Area Health Authority* (1987), where it was not possible to prove the necessary link and, despite a possible but unproven link with the problems of the equipment monitoring blood oxygen levels, the claimant was unable to recover compensation (see p.61 for facts).

Strict application of these rules could lead to injustice and the courts have taken some limited steps towards mitigating this. In *Bonnington Castings Ltd v Wardlaw* (1956), it was held that the claimant can succeed if it is possible to establish that the breach was a material cause of the damage, even though it was not the only cause.

Bonnington Castings Ltd v Wardlaw (1956)

Mr W worked in an atmosphere in which he inhaled silica dust. As a result he contracted pneumoconiosis. The court, awarding him damages against his employers for breach of the duty of care, was prepared to divide the dust into 'innocent' dust, in respect of which the employers were not in breach, and 'guilty' dust from the employers' failure to maintain dust extraction equipment to an appropriate standard. Mr W did not have to prove whether it was the 'innocent' dust or the 'guilty' dust which was responsible for his condition.

> Lord Reid said that all that was necessary was that the claimant should prove 'on the balance of probabilities the breach of duty caused or materially contributed to his injury'.

In the later case of *McGhee v National Coal Board* (1972) the defendants were held liable on the basis that their breach of duty materially increased the risk to the claimant and was therefore a material cause.

McGhee v National Coal Board (1972)

Mr McGhee worked in a brick-kiln and contracted dermatitis as a result of his exposure to brick dust. The defendants were not liable for the exposure to brick dust during working hours, but Mr McGhee's exposure was unnecessarily prolonged by the defendant's negligent failure to provide adequate washing facilities. The defendants were held to be liable as their failure made the injury to Mr McGhee more probable.

The law in this area was considered in detail by the House of Lords in 2002.

Fairchild v Glenhaven Funeral Services Ltd & Others (2002)

Mr Fairchild was employed at different times and for varying periods by a number of employers including the defendants. During his employment Mr Fairchild inhaled substantial quantities of asbestos fibres which are known to cause mesothelioma (a fatal form of lung cancer). While the risk was known, the actual cause of the disease is not understood. It could be one fibre of asbestos dust, a few fibres or many fibres. It is known that the risk increases with the amount of fibres inhaled. The disease can develop over a period of 30 to 40 years after exposure. Mr Fairchild died and his widow sued the defendants, alleging that they had been in breach of their duty of care to protect Mr Fairchild from exposure to asbestos fibres. The problem was that it was impossible to say when the disease had been triggered. Both defendants admitted that the exposure had occurred but argued that on the basis of the 'but for' test, the claimant had to prove in which employment the disease had been triggered. This could not be done and therefore neither employer could be found to be liable as either could have been. The claimant lost in the Court of Appeal and the case went, with two similar cases, to the House of Lords.

The judges were agreed that it would be unjust were the defendants able to escape liability for breach of duty because it was scientifically impossible to prove who was in fact responsible. The judges recognised that this would impose injustice on the innocent employer but, on policy grounds, the need to compensate the victim for a disease which could only have been caused by a breach of duty outweighed any injustice to the employers. The breach of duty by each employer had materially increased the risk that Mr Fairchild would develop the disease. This was a sufficient causal link and the defendants were liable.

Fairchild is clearly a policy decision and the judges were at pains to say that the decision depended on the very special circumstances of the case. It does, however, confirm that a breach of duty which materially increases the risk of injury is enough to create a causal link between the injury and the breach of duty.

It might be thought that the decision in *Wilsher v Essex Area Health Authority* (1987) would be decided differently today but there is a crucial difference between Wilsher and Fairchild. In Wilsher the cause of the baby's visual impairment was unknown save that there were six different possible causes. In Fairchild there was only one possible cause, the problem was that it was unknown which employer was responsible.

> Look back to the Introduction to the book. Do you believe that the 'but for' test means that the law fails to give justice to some victims?

The 'but for' test and loss of a chance

In cases concerning a claim for breach of contract, it is well established that damages can be assessed by reference to the lost chance of securing a valuable advantage (*Chaplin v Hicks* [1911]). The position is not so clear-cut in relation to the tort of negligence.

In 1987, following *McGhee*, it seemed that the courts might be prepared to deal with claims on the basis of the chance of loss rather than on 'all or nothing'. *Hotson v East Berkshire Health Authority* (1987) concerned a claim by a boy who had fallen out of a tree and suffered an injury to his hip. When he reached hospital, treatment was badly delayed. As a result of all this, the boy was left with substantial disability.

The boy claimed compensation from the hospital authorities. It was found, by the trial judge, that immediately after the accident there was a 75 per cent chance that the boy would suffer disability; this had been changed into a 100 per cent certainty by the delay in treatment. The trial judge therefore awarded the boy 25 per cent damages against the hospital which had destroyed his chance of full recovery.

On appeal to the House of Lords, the judges held that the issue was simply one of causation on the balance of probabilities and that on the balance of probabilities, the disability was caused by the fall and therefore the hospital was not liable. The judges expressly left open the possibility that had the percentage chance of full recovery been greater, the decision might have been different.

Remoteness of damage

The victim of negligence must establish that it was reasonably foreseeable that the wrongdoer's act or omission would cause damage to someone. A problem can arise, however, when the consequences of the wrongful act are not quite as might have been anticipated. As has already been seen, the courts try to avoid 'indeterminate liability' and to this end, rules have been formulated to decide for what damage the defendant should be liable.

In most cases, the consequences are as might have been foreseen; for example, it is not unexpected that a car and the people in it will suffer damage and injury if another driver negligently causes an accident. The facts of the two leading cases on the issue of remoteness illustrate the difficulties that can arise.

> ***Re Polemis and Furness Withy & Co Ltd*** (1921)
> The *Polemis*, a cargo ship, was being unloaded when a wooden plank was dropped into the hold. The plank struck a spark which ignited petrol vapour which had accumulated in the hold. The resulting fire destroyed the ship.
>
> ***The Wagon Mound***, more correctly cited as ***Overseas Tankship (UK) Ltd v Morts Dock & Engineering Co, the Wagon Mound*** (1961)
> The *SS Wagon Mound* was moored in Sydney Harbour. As she was bunkering (taking on oil), oil was negligently spilled into the waters of the harbour. The *Wagon Mound* upped anchor and sailed away, leaving the oil drifting towards a wharf where welding work was being carried out on another ship. The welders were told that it was safe to carry on

> welding as the oil would not ignite. What was not anticipated
> was that a piece of molten metal from the welding would
> fall onto cotton waste and ignite the waste which in turn set
> fire to the oil. The ship which was being repaired and the
> wharf were damaged.

In *Re Polemis* the original decision was that the damage caused by
dropping a plank of wood could not reasonably have been anticipated.
When the matter was heard on appeal, however, Lord Scrutton said,

> if the act would or might probably cause damage, the fact that the
> damage it in fact causes is not the exact kind of damage one would
> expect is immaterial, so long as the damage is in fact directly
> traceable to the negligent act, and not due to the operation of
> independent causes having no connection with the negligent act.

Although the judges agreed that the consequences could not have
been foreseen, it was foreseeable that some damage, for example a
dent in the ship, would be caused by the negligent act and therefore
the employers of the careless dock worker were liable for the loss of
the ship.

Re Polemis is no longer regarded as good law because of the decision
in *The Wagon Mound*, when the judges recognised the injustice which
the rule in *Re Polemis* could cause and attempted to formulate more
suitable rules. *Re Polemis* had imposed liability for 'the direct and
natural' consequences of a negligent act, regardless of whether or not
those particular consequences had been reasonably foreseeable. In
The Wagon Mound [No 1] Lord Simonds said,

> the essential factor in determining liability is whether the damage
> is of such a kind as the reasonable man should have foreseen.
> Thus foreseeability becomes the effective test.

The owners of the *Wagon Mound* were not liable for the damage to
the wharf as the possibility of such damage being caused by fire was
not reasonably foreseeable.

In later cases, the courts have endeavoured to find some principles
which will help to determine whether or not unexpected consequences
are in fact reasonably foreseeable while still acknowledging the need
for some limitation of liability for such consequences.

One of the principles acknowledged by the courts has become
known as 'the egg-shell skull' principle, whereby once the possibility

of damage is foreseen, the defendant must take his victim as he finds him. This means that the defendant may be liable where the consequences to the claimant are more serious than might have been anticipated because of some idiosyncracy peculiar to the victim. *Robinson* and *Smith* are the two key cases here.

> **Robinson v Post Office** (1974)
> Mr R slipped on an oily ladder and cut his leg. When he went to the doctor he was given a tetanus injection to which he was allergic. As a result he suffered from encephalitis.

In *Robinson v Post Office*, although the claimant's allergy was not actually foreseen, it was reasonably foreseeable that he would be given the injection and that he might prove to be allergic to it, therefore he recovered full compensation.

> **Smith v Leech Brain & Co Ltd** (1961)
> Mrs S's husband was employed by the defendants. His job meant that he had to lower articles into a tank which contained molten metal. The larger items were lowered by an overhead crane while Mr S sheltered behind a sheet of corrugated iron. An accident occurred and Mr S was struck on the lip by a piece of molten metal. He eventually died of cancer. Forensic evidence showed that the original burn had activated pre-cancerous cells and thus triggered the development of the cancer from which he died.

Although it is not reasonably foreseeable that a person may suffer a particular result from a negligent action, the fact that injury, in the case of Mr S a burn, is foreseeable means that the defendant is liable for all the consequences of that injury including, in this particular case, the death of Mr S from cancer.

Remember that slightly different rules apply where the injury complained of amounts to nervous shock suffered by a secondary victim. (*Page v Smith* [1995].)

Where the injury is not caused by a series of actions which are foreseeable, the defendant's liability may well depend on whether the general nature or type of injury is in fact foreseeable.

> ### *Hughes v Lord Advocate* (1964)
> The Post Office had been working on repairing cables. They got access to the cables by means of a manhole. When they went for a break, the men left the manhole open but covered by a tent and drew up the ladder so that others could not gain access. There were red paraffin lamps around the manhole warning of the danger. Hughes (aged 10) and another boy were playing around the area and knocked one of the paraffin lamps into the hole, causing an explosion. Hughes was seriously burned by the flames when he fell into the hole.

The precise sequence of events may not be foreseeable, but in circumstances like those in *Hughes v Lord Advocate*, it was foreseeable that a child might be burned by the lamp. The child was in fact injured by being burned and the defendants were therefore liable. Lord Guest said,

> it is sufficient if the accident which occurs is of a type which should have been foreseeable by a reasonably careful person.

Although it may seem that the position is clear, in *Doughty v Turner Manufacturing Co Ltd* (1964) some problems were raised. The facts were similar to those of *Smith v Leech Brain* in that the victim was injured by an explosion of molten liquid. In *Doughty v Turner* the explosion was caused by an unforeseeable chemical change caused when a lid inadvertently fell into a vat. As the chemical change was unforeseeable in the light of knowledge at that time, the defendants were not liable.

Once the risk of injury is established, it seems that the usual rules as to the proof of breach of duty apply so that the state of scientific knowledge at the date of the accident becomes relevant.

> ### *Tremain v Pike* (1969)
> In this case a water trough, used by Mr T in the course of his employment as a dairyman to wash his hands, was shown to be contaminated by rats. As a result Mr T contracted Weil's disease, which he alleged was due to the defendant's negligence in failing to take precautions against such infection. It was held, however, that the defendants had taken all reasonable precautions in the light of knowledge at the time of the extent of the risk of infection, and they were therefore not liable.

Intervening acts of a third party

In some cases, more than one incident occurs. The effect of a second or subsequent incident on the liability of the original wrongdoer varies according to the particular circumstances.

Where the two incidents combine to cause the claimant's injury or damage, it is a relatively straightforward matter for the total damages payable to the claimant to be assessed and then apportioned between the various defendants. The Civil Liability (Contribution) Act 1978 contains provisions which mean that whichever wrongdoer the claimant sues, that wrongdoer can obtain a contribution reflecting the responsibility of the other wrongdoer.

> You are in a car which has stopped in a line of traffic. You have not put the handbrake on. Suddenly the car behind you collides with your car and pushes it into the car in front. The accident was caused by a car which had gone into the back of the vehicle behind yours. You have received a letter from the owner of the car in front of you claiming the cost of repairs. How will the court decide who is liable to pay for what?

The situation is less straightforward where the incidents are not linked in any way, and each causes its own type of damage.

If the adverse effects of the second incident are effectively wiped out by the first, the claimant may find that a wrongdoer escapes liability.

Performance Cars Ltd v Abraham (1962)
A vehicle driven by Mr A collided with the claimant's Rolls Royce, denting the bodywork which consequently required a re-spray. Mr A in fact escaped liability for the cost of the repair as the car had previously been damaged in the same place, and a respray was already required because of the first accident.

A second incident can have a similar effect, wiping out liability for the first incident where the damage caused by the second incident overwhelms that caused by the first.

> ### Carslogie Steamship Co Ltd v Royal Norwegian Government (1952)
>
> A ship was damaged by a collision caused by the defendant's negligence. The ship was repaired to make it seaworthy and then sent across the Atlantic Ocean for a more permanent repair to be made. On the way the ship was damaged very severely by stormy weather, and as a result had to spend 51 days in dry dock instead of the 10 days originally estimated. It was held that as the repairs caused by the storm damage would in any event have taken the full 51 days, there could be no liability on the part of the defendant for the loss of use of the ship.

In *Carslogie* it is clear that the second incident was an 'innocent' cause – in other words, the weather. If the second incident is itself a tort, the situation will be different as the second wrongdoer 'takes the victim as he finds him', in other words, the second wrongdoer will be liable for the additional damage that has been caused.

> ### Baker v Willoughby (1970)
>
> Mr B was injured in a car accident due to the negligent driving of Mr W. As a result, Mr B was left with a permanently stiff ankle. Before the trial of his claim against Mr W, Mr B was shot in the same leg which then had to be amputated. Mr W argued that his liability should be limited to the loss caused by the first accident coming to an end once the later incident occurred and increased Mr B's loss; the amputation and any after-effects were not his responsibility. The court held that this was not the case – Mr W was liable for damages which reflected the loss caused by a permanently stiff leg. The gunman, if caught and sued, would have been liable for the additional loss caused by the amputation.

The reasoning in *Baker v Willoughby* was criticised by the House of Lords in the later case of *Jobling v Associated Dairies Ltd* (1981): these were the facts of the case.

Jobling v Associated Dairies Ltd (1981)

Mr J was the manager of a shop belonging to the defendant. In 1973 he slipped on the floor of a meat refrigerator and damaged his back. The defendants were liable for the fall. As a result of the accident, Mr J's earning ability was cut by 50 per cent. In 1976 Mr J became totally disabled by the onset of spondylotic myelopathy which was not in any way related to the accident. He claimed that the defendants should pay damages on a basis which ignored the onset of his illness and the effect that the illness had on his earning capacity. The court held that he was only entitled to be compensated for loss of earning capacity from 1973 to the time when he became incapable of working because of the illness.

Lord Keith said, during the course of his judgment:

In the case of supervening illness, it is appropriate to keep in view that this is one of the ordinary vicissitudes of life, and when one is comparing the situation resulting from the accident with the situation, had there been no accident, to recognise that the illness would have overtaken the plaintiff in any event, so that it cannot be disregarded in arriving at proper compensation, and no more than proper compensation.

The House of Lords did not overrule *Baker v Willoughby*, acknowledging that the decision was correct on the facts although no legal principle for this was given.

It has been suggested that the reasoning in *Baker v Willoughby* applies where the supervening event is a tort and that *Jobling v Associated Dairies Ltd* applies where the supervening event is non-tortious. However, on 13 June 2000 a case came before the Court of Appeal which has left the law in this area in even more confusion than it was before.

Heil v Rankin & Anor (2000)

Lord Justice Otton ruled that

there was no general rule that, when assessing damages for personal injury, future tortious acts had to be ignored even if they were a foreseeable, indeed likely, source of early termination of the claimant's employment.

The case concerned a police officer who, as a result of a car accident in 1993, suffered post-traumatic stress disorder and

> who was discharged from the police force. In assessing the damages payable by the defendant, the court held that the amount of damages should take account of the fact that some other incident, probably tortious, would in any event have led to early retirement. This is one of the 'viscissitudes' of life for a police officer and must be taken into account.

There can be no doubt that the courts are still searching for a general principle and that further developments can be expected.

Breaking the chain of causation (*novus actus interveniens*)

In some circumstances, the defendant's negligence has clearly been a part of the sequence of events which have led to the claimant's injury, but may not itself have been a direct cause of the damage. In such cases the court has to decide whether the wrongdoer is liable for all the consequences or whether the other acts have 'broken the chain of causation'.

In *Lord v Pacific Steam Navigation Co Ltd (The Oreposa)* (1943) Lord Wright highlighted the difficulties in deciding this issue when he said

> To break the chain of causation it must be shown that there is something unwarrantable, a new cause which disturbs the sequence of events, something which can be described as either unreasonable or extraneous or extrinsic.

A simpler way to state the matter is to ask whether there was 'such a direct relationship between the act of negligence and the injury that the one can be treated as flowing directly from the other'. (*The Oreposa* [1943] *per* Wright LJ)

A sensible starting point is to ask whether the subsequent act was 'reasonable' in the sense that it was part of the ordinary acts which could have been expected to arise from the original tortious act. If the subsequent act is both reasonable and foreseeable, the wrongdoer will be liable; if it is neither reasonable nor foreseeable, the defendant is unlikely to be liable.

Where the intervening act is performed by a third party in response to an emergency or dilemma created by the original wrongdoer, provided the third party behaves reasonably the act by the third party will not break the chain of causation – even if with the benefit of hindsight, it was ill-advised. In *Haynes v Harwood* (1935) Lord Greer said there will be no break in the chain if the intervention 'is the very kind of thing which is likely to happen if the want of care which is alleged takes place'.

> ***Haynes v Harwood* (1935)**
> A horse-drawn van was left unattended in a busy street. A lad threw stones at the horses which bolted. The claimant was injured as he tried to bring the horses to a halt. The driver was liable for the injuries which had resulted from his original negligent act in leaving the van unattended.

Although the concept of an intervening act is dealt with as a separate topic, the reader will realise that the cases are closely connected to, and decided by reference to, the rules already discussed, i.e. causation and remoteness of damage, the element of foreseeability being very relevant.

SUMMARY

Breach of duty of care

- all actions are judged by the standard of the 'reasonable man'

- the reasonable man balances the risks caused by the act or omission against:
    the likelihood of damage happening – *Bolton v Stone* (1952)
    the severity of any damage or injury which may be caused – *Paris v Stepney Borough Council* (1952)
    the cost and practicability of any precautions – *Latimer v AEC Ltd* (1952)

- the reasonable man is presumed to be
    competent in relation to the task being undertaken – *Wilsher v Essex A.H.A.* (1987)
    up to date with recent changes – *Crawford v Charing Cross Hospital* (1953)

Causation and damage

'But for' test

- would the damage have occurred if negligence had not occurred? – *Barnett v Chelsea & Kensington HMC* (1969), *Wilsher v Essex A.H.A* (1987)

- was the negligence a material cause of the damage? – *Bonnington Castings v Laidlaw* (1956)

- did the negligence materially increase the risk of damage – *McGhee v N.C.B.* (1972)

Loss of a chance

- the courts may be prepared to allow a claim when a chance of recovery or lessening the consequences is high and is lost because of negligence

- balance of probability test applies – *Hotson v East Berks A.H.A.* (1987)

Remoteness

- possibility of damage must be reasonably foreseeable – *The Wagon Mound* (1961)

- egg-shell skull principle applies – if damage is foreseeable, defendant takes claimant as the claimant is – *Robinson v Post Office* (1974), *Smith v Leech Brain* (1961)

- damage must be of type or kind that is reasonably foreseeable – *Hughes v Ld Advocate* (1964), *Doughty v Turner Manufacturing* (1964)

Intervening acts of third party

- if two or more incidents combine to produce the damage, all wrongdoers are liable

- if second incident is wiped out by the effect of the first, second wrongdoer escapes liability – *Performance Cars v Abraham* (1962)

- if second incident wipes out the effect of the first, the first wrongdoer escapes – *Carslogie Steamship Co v Norwegian Government* (1952)

- if second incident increases the damage, first wrongdoer remains liable for damage caused by first incident, second wrongdoer liable for the further deterioration – *Baker v Willoughby* (1970), *Jobling v Assoc. Dairies* (1981)

Breaking the chain of causation

- has something happened for which defendant should not be liable?

- was second act something which could be expected to arise as a consequence of the first? If so, chain is unbroken – *Haynes v Harwood* (1935)

QUESTIONS

1. Yasmin was riding her bicycle at night along a main road. The bicycle was not fitted with rear lights. Yasmin swerved into the path of a car

coming fast behind her and was knocked under the wheels of the car. She was taken to hospital where, owing to a major incident which meant the hospital was exceptionally busy, she was left waiting on the trolley, without having been examined, for several hours.

When she was eventually examined, it was found that she had a badly injured hip. As a result of the injury Yasmin will be unable to continue her career as a dancer. It is, however, certain that had she been examined earlier, it might have been possible to prevent permanent disability.

Yasmin wants to obtain compensation for her injuries. Advise her as to any claim she may have in negligence. (OCR 1998)

2. Eddie has recently started a course on bricklaying at his local college. Fiona, who lives next door to Eddie, asks him to build a wall between her garden and the pavement. He agrees to do so and says that he will not accept payment.

   About six weeks after the wall is completed, it collapses onto the pavement injuring Gerald, a passer-by. When the accident is investigated, it appears that the bricks were not laid properly and that, because of this, the wall was bound to collapse.

   Gerald wishes to claim damages for his injuries from Eddie. Consider his likely chances of success. (You do not need to discuss the possibility that Fiona may also have liability.) (OCR January 2002)

3. To what extent do the rules relating to causation and remoteness of damage achieve the aim of compensating a plaintiff for loss or injury? (Oxford 1996)

4. In an action for negligence 'it can be difficult to untangle the web of circumstances to pinpoint liability'. (Harpwood, *Principles of Tort Law*, Cavendish 1997).

   Consider to what extent the rules relating to causation ensure that liability is appropriately pin-pointed where there are several possible causes of the damage. (OCR 1999)

5. 'One of the purposes of the law of torts is said to be to encourage people to take care in what they do and to discourage activities that are dangerous to others.'

   Do the rules that courts apply in determining the standard of care in negligence achieve this aim? (Oxford 1997)

6. The reasonable man has been described as possessed of 'all solid virtues' and 'devoid of any human weakness.' (A. P. Herbert, *Uncommon Law*)

   Is this concept of the reasonable man appropriate for determining the standard of care of negligence? (Oxford 1995)

4 Negligence and dangerous premises

The Occupiers' Liability Acts 1957 and 1984

Although the problems posed by dangerous premises are addressed in this chapter, it is important to bear in mind that many of the matters already discussed will be relevant to this. We will come back to this point later.

The essence of the problem connected with dangerous premises is to identify those persons to whom a duty of care is owed, the person who owes that duty and the extent of the duty. This chapter starts by considering the distinction between lawful and unlawful visitors and discussing the identity of the person who owes the duty. It will go on to discuss the nature of the duty owed to particular categories of visitors.

Lawful and unlawful visitors

Until recently the occupier of land and premises could escape liability for negligent injury caused to someone on that land or in those premises by establishing that the person had no right to be there. This is an example of the maxim discussed under the heading 'Participation in an unlawful act (*ex turpi causa non oritur actio*)' in Chapter 5 (see pp. 106–107). A person classified as a trespasser was historically given no protection.

Problems could arise in respect of lawful visitors as the duty of care owed by an occupier varied according to the nature of the permission which allowed the person to enter the land. Parliament acted, following the recommendations of the *Third Report of the Law Reform Committee* (Cmd 9305) 1954, which dealt with some of these problems, and then passed the Occupiers' Liability Act 1957.

The Act ensures that any visitor with either express or implied permission or lawful authority to be on the land has the benefit of the protection of the Act. It is not difficult to identify such categories of visitors. Persons who have received a specific invitation are obviously included as are those who have paid for the right of entry, for example to a theme park or to a cinema. Others included are those who visit premises as a result of implied permission, for example a person delivering milk which has been ordered or a person delivering the post, or the fire brigade summoned to deal with a fire emergency. Lawful authority will extend to the police and other persons exercising rights granted by a warrant.

It might seem that casual visitors, for example canvassers on behalf of a political party, door-to-door salespersons and those seeking religious converts, are excluded but this will depend on the circumstances. As a general rule, any person has the right to come as far as a front door unless steps are taken to prevent this, for example by means of a locked gate or a notice forbidding entry. Once at the door, however, such persons must leave as soon as the occupier asks them to do so, although reasonable time for compliance must be allowed.

Unlawful visitors were given some protection by the Occupiers' Liability Act 1984 which was passed following a Report by the Law Commission published in 1976 (*Report on Liability for Damage or Injury to Trespassers and Related Questions of Occupiers Liability*, Law Commission, No 75, Cmnd. 6428). Although it is usual to refer to unlawful visitors as 'trespassers' the Act does in fact extend to persons exercising a private right of way over the land who were not clearly protected by the 1957 Act. 'Trespassers' are those who come onto the land unlawfully (without permission or authority) or who remain on land after having been asked to leave. (For more details about this, see Chapter 6, pp. 118–120.)

Make a list of all the people who have come to your home over the past week and decide whether or not they are lawful visitors and whether they have express or implied permission to be there.

By whom is the duty of care owed?

The Occupier

The title of both Acts refers to the 'Occupier'. In many cases this will be a person who is easily identified as having control over the premises and who is easily seen to have responsibility for the safety of visitors. In some cases it is neither easy to identify such person nor is the necessary degree of control obvious.

The facts of *Wheat v E Lacon & Co Ltd* (1966) illustrate the problem and show that occupation, for the purposes of the Act, can be by a person who is not in fact to be found on the premises if such a person has a sufficient degree of control.

> ### *Wheat v E Lacon & Co Ltd* (1966)
>
> Mr and Mrs R were the managers of a public house owned by the defendant brewery. Mrs R ran a private bed and breakfast business on the first floor of the public house using rooms which were part of the dwelling used by her and her husband. Mr and Mrs W were guests. At about 9 p.m., just as it was getting dark, Mr W fell down the stairs in the private dwelling and died. He fell because the handrail was too short and did not reach the foot of the stairs and because someone had removed the light bulb from the light at the top of the stairs. Obviously someone owed a duty of care to Mr W to ensure his safety while using the premises. But was this Mr and Mrs R or the defendant brewery?
>
> On examining the details of the legal agreement whereby Mr and Mrs R occupied the premises and ran the public house, it was held by the courts that the brewery was clearly in control of the public part of the premises, in other words it was the occupier; given that Mr and Mrs R were granted merely a licence to occupy the other part of the premises, the brewery retaining the right to do any necessary repairs, the brewery was the occupier of that part of the premises also and therefore the duty of care was owed to Mr W by the brewery.

Landlords

A landlord who has let premises and who retains no control over the state of repair of those premises will not usually be regarded as having control and therefore will not usually be in occupation. A landlord who retains control over 'common parts' such as the communal stairs and hallways used by all tenants, will be in occupation of those common parts.

Where the landlord has a duty or contractual obligation to the tenant to maintain and repair premises, s.4 Defective Premises Act 1972 (formerly s.4 Occupiers' Liability Act 1957) makes it clear that the landlord owes a duty to all persons who might reasonably be expected to enter the premises to ensure that they are reasonably safe provided the landlord knows or ought to have known of the defect which has caused the danger. The landlord's duty to maintain and repair may arise from the agreement with the tenant or from statute. The Landlord and Tenant Act 1985 (as amended by the Housing Act 1988) imposes a duty on a landlord in relation to the repair of a dwelling let for a period of less than seven years. A landlord is not liable if the tenant has failed to carry out necessary repairs under the tenant's covenant to keep the premises maintained and repaired.

Independent contractors

Where an independent contractor has been employed by an occupier who has taken reasonable care to ensure the contractor's competence to do the job to a safe standard and who has taken reasonable steps to ensure that the work has been properly done, the contractor will be regarded as liable on the usual principles of negligence, the duty owed by the occupier having been discharged by the care taken to choose, appoint and check on the contractor (s.2(4)(b) Occupiers' Liability Act 1957). The duty to check on the work is only to do what the employer can reasonably be expected to do. Cases which illustrate the courts' approach are *Haseldine v Daw* (1941) and *Woodward v Mayor of Hastings* (1954).

> ### *Haseldine v Daw* (1941)
> Mr D owned a block of flats and employed independent engineers to maintain and repair the lift. Mr H was injured when the lift fell to the bottom of the shaft after being negligently repaired. *Held*: Mr D had done all that he reasonably could to ensure the safety of the lift and had discharged the duty which he owed to visitors. He was not expected to have the technical expertise to double-check on the work done by the contractors and he was not liable to Mr H.

> ### *Woodward v Mayor of Hastings* (1954)
> A schoolboy slipped and fell on an icy step. The step had been cleaned negligently by a cleaner. It was not clear that the cleaner was an independent contractor but it was held that even if s/he had been, the school was still liable as no expert knowledge was needed to check whether or not the cleaning had been properly done.

An independent contractor may also be liable as occupier if the evidence shows a sufficient degree of control over the land or premises by the contractor. Note that an employer may be liable alongside the independent contractor where the activity being undertaken is especially hazardous. For a full discussion of this point see Chapter 8, page 182–183.

> You are at home when there is a knock at the door. The person standing there asks if you want your driveway re-laid. As you have been thinking of having this done for some time and the price seems to be a bargain you agree to have the work done. Once it is finished, the drive is very uneven and as a result the person delivering the milk has fallen and broken her ankle. Are you or the contractor liable to the injured person?

Lawful visitors

The statutory duty

The duty is set out in s.2 of the Occupiers' Liability Act 1957 which provides:

(1) An occupier of premises owes the 'common duty of care' to all his visitors, except in so far as he is free to and does extend, restrict, modify or exclude his duty to any visitor or visitors by agreement or otherwise.

(2) The common duty of care is a duty to take such care as in all the circumstances of the case is reasonable to see that the visitor will be reasonably safe in using the premises for the purposes for which he is invited or permitted by the occupier to be there.

Figure 4.1: Occupiers' liability

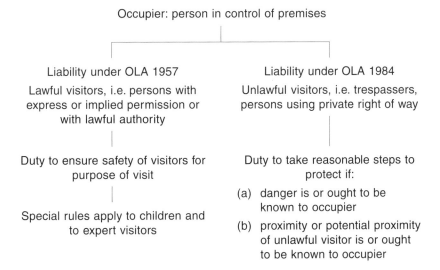

Occupier: person in control of premises

Liability under OLA 1957	Liability under OLA 1984
Lawful visitors, i.e. persons with express or implied permission or with lawful authority	Unlawful visitors, i.e. trespassers, persons using private right of way
Duty to ensure safety of visitors for purpose of visit	Duty to take reasonable steps to protect if:
Special rules apply to children and to expert visitors	(a) danger is or ought to be known to occupier (b) proximity or potential proximity of unlawful visitor is or ought to be known to occupier

The provisions of s.2 make it clear that some of the problems raised by the common law tort of negligence have been dealt with by the Act; there can be no argument as to the existence of a duty of care, thus the rules developed following *Donoghue v Stevenson* (see Chapter 2, pp. 29–30) do not need to be considered. It is not quite so simple to find out what the appropriate standard to fulfil the duty should be, but again the Act helps as it sets out, in s.2(2), what must be achieved. An occupier must take reasonable care to ensure the safety of visitors. This does not mean that an occupier will have liability whenever a visitor is injured; the duty is not absolute nor does the Act impose strict liability. The circumstances will always be very relevant.

Attention focuses on what steps the occupier takes to warn visitors of dangers or to prevent them from coming into the area of danger. In *Sawyer v H and G Simonds Ltd* (1966) the defendants were held to have taken reasonable steps to ensure the safety of visitors to their public house when it was found that there was an adequate system in place to ensure that broken glass was cleared up quickly. In *Martin v Middlesborough Corporation* (1965), failure to clear up a broken bottle in a school playground led to a finding of breach of duty by the education authority which had failed to put in place an adequate system for the disposal of bottles.

The duty may be discharged by giving a warning, provided this is sufficiently precise to enable the visitor to understand the nature of the danger and thus take steps to ensure his own safety. Section 2(4) of the Act specifically provides that a warning may suffice provided 'in all the circumstances it was enough to enable the visitor to be reasonably safe'.

> ### *Roles v Nathan* (1963)
> Douglas and Joseph Roles were chimney sweeps. The flues on which they were working were very long and a boiler engineer had been consulted. The engineer had advised that there should be no work done on the flues while the fire was lit because of the risk of carbon monoxide poisoning. The sweeps disregarded the expert advice which they had received and worked on the flues while the fire was lit, both men dying as a result of the build-up of carbon monoxide. The court held that the warnings had, in the circumstances, been sufficient to enable the sweeps to ensure their own safety and that the duty imposed by the Act had been discharged.

A warning sign may be effective but only if it contains enough information to alert the visitor to the nature of the danger. A warning that a floor is wet and therefore slippery may be enough. The character of the visitor must also be taken into account – not every one can read English, not every one is sighted and children may well fail to appreciate just how seriously the warning is meant. Obviously the notice must be clearly visible; for example it must not be obscured by vegetation, and it must be legible, and be repainted as necessary.

Expert visitors

The sweeps in *Roles v Nathan* were said to have been influenced by the fact that they regarded themselves as experts. The Act provides in s.2(3)(b) that

> an occupier may expect that a person, in the exercise of his calling, will appreciate and guard against any special risks ordinarily incident to it, so far as the occupier leaves him free to do so.

The court in *Roles v Nathan* found that it was reasonable to expect the sweeps, as specialists, to guard against the dangers arising from the blocked flues they had gone to sweep.

An occupier may be liable, even to an expert, for failure to make the expert aware of pertinent facts. The fact that the visitor is an expert is not of itself sufficient to free the occupier from liability. The expert can be expected to guard against the ordinary risks associated with the practice of the profession, but if the expert is injured as a foreseeable consequence of negligence by the occupier, the occupier will be liable. The following two cases are relevant here.

> **Salmon v Seafarer Restaurants Ltd (1983)**
> A fire in a fish and chip shop melted a seal on a gas meter which allowed gas to escape. An employee of the defendants negligently forgot to turn off a gas burner under a fat heater when he went home and as a result the fat overheated and caught fire. Mr S, a fireman, was injured. As the fire had been caused by negligence and Mr S had suffered injury as a consequence, he was entitled to compensation.
>
> **Ogwo v Taylor (1987)**
> Mr T used a blow-lamp to burn off paint on the eaves of his house and negligently set fire to the house. Mr O, a fireman, was injured while trying to put the fire out. As he had suffered injury because of Mr T's negligence, Mr O was entitled to compensation.

> You have noticed that the paving in the garden of your house is cracked and wobbly. The person who cleans your windows falls from the ladder when the paving on which it is balanced moves. Are you liable for payment of compensation to the window cleaner?

Children

Section 2(3)(a) of the 1957 Act provides that 'an occupier must be prepared for children to be less careful than adults'. An occupier must therefore make sure that children of all ages are safe in using premises they are allowed to visit bearing mind that risks which are obvious to an adult may not be appreciated by a child.

Children, some parents say, are drawn to danger like bees to a honeypot. This has been recognised by the courts, which have held that an occupier who has on the premises something which attracts a child (an allurement) owes a duty to ensure the child's safety.

> ### *Glasgow Corporation v Taylor* (1922)
> A child was poisoned when he ate berries which looked like cherries growing on a shrub in a public park. The Corporation knew that the plant was dangerous and the court held steps should have been taken to make sure that children could not get close enough to pick and eat the berries.

Occupiers are, however, entitled to assume that very young children will be properly supervised by those caring for them.

> ### *Phipps v Rochester Corporation* (1955)
> The claimant, aged five, went picking blackberries with his seven-year-old sister on a building site occupied by the Corporation. As they were crossing the site, the claimant fell into a deep trench and broke his leg. The claimant received no compensation as the court held that, even though the child was a lawful visitor, it was reasonable for the Corporation to assume that such a young child would only be allowed onto such a site if the parents were satisfied that no danger existed. The danger of the trench would have been obvious to the parents.
>
> ### *Simkiss v Rhondda Borough Council* (1983)
> A girl aged seven slid down a steep slope on a blanket and hurt herself. As he gave evidence, her father stated that he

had not considered the slope to be dangerous. The court held that the council had no reason to believe that the slope was dangerous, when a parent did not take steps to keep his child away; it would be wrong to impose a higher duty on an occupier than on a parent.

> At what age, in your opinion, is a child old enough to be free of supervision by its parents? What factors would be relevant to decide this?

In the past the concept of 'allurements' has sometimes been of use to children who might have been viewed as trespassers. Where an occupier is aware that children are coming onto land, attracted by something on it which is dangerous, the children may be viewed by the courts as licensees (a category of lawful visitor) if the occupier takes no steps to keep them out and thus the occupier will be liable if the children are injured.

> *Cooke v Midland Great Western Railway of Ireland* (1909)
> Children regularly played on an unlocked railway turntable on the defendants' premises near to a road. The claimant, aged four, was injured while playing on the turntable. The defendants were held to have acquiesced in the presence of children on the site to the extent that the children had to be regarded in law as licensees to whom a duty of care was owed. The claimant recovered damages for his injuries.

Unlawful visitors

The statutory duty

The duty is spelled out in s.1(3) Occupiers' Liability Act 1984 as follows:

An occupier … owes a duty to another (not being his visitor) … if

(a) he is aware of the danger or has reasonable grounds to believe that it exists;

(b) he knows or has reasonable grounds to believe that the other is in the vicinity of the danger concerned or that he may come into the vicinity of the danger (in either case, whether the other has lawful authority for being in that vicinity or not); and

(c) the risk is one against which, in all the circumstances of the case, he may reasonably be expected to offer the other some protection.

By s.1(4) the Act provides that the duty 'is to take such care as is reasonable in all the circumstances of the case to see that [the trespasser] does not suffer injury on the premises by reason of the danger'.

The Act further provides that the duty may be discharged by taking reasonable steps to give a warning of the danger (s.1(5)). As in the case in respect of the Occupiers' Liability Act 1957, the warning must be clear and sufficient to alert the trespasser to the danger.

The obvious defence is that the defendant took all reasonable steps to fulfil the duty owed to visitors or trespassers. Other defences of particular relevance are those of contributory negligence and voluntary assumption of risk. For a full discussion of these issues in relation to negligence see Chapter 5.

The duty to trespassers

In *Addie (Robert) & Sons (Collieries) Ltd v Dumbreck* (1929) Lord Hailsham set out the following rule which held for many years:

> Towards the trespasser the occupier has no duty to take reasonable care for his protection or even to protect him from concealed danger. The trespasser comes on to the premises at his own risk. An occupier is liable only where the injury is due to some wilful act involving something more than the absence of reasonable care. There must be something done with the deliberate intention of doing harm to the trespasser, or at least some act done with reckless disregard of the presence of the trespasser.

The ruling by the House of Lords was subject to a lot of criticism over the years, especially in cases involving child trespassers. The judges on occasion tried to find a way to mitigate the hardship the rule caused, for example, as has been seen, by treating regular child trespassers as licensees. The Court of Appeal tried to impose liability where the presence of a trespasser ought to have been foreseen (*Videan v British Transport Commission* [1963] and *Kingzett v British Railways Board* [1968]), but its decisions were overturned by the House of Lords which reaffirmed the position set out in *Addie v Dumbreck*. It was not until 1972 that the position changed as the House of Lords exercised its powers under the Practice Direction 1966 to avoid the precedent it had set in 1929.

In *British Railways Board v Herrington* (1972) the House of Lords held that a 'duty of common humanity' was owed by an occupier to take reasonable steps to avoid an accident to a trespasser if they knew that there was a likelihood that trespassers were at risk.

> ### British Railways Board v Herrington (1972)
> An electrified railway crossed common land regularly used by local people. The line was fenced off by a wire fence which was not in a good state of repair. Local people had, as the Railways Board knew, got into the habit of going through a hole in the fence and crossing the line. Children had been seen doing the same thing and the local station master had been told. The claimant, a child of six years, went onto the line and was injured by a live rail. The House of Lords held that the child was entitled to damages on the basis of the duty of common humanity.

The Act does not refer to the duty of common humanity but it is believed that this duty provides a minimum level of protection and will be relevant when the court assesses the reasonableness or otherwise of the occupier's actions.

The Act applies only in relation to personal injury and the defences of consent and contributory negligence are available to the occupier.

The extent of the duty owed to a non-lawful visitor

We have already seen that s.1(3) requires an occupier to protect persons from dangers of which the occupier is aware when the occupier is also aware that a trespasser may come into the vicinity of the danger. The duty extends only to offering protection when it is reasonable to do so.

The Act itself is not very helpful in deciding when such a duty may arise but case law helps. In *White v St Albans City Council* (1990) the Court of Appeal held that when an occupier has taken precautions to make a site secure this does not, of itself, mean that the occupier either knows or has reason to believe that a trespasser may come onto the land.

> ### White v St Albans City Council (1990)
> Mr W took a short cut over land owned by the Council. He fell from a narrow bridge, which was fenced off, into a neighbouring car park and was injured. *Held*: there was no evidence that the Council had known or had reason to believe that anyone used the land as a short cut and the Council was not liable.

In *Swain v Natui Ram Puri* (1996) the Court of Appeal held that a claimant must establish actual knowledge of facts from which it could be inferred that the occupier had reasonable grounds to believe that someone may come into danger.

While these cases help to explain the meaning of s.1(3)(a) and (b), they are of little help in deciding when it would be reasonable for the occupier to provide protection. This was considered by the Court of Appeal in *Ratcliff v McDonnell* (1999).

> ### *Ratcliff v McDonnell* (1999)
> A 19-year-old student went drinking with friends. They decided to go swimming in the pool at the college which R attended. R knew that the pool was closed for the winter and that swimming was banned. There were signs at the pool which said it was closed and the gate was locked but R ignored all this and, having climbed over the fence, he dived into the pool. He hit his head on the bottom and was very seriously injured. *Held*: the college had done all it reasonably could to ensure that R was aware of the danger. The college was not liable for R's injuries. (This case is also a good example of the defence of contributory negligence – see Chapter 5.)

More recently the problem has been discussed by the House of Lords.

> ### *Tomlinson v Congleton Borough Council & Others* (2003)
> The defendants owned a park which was open to the public. A lake had been created by flooding a disused quarry. The lake was bordered by 'beach' areas used by the public for picnics. Swimming was prohibited but the defendants were aware that some people ignored the ban and were abusive to park rangers when they tried to stop the swimming. On a very hot day Mr T, aged 18, decided to cool off in the water. He waded into the lake until the water was just over knee height and then threw himself forward into a shallow dive. He struck his head on the smooth sandy bottom and broke his neck. As a result, he became paralysed and unable to walk. He claimed damages from the defendants under the Occupiers Liability Act 1984 on the basis that the

defendants were aware of the danger and had not done all that was reasonable to protect him. The judges unanimously held that he was not owed a duty under the Act and, even if he were, the defendants had done all that was reasonable.

The reasons for the decision are interesting. Lord Hoffmann emphasised that the danger must arise out of the state of the premises and in this case the only dangers were those which arise in relation to any area of deep water – the risk of drowning and a very small risk of injury from diving. The defendant had taken steps to prevent such accidents by banning swimming. The Lords were satisfied that s.1(3)(a) and (b) were satisfied and turned to give s.1(3)(c) detailed consideration. In deciding whether or not it was reasonable to offer protection, the judges said that the following must be taken into account:

- the likelihood of injury

- the seriousness of any injury which might happen

- the social value of the activity

- the cost of preventative measures.

In this case the risk of injury was extremely small and the financial cost of prevention was insignificant. The most important factor was the social value of the activities which would have to be prohibited in order to eliminate the risk. These would mean that all access to the beach areas would be blocked. In ruling that there was no duty to take such steps, Lord Hobhouse said

> The law does not require disproportionate or unreasonable responses … it is not … the policy of the law to require the protection of the foolhardy or reckless few to deprive, or interfere with, the enjoyment by the remainder of society of the liberties and amenities to which they are rightly entitled.

Lord Scott said

> Of course there is some risk of accidents arising out of the *joie de vivre* of the young. But that is no reason for imposing a grey and dull safety regime on everyone.

On the facts the only danger arose from the obvious risk associated with diving in shallow water. The fact that people choose to ignore warnings cannot impose a duty on an occupier to take steps to protect them from dangers which are perfectly obvious.

Unfair Contract Terms Act 1977

Although the Occupiers' Liability Acts recognise that a warning may be sufficient to discharge the duty imposed on the occupier, the Unfair Contract Terms Act 1977 limits the effectiveness of such notices. By s.2(1) of the Act,

> A person cannot by reference to any contract term or to a notice given to persons generally or to particular persons exclude or restrict his liability for death or personal injury resulting from negligence.

The Act, among other matters, applies to premises occupied for the purposes of business by the occupier. Where there is no business liability, the Act does not apply and a warning notice may suffice according to the common law rules.

The Act also operates to limit the scope of the defence of voluntary assumption of risk. By s.2(3) it is provided that,

> where a contract term or notice purports to exclude or restrict liability for negligence a person's agreement to or awareness of it is not of itself to be taken as indicating his voluntary acceptance of any risk.

It seems therefore that the occupier will still have to prove that the notice conveyed a sufficient warning to the visitor to enable the visitor to take steps to ensure their own safety from the danger.

Defective Premises Act 1972

The Act imposes duties on people doing work for or in connection with the provision of dwellings

> to see that the work which he takes on is done in a workmanlike or, as the case may be, professional manner, with proper materials

and so that as regards that work the dwelling will be fit for habitation when completed. (s.1(1))

The Act does not apply to new dwellings which are covered by other approved schemes – for example the National House Building Council runs a scheme under the trademark 'Buildmark' which effectively guarantees a new dwelling for ten years.

The duty imposed by the Act is owed to 'persons who might reasonably be expected to be affected by defects in the state of the premises created by the doing of the work'.

SUMMARY

Visitors

*   lawful visitor – anyone with express or implied permission or with lawful authority

*   non-lawful visitor – anyone without permission, people lawfully exercising a private right of way

*   occupier: the person in control of the land/premises – *Wheat v E Lacon & Co Ltd* (1966)

Occupiers' Liability Act 1957

*   applies to lawful visitors only

*   duty on occupier to ensure that visitors are reasonably safe in using the premises for the purpose of the visit – OLA 1957 s.2

*   special rules – expert visitors
        expected to take care for own safety in connection with their expertise – OLA 1957 s.2(3)(b) – *Roles v Nathan* (1963)
        occupier liable for injury caused by occupier's negligence – *Salmon v Seafarer Restaurants Ltd* (1983), *Ogwo v Taylor* (1987)

*   special rules – children
        less careful than adults – OLA 1957 s.2(3)(a)
        concept of allurements – *Glasgow Corp. v Taylor* (1922), *Cooke v Midland Great Western Railway of Ireland* (1909)
        need for supervision of young children – *Phipps v Rochester Corp* (1955), *Simkiss v Rhondda BC* (1983)

Occupiers' Liability Act 1984

*   applies to non-lawful visitors only

- occupier has duty to ensure that reasonable precautions taken to protect non-lawful visitors against known risks where presence of non-lawful visitor known or should be anticipated – OLA 1984 s.1(3) and s.1(4), *Tomlinson v Congleton BC* (2003)

- duty of common humanity – *BRB v Herrington* (1972)

QUESTIONS

1. Jay owns and is modernising an old house, doing most of the work himself. Last week Sally, a visitor aged seven, wandered into the front room to see what Jay had done since her last visit and broke her leg when she fell through a hole where Jay had removed the floorboards.

   Last winter, Jay was attempting to thaw frozen water pipes in the loft with a blowtorch. When he left the lighted torch unattended a fire started and Helen, a fire-fighter, was seriously burned while putting out the fire.

   Jay employed Shoddy Builders, independent contractors, to repair the drains. The Post Office is now refusing to deliver mail to Jay since one of the postmen, Pat, fell in the dark into the trench in front of Jay's front door which was dug but left uncovered by Shoddy Builders.

   Advise Jay of any potential claims which Sally, Helen and Pat may have against him in respect of their injuries. (OCR 1998)

2. Indira, aged three years, has been taken by her parents to the local zoo. She is very excited and runs from one enclosure to the other. The chimpanzees' enclosure consists of a wire cage with a second wire mesh fence one metre away to stop people from getting too close. There are notices warning the public that the animals in the enclosure are dangerous. Indira runs ahead of her parents and before they realise what is happening, she manages to climb through the bars of a gate in the outer fence. She rushes up to the cage itself and tries to stroke one of the chimpanzees. The chimpanzee grabs her by the arm and bites her. Indira is taken to hospital where the doctors tell her parents that her arm has been very badly injured. She will never be able to use it properly and it will be badly scarred.

   About three months ago Gareth, who had been drinking at the local public house, was on his way home when he decided to visit the lions. The zoo was closed but he managed to scale the perimeter fence and make his way to the lion enclosure where he climbed over another fence into the enclosure. He was badly mauled by two lions. Gareth has survived but will be disabled and scarred for the rest of his life.

   Advise the zoo about what claims, if any, Indira and Gareth may have for compensation. (Oxford 1996)

3. The Occupiers' Liability Acts 1957 and 1984 are intended to ensure the safety of those who come onto premises belonging to someone else. Discuss whether the Acts achieve this aim. (OCR January 2002)

4. To what extent can the view that the Occupiers' Liability Acts 1957 and 1984 impose an unfair burden on an occupier of land to ensure safety be justified? (Oxford 1997)

5   Negligence – defences, remedies and policy issues

Defences

Contributory negligence

The doctrine

Common sense suggests that, in some cases, the alleged victims of an accident have only themselves to blame, or they are at least partly responsible for their own loss. It might seem that this should already have been considered in relation to 'intervening acts' but the law does in fact make specific provision for such issues.

Historically, if a victim could be shown to have contributed to or increased his own misfortune, no compensation would be due from a defendant who had actually been negligent despite the injustice that this might cause. There was no means whereby the courts could say that both parties were somewhat to blame and apportion the damages to reflect the appropriate degree of blameworthiness.

The position was eventually remedied by Parliament which passed the Law Reform (Contributory Negligence) Act 1945. In s.1 the Act provides:

> Where any person suffers damage as the result partly of his own fault and partly of the fault of any other person or persons, a claim in respect of that damage shall not be defeated by reason of the fault of the person suffering the damage, but the damages recoverable in respect thereof shall be reduced to such extent as the court thinks just and equitable having regard to the claimant's share in the responsibility for the damage

The practical effect of the Act is to enable judges to work out the total sum to which the claimant would be entitled were the defendant wholly to blame, and then to reduce that sum by a percentage which fairly reflects the degree of blame which attaches to the claimant.

The Act uses the phrase 'contributory negligence' and it might be thought that the rules discussed in Chapter 2 would apply to set a standard by which the claimant's actions might be judged. This is not in fact the case, as Lord Denning explained in *Jones v Livox Quarries Ltd* (1952), when he said:

Contributory negligence does not depend on the existence of a duty. Although contributory negligence does not depend on a duty of care, it does depend on foreseeability. Just as actionable negligence requires the foreseeability of harm to others, so contributory negligence requires the foreseeability of harm to oneself. A person is guilty of contributory negligence if he ought reasonably to have foreseen that, if he did not act as a reasonable, prudent man, he might be hurt himself; and in his reckonings he must take into account the possibility of others being careless.

Jones v Livox Quarries Ltd (1952)
Mr J was employed by the defendants and, in defiance of instructions given by his employers, stood on the back of a vehicle called a traxcavator which was going to the works canteen. The driver of the vehicle was unaware that Mr J was on the back. As the vehicle came to a near stop, another vehicle, a dumper, collided with the rear of the traxcavator, injuring Mr J. Mr J was found to be 5 per cent to blame for his injuries as he had disobeyed the clear instruction given by his employers and the damages to which he was entitled were reduced by that percentage.

Road traffic accidents

The increased use of cars and other vehicles has led to a number of cases in which the doctrine of contributory negligence has been considered in relation to road traffic accidents. In *O'Connell v Jackson* (1972), it was decided that failure to wear a crash helmet on a motor cycle could amount to contributory negligence. In the later case of *Froom v Butcher* (1975) Lord Denning found that failure to wear a seat belt could have a similar effect, and suggested that the victim's share of the blame should be assessed by reference to the degree of protection which wearing the belt would have given in relation to the injuries actually suffered. A passenger who knows that the driver of a car has been drinking may also be liable for contributory negligence (*Owens v Brimmell* [1977]).

A person who is not wearing a seat belt is injured in an accident.
By what percentage should his damages be reduced if:
(a) the injuries would have been the same;
(b) the injuries would have been less serious;
(c) the injuries would have been prevented?

Emergencies

The courts recognise that a victim may act in an emergency in a way which with hindsight is not the best way, and which might not have been the case had the victim had time to think. In such cases, the courts take into account the state of alarm in which the victim is placed, and ask, 'Was the response a reasonable one to a reasonably perceived danger?' If the answer to the question is 'Yes, although it might have been better or more sensible to do something else', then the victim is not guilty of contributory negligence. If, however, the answer to the question is 'No', then the victim may well be found at least partly to blame.

> ### *Jones v Boyce* (1816)
> The claimant was an outside passenger on a coach. A rein broke due to the negligence of the owner of the coach and horses, and one of the horses became uncontrollable. As the coachman tried to control the coach the claimant, believing that it was about to overturn, jumped for safety and broke his leg. It was argued that there had been no need for him to jump and, as the coach did not in fact overturn, it might seem that he had overreacted. The court found that the claimant's fear was reasonable in the circumstances and that his response was also reasonable. He was compensated in the sum of £300.
>
> ### *Sayers v Harlow UDC* (1958)
> Mrs S was going from Harlow to London by bus with her husband. As they were waiting at the bus stop, Mrs S decided to pay a visit to the public toilets. She went into a cubicle and closed the door. Only then did she realise that she could not get out. She shouted for a while but no one heard her so she decided to try to escape. As she was trying to climb up to squeeze through the small gap at the top of the door, she put her weight on the toilet roll holder which gave way throwing her to the floor and injuring her. The court held that it was reasonable for her to try to escape but she had been careless in the way in which she tried and her damages were reduced to take account of her own carelessness.

Children

A child can be guilty of contributory negligence but this obviously depends very much on the age of the child concerned and the particular circumstances. In *Gough v Thorne* (1966) Lord Denning said:

> A very young child cannot be guilty of contributory negligence. An older child may be; but it depends on the circumstances. A judge should only find a child guilty of contributory negligence if he or she is of such an age as reasonably to be expected to take precautions for his or her own safety: and then he or she is only to be found guilty if blame should be attached to him or her.

Voluntary assumption of risk (*volenti non fit injuria*)

If contributory negligence on the part of the victim is established, the damages can be apportioned; if it is established that the victim consented to the risk of injury, he or she will receive nothing.

In order to succeed, the defendant must show that the victim knew of the risk and was able to exercise free choice in deciding to take the risk of injury. It is not enough simply to show that the victim knew that the risk existed. Each case will depend on its own particular facts but some situations have given rise to views which provide some guidance.

Employees

In the case of an employee who has been injured at work, the defence appears to be easily established: if the risk was not acceptable, the employee was free to leave the job. The courts have taken a realistic view that this is not always the case; an employee may be under pressure for all sorts of reasons to keep the job and may anticipate that if a complaint is made about unsafe working practices, dismissal is the likely outcome. Although the Employment Rights Act 1996 s.44 gives an employee who makes such a complaint protection from being 'subjected to any detriment', and enables a claim to be brought before the Employment Tribunal, this does not in fact mean that the employee will get the job back, and any compensation will be calculated in a way similar to that for unfair dismissal.

Even with this additional protection (which was originally introduced in 1993 by earlier legislation) it is likely that the courts will continue to maintain the view that an employee may be under sufficient pressure to stay in an unsafe job. In *Smith v Baker* (1891) Lord Herschell, while acknowledging that an employee 'no doubt voluntarily subjects himself to the risks inevitably accompanying [the job]', said that it could not be the case that by 'mere continuance in service, with knowledge of the risk' the employee should be taken to have consented to it.

> ### Smith v Baker (1891)
> The victim was a driller working to create a railway cutting. As he drilled the rock face at the bottom of the cutting, a crane swung to and fro at the top carrying large stones. He knew that there was a risk that a stone could fall and injure him but was given no warning when the crane was to be used. A stone fell and injured him. The court held that his employers were liable.

It should not be thought that the defence can never apply in the employment situation. An employee who freely chooses to adopt an unsafe practice may well find that any claim for compensation is unavailable. In *Imperial Chemical Industries Ltd v Shatwell* (1964) Lord Reid took the view that if the claimant was a willing party to a risk created by a fellow worker (for which the employers would have vicarious liability), 'He cannot complain of the resulting injury ... against the fellow servant or against the master.'

> ### ICI Ltd v Shatwell (1964)
> George and James Shatwell were both qualified shot-firers employed by ICI. In order to save time, George suggested to James that they revert to a dangerous practice which, as they both knew, had been banned by ICI the previous year. ICI had also taken disciplinary action against another shot-firer who had broken the new rules. There was an explosion injuring both George and James. George sued for compensation. The court held that George had freely consented to the risk and his claim failed.

Transport

In relation to transport matters, the Road Traffic Act 1988 s.149 specifically excludes the defence of consent where a driver of a vehicle is insured compulsorily and is sued by a passenger protected by that insurance. The defence may be used against passengers in other forms of transport. In *Morris v Murray* (1991) a passenger in a light aircraft being flown by a friend with whom he had been drinking all afternoon (the friend having consumed the equivalent of 17 whiskies), was held to have consented to the risk that the pilot was incapable of flying the aircraft properly and lost his claim for compensation for injuries caused when the aircraft crashed.

Spectators and participants in sporting events

A person who goes to watch a sporting event is entitled to assume that participants will exercise a reasonable degree of care and skill but consents to those risks which are inherent in the nature of the sport. (For an example see *Wooldridge v Sumner* (1963), p. 65, in which the injured spectator lost his claim on the grounds that he had consented to the risk which in fact caused the injury.)

A participant in a sporting event similarly consents to the risks inherent in the sport but not to a 'reckless disregard of safety'. (*Harrison v Vincent* [1982] – a claim brought by a participant in a motor-cycle and side-car race.)

Figure 5.1

Contributory negligence	Voluntary assumption of risk
Governed by Law Reform (Contributory Negligence) Act 1945	Also known as *volenti non fit injuria*
(a) A partial defence	(a) A complete defence
(b) Allows court to share blame between claimant and defendant	(b) Claimant solely to blame
(c) Test: ought claimant to have recognised potential risk and acted to reduce or eliminate it?	(c) Test: (1) Was claimant aware of the risk? (2) Did claimant freely decide to take the risk?

Exclusion of liability

Until comparatively recently, a person could be protected from liability caused by their negligence provided the victim was aware that an exclusion clause relating to such matters was part of the agreement between them.

The widespread use of such clauses was recognised as causing injustice and led to the Unfair Contract Terms Act 1977 which provides,

> s.1(1) A person cannot by reference to any contract term or to a notice given to persons generally or to particular persons exclude or restrict his liability for death or personal injury resulting from negligence.

(2) In the case of other loss or damage, a person cannot so exclude or restrict his liability for negligence except in so far as the term or notice satisfies the requirement of reasonableness.

The Act, in s.11, gives guidance as to those matters which the court must consider when deciding whether or not the provision excluding liability for loss or damage other than death or personal injury is reasonable. Such matters include the resources available to meet any liability should it arise, and the availability of insurance.

If an agreement or notice is reasonable, then liability can be effectively excluded or limited.

(For a fuller discussion of these issues, reference should be made to a textbook on consumer protection or contract law.)

Participation in an unlawful act (*ex turpi causa non oritur actio*)

A person who participates in an unlawful act and who suffers injury as the result of someone else's negligence, may find that any claim for compensation is defeated by this doctrine. The law is not clear on what will be regarded as an unlawful act. A crime is likely to be regarded as unlawful for these purposes, but in *R v Horseferry Road Justices ex p. Independent Broadcasting Authority* (1987) it was held that breach of statutory duty may or may not be a crime, but the victim's claim for compensation will not be barred. Where the unlawful act amounts to a tort, it is unlikely that the defence will be successful but the court may decide otherwise on the basis of public policy. In *Euro-Diam v Bathurst* (1990) Lord Kerr explained the approach by saying that the doctrine would apply

> if, in all the circumstances, it would be an affront to the public conscience to grant the plaintiff the relief which he seeks because the court would thereby appear to assist or encourage the plaintiff in his illegal conduct or to encourage others in similar acts.

This view was apparently contradicted in *Revill v Newbery* (1996) when the claimant had been shot while attempting to enter the defendant's allotment shed in order to steal. This involved the criminal offence of attempted burglary for which the claimant had received an appropriate sentence and the tort of trespass to land. The Court of Appeal held that in the circumstances the claimant was entitled to compensation:

> It is one thing to deny a plaintiff any fruits from his illegal conduct, but different and far more far-reaching to deprive him even of

compensation for injury which he suffers and which otherwise he
is entitled to recover at law. (*per* Evans LJ)

It is clear that where the damage suffered by the a defendant is the
direct result of their own illegal act, it is unlikely that damages can be
recovered. This seems rather confusing but is explained by the facts
of *Clunis v Camden & Islington AHA* (1998).

> **Clunis v Camden & Islington Area Health Authority (1998)**
> Mr C had been convicted of manslaughter on the ground
> of diminished responsibility. He alleged that the defendant
> had been negligent in the way in which his mental health
> had been assessed. He argued that had the assessment been
> properly done, he would not have been released from
> hospital and would not have killed his victim.
>   As the injury he had suffered was punishment for a crime
> which he had committed, to allow his claim might be seen
> as enabling a criminal to profit from his crime. His claim
> was dismissed.

The position in law is confused. Probably all that can be said with
any degree of accuracy is that each case will be decided on its own
particular facts.

Limitation periods

For a full discussion of the relevant law see Chapter 11, pp. 221–223.
Generally an action based on alleged negligence must be begun within
six years of the incident which caused damage to property and within
three years of the incident which caused personal injury. It is possible
for an action to be brought after the time limit has expired but this
depends on the court being prepared to grant special permission.

Remedies

Damages

A person who succeeds in bringing a claim in negligence will usually
be seeking compensation for the damage sustained. The rules relating
to the calculation of damages are complex. What follows is a brief
outline of the various types of damage which may be recovered.

The purpose of an award of damages is to put the victim in the
position that they would have been in had the tort not occurred. It is

obvious that, in many cases, the victim would far rather that the negligence had not happened, as in reality there can sometimes be no restoration of the position which would have been. The award seeks to allow the victim to return to a state as near as possible to the original, for example by ensuring that sufficient money is available to enable a victim to obtain the most up-to-date treatment for, or equipment needed to cope with, the position in which the victim is left.

Damages may be classified as 'general' (those losses which cannot be quantified in exact financial terms) and 'special' (those losses which can be exactly quantified in terms of money). Damages are awarded under various heads, for example medical and other expenses, loss of earnings, pain and suffering and damage to property.

Nominal damages

Where the actual loss suffered by the victim is very small or non-existent, nominal damages may be awarded. This is a small sum which recognises that the victim has suffered a wrong at the hands of the defendant, and will not usually be awarded in a case involving negligence.

Contemptuous damages

Contemptuous damages are a derisory sum, usually the smallest coin in the realm (presently 1p), to mark the court's view that the action should not have been brought in the first place.

Aggravated damages

Aggravated damages allow the court to take into the reckoning the way in which the victim's injuries occurred – were the actions of the defendant made worse from the victim's point of view by the injury to their self-respect and pride caused by the defendant? Aggravated damages are still designed to compensate the victim, not to punish the defendant.

Exemplary damages

Exemplary damages are used in the rare cases where the court seeks not only to compensate the victim but also to punish the defendant. A public official who has behaved oppressively, arbitrarily or unconstitutionally may find that exemplary damages are awarded to the victim, as will a defendant who has calculated that profits to be made outweigh any compensation which might be payable.

The role of policy

We have already seen one example of the way in which policy can influence a decision about damages (*Clunis v Camden & Islington AHA* [1998]). Other policy issues have arisen in cases where a child has been born after one of its parents had undergone a negligent operation of sterilisation. The question is whether damages should be recoverable when the injury complained of is the birth of a baby. There have been three recent cases in which this problem has been considered. In *McFarlane v Tayside Health Board* (1999) the House of Lords held that no damages could be payable for the costs of bringing up a healthy child after a failed sterilisation. A number of reasons were given:

- it would not be fair, just and reasonable to impose liability on the doctor

- the extent of the potential liability was disproportionate to the duties undertaken by the doctor

- the benefits to parents of bringing up a healthy child are incalculable but are likely to exceed the costs

- it would be unreasonable to relieve the parents of the cost of raising their own child

- the law must treat the birth of a normal, healthy baby as a blessing, not a detriment.

The second case, *Parkinson v St James & Seacroft University Hospital NHS Trust* (2001), concerned the birth of a disabled child after a failed sterilisation. In this case the Court of Appeal held that the parents were entitled to recover the costs of raising a disabled child but only the additional costs caused by the disability.

The most recent case is *Rees v Darlington Memorial Hospital NHS Trust* (2002).

> **Rees v Darlington Memorial Hospital NHS Trust (2002)**
> Ms R was a disabled woman who chose to be sterilised as she knew that she would be unable to cope with looking after a baby. She had made her reasons clear to her surgeon. The sterilisation failed and she gave birth to a healthy child. The Court of Appeal allowed the claim to cover the costs caused by Ms R's inability to look after the child properly by herself. The majority treated this as allowing a legitimate extension of the principles set out in *Parkinson*.

It is clear, from the judgments in the three cases, that the judges found it morally wrong to allow compensation for the birth of a healthy child but they were prepared to take a different view in the face of disability. Lord Justice Waller, giving a minority judgment in *Rees*, disagreed with the majority, holding that the disability of the mother made no difference. He said

> It is the fact that ... benefits of having a healthy child are incalculable which it seems to me leads to the result that the court simply should not give damages for the birth of that child.

It will be interesting to see how this issue is dealt with in the future.

Death

Where a victim of negligence has died, their right of action may well survive them and an action can be brought on their behalf by their personal representatives. Dependants of the deceased person can sue for their own loss by virtue of the Fatal Accidents Act 1976. A relatively small sum is payable to dependants for bereavement (at the time of writing up to a maximum of £7,500), but larger sums may be awarded to cover actual and future financial loss.

Injunction

An injunction is an order of the court addressed to a specific person requiring or compelling that person to do or refrain from doing certain actions which cause the victim damage. Breach of an injunction amounts to contempt of court and can be punished by imprisonment. Such orders are rare in relation to the tort of negligence. For further details, see Chapter 6, pp. 132–136.

Justice, policy and other issues

The idea of justice

The ethical principle of justice is defined by the Shorter Oxford Dictionary as

> The quality of being (morally) just or righteous; the principle of just dealing; just conduct; integrity; rectitude.

The word 'just' is defined in this context as meaning,

1   what is morally right, righteous;

2   upright and impartial in one's dealings;

3   consonant with the principles of moral right; equitable; fair.

The development of the law of negligence can be seen to be attempting to give effect to this principle. In relation to the tort, the principle may not be openly acknowledged but it is likely that it played a part in the decision which allowed Mrs Donoghue to obtain compensation from the manufacturers of the bottle of ginger beer. Had the courts decided otherwise, the person responsible for her injuries would have 'got away with it' – something which would be morally wrong in the opinion of many people.

The principle can also be seen to influence the development of the rules relating to nervous shock although it can be argued that economic policy has limited the influence of the principle in this area – in other words the 'floodgates argument'.

The danger of opening the floodgates

In the past the judges denied that they made the law or that policy issues had any influence on their decisions. As has been seen, modern judges are prepared to acknowledge the role of the judiciary in developing the law and to admit the relevance of policy. The tort of negligence provides good examples of this change.

With the creation of the neighbour test in *Donoghue v Stevenson* in 1932, Lord Atkin provided a flexible principle which largely achieved his aim of creating a basic principle which could be applied in all cases. The tort of negligence since then has grown in importance. It has not always been a smooth development. This can be seen by the creation of Lord Wilberforce's 'two-stage' test in *Anns v Merton London Borough Council* (1978) after which it seemed that a duty of care would always be owed unless there was good reason to hold otherwise. The floodgates were opened but were closed again in 1990 when *Anns* was overruled by the House of Lords in *Murphy v Brentwood District Council.*

The application of the neighbour test is also the basis of the development of the rules relating to compensation for nervous shock. In *McLoughlin v O'Brian* (1983) the majority of the House of Lords used the neighbour test alone to decide that a secondary victim could recover damages. The influence of the principle of justice may well have played a part in the decision. Again the floodgates opened to the extent that it was even possible to obtain compensation for nervous shock caused by watching one's home burn down (*Attiah v British Gas plc* [1988]). With the potential of thousands of claims arising from the Hillsborough disaster, and an awareness of the economic and other problems that this would cause, the House of Lords again acted to limit the flood of claims, not by overruling the earlier case of *McLoughlin v O'Brian* but by refining the requirements to be satisfied by potential claimants (*Alcock v Chief Constable of South Yorkshire* [1991]). This process has continued with *McFarlane v EE Caledonia Ltd* (1994), *Page v Smith* (1996) and *White v Chief Constable of South Yorkshire* (1999).

Law reform

The work of the various law reform bodies has been relevant to the development of the tort of negligence. The Occupiers' Liability Act 1957 resulted from a report by the Law Reform Committee; the Occupier's Liability Act 1984 came from a report by the Law Commission.

Recommendations are not always adopted. The Pearson Report published in 1978 (Report of the Royal Commission on Civil Liability and Compensation for Personal Injury) set out detailed proposals to deal with injustices caused by the need to establish fault in order to obtain compensation for personal injury. The main recommendation was the introduction of a 'no fault' scheme which would in time eliminate the need for court action in most cases where personal injury had occurred. The Report is still the subject of debate, particularly in relation to injuries resulting from medical negligence, but to date the chances of it being implemented are not good, despite the support of influential bodies such as the British Medical Association.

Many of the difficulties of the system which were actually identified by Pearson have been dealt with by piecemeal reforms of, for example, the social security system and, most recently, of the court system and legal aid.

Nervous shock

In 1998 the Law Commission published a report on the reform of the law relating to nervous shock (Law Com. No. 249). The proposal is to modify the Alcock criteria by removing the requirement for the claimant to prove proximity in time and space. It would also no longer be necessary for perception of the incident to be by means of the claimant's own unaided senses. Although it would be necessary to prove close ties of love and affection, the law should provide a list of relationships where this will be presumed. The Law Commission suggests that psychiatric illness should be recognised even when it has not been caused by a sudden trauma which would open the doors to claims by those who suffer in the long term as a result of the injuries to the primary victim. Whether or not these proposals will ever become law is not yet clear but should they do so, progress will have been made to deal with the present perception that secondary victims are not treated fairly by the law.

SUMMARY

Defences

Contributory negligence

- governed by Law Reform (Contributory Negligence) Act 1945

- allows damages to claimant to be reduced to take account of claimant's share of responsibility for injury/damage – s.1

- defined as failure to take reasonable care for one's own safety – *Jones v Livox Quarries Ltd* (1952)

Voluntary assumption of risk

- defeats any claim by claimant if defendant can show that claimant voluntarily agreed to the risk

- note courts reluctant to find employees have voluntarily assumed risk – *Smith v Baker* (1891) – but will do so in appropriate case – *ICI v Shatwell* (1964)

- cannot be used to defeat claim by person covered by compulsory third party insurance (Road Traffic Act 1988 s.149) but applies to other forms of transport – *Morris v Murray* (1991)

Participation in unlawful act

- generally a wrongdoer who suffers injury resulting from someone else's negligence while the wrongdoer is acting unlawfully will be unable to claim compensation

- note *Revill v Newbury* (1995) in which would-be burglar successfully obtained damages from allotment keeper who shot him

- a wrongdoer who suffers only because of his own unlawful act will not be able to claim damages – *Clunis v Camden & Islington AHA* (1998)

Limitation

- action for negligence must be brought within six years for damage to property, within three years if the claim includes a claim for personal injury – Limitation Act 1980

- court can allow claim to be brought later in special circumstances

Remedies

Damages

- intended to put claimant as far as money can do so back to the position they were in before the negligent act

- general damages – losses which cannot be quantified exactly in terms of money, e.g. pain and suffering

- special damages – losses upon which it is possible to put an exact value, e.g. cost of repair of damages to property

- contemptuous damages – nominal amount to mark court's view that claim should not have been brought

- aggravated damages – include element of punishment of defendant for making a bad situation worse than it need have been

- note influence of policy issues – *McFarlane v Tayside Health Board* (2000), *Parkinson v St James & Seacroft University Hospital NHS Trust* (2001), *Rees v Darlington Memorial Hospital NHS Trust* (2003)

Death

- Dependants of someone killed by negligence have claim in their own right – Fatal Accidents Act 1976

Injunction

- rare in negligence case

- order requiring defendant to stop doing something

- breach of injunction is contempt of court and punishable by, e.g. a fine or imprisonment

Justice, policy and other issues

Justice

- the requirement of fairness – not allowing a person 'to get away with it'

- can be seen in rules relating to duty of care

Policy

- modern judges admit to being influenced by policy to avoid 'opening the floodgates'

- can be seen in rules relating to economic loss and rules relating to nervous shock

Law reform

- Law Commission and other reform bodies suggest changes which may or may not be adopted by Parliament

- examples of reports which have been adopted include Occupiers' Liability Acts 1957 and 1984

- examples of reports which have *not* been adopted include Pearson Report on Compensation for Personal Injury

QUESTIONS

1. James is driving his car slowly along a narrow country lane. As he approaches a bend another car, being driven very fast by Susan, comes round the bend on the wrong side of the road. Both cars are damaged beyond repair as a result of the accident. James and Susan are not badly hurt but Susan's passenger Peter, is seriously injured. The police give both James and Susan a breath-test and find that Susan was driving with an excessive amount of alcohol in her blood. Susan tells the police that she had drunk three double whiskies about two hours earlier. Peter had been with her but never drinks alcohol. A witness confirms that James was driving slowly but that, although it was dark, the lights on his car were not on.

   Consider what claims, if any, James and Peter may have against Susan in tort. Do not discuss Susan's potential criminal liability. (Oxford 1996)

2. Billy recently saw a film on mountaineering and decided to take up the sport. He visited a local climbing centre run by Ann. On his first visit, he and Ann agreed a programme of instruction and Ann made it clear that he was not to use any equipment without proper supervision by a member of the centre's staff.

   Last week, when Billy appeared at the centre, all the staff were having their coffee break. Rather than wait five minutes, Billy decided to have a go at the climbing wall by himself. He was about 3 metres up when his foot slipped and he fell, as a result of which he broke his shoulder. On investigation by Ann, it appears that Billy was not wearing proper shoes for climbing, which would have been checked by a member of staff had he waited. Ann has admitted that the centre was negligent as the staff did not keep a proper eye on what was going on. Billy wants to claim damages for his injury.

Discuss the issues which would be considered by a court in assessing his likely chances of success. Do not discuss the issue of vicarious liability. (OCR Jan 2003)

3. The defences of *volenti non fit injuria* and contributory negligence are sometimes thought to be very similar. By means of a detailed analysis of both defences, explain whether or not you agree with this view. (Oxford 1997)

6 Torts protecting land

This part of the law protects a person's interest in land. The tort of trespass to land protects a person's right to decide who may come onto or use their land. This can be used to prevent an invasion of privacy. The tort of nuisance protects a person's right not to have the use of their land interfered with by activities on nearby land – an important tort in dealing with problems caused by so-called 'neighbours from hell'. The third tort in this group is named after a nineteenth-century case – *Rylands v Fletcher* – and gives protection against the escape of dangerous substances stored on land.

While the common law gives a substantial degree of protection, the procedure in the courts is slow and expensive. As the importance of the environment has increased, alongside a greater awareness of rights of privacy, Parliament has acted to provide simpler, quicker and cheaper remedies which will be looked at where appropriate.

Before looking at the individual torts, it is useful to consider the meaning of 'land' which is particularly relevant to trespass and to nuisance.

The meaning of 'land'

Many people would say they know what 'land' is but would be in difficulty if asked to define it. In law, 'land' refers to a complex bundle of rights in relation to land as well as the soil itself and buildings placed on it. The most important right is the right to possession, but possession of what? 'Land' includes not only the surface of the soil and any buildings placed on it but also the sub-soil and rights to exploit any minerals, such as gravel, clay or sand, which are in the sub-soil. Riparian rights include the right to exploit water on the land or flowing through it whether on the surface or beneath it. The right to use the land for the raising of crops or grazing livestock are included as are rights to exploit wild life. Timber carries with it rights to harvest the trees which can have substantial tax benefits. 'Land' also includes the airspace above the surface, in theory out to infinity but in reality to the extent that is reasonable, aircraft having the right to pass over the land at a reasonable height having regard to the conditions (Civil Aviation Act 1982).

Trespass to land

Definition

Trespass to land occurs where someone without lawful authority or justification

(a) enters land in possession of another; or

(b) stays on land having been asked to leave or after any permission has come to an end; or

(c) puts anything on, over or under land.

Who can sue?

The simple answer to this is 'the person in possession'. This usually means someone who is in occupation of the land by virtue of ownership or tenancy. A lodger will not be regarded as a person with an interest in land nor will a visitor to a public house. Possession must be of a formal nature recognised by the law. In *Khorasandjian v Bush* (1993) it was held that a child living with her parents could qualify but this case has since been overruled in *Hunter v Canary Wharf Ltd* (1997).

In some rare cases a trespasser may sue. For example, a person occupying land as a squatter has no legal rights against the true owner but may successfully enforce rights against anyone else who tries to interfere with the squatter's occupation.

The act of trespass

The most common form of trespass is entry onto land without lawful justification. Lawful justification can arise in a number of ways, the most usual being express permission given to a visitor. Express permission to enter land for a specific purpose is limited to that purpose, for example to watch one performance of a play.

Permission to enter can be implied, for example to those who come onto the land to deliver post or milk. If the gate is unlocked, door-to-door salespersons, religious or political canvassers or others may come as far as the front door in order to see if the owner of the land is interested in what they have to offer. Permission is also implied in relation to land such as shops and hospitals, to which the public are admitted. The permission can be withdrawn if the right is abused. A shopkeeper may withdraw permission from someone suspected of being a thief and a hospital can withdraw permission from visitors creating a disturbance.

> The manager of the local shopping centre has received complaints
> from a number of the shop owners that a gang of people regularly
> comes into the centre in order to steal and generally create a
> nuisance for other customers. What steps can the manager take,
> using the civil law to deal with the problem?

The entry must be intentional in the sense that the trespasser intended to go onto that particular land. It is not necessary for the trespasser to intend to trespass. A person going home the worse for drink might mistake the address and try to get into a neighbour's house. In this case the entry is intentional and trespass has been committed. Entry by a parachutist accidentally blown onto the land by the wind is unintentional and there is no liability for trespass.

Invasion of airspace can occur when a sign protrudes over the boundary (*Kelsen v Imperial Tobacco Co* (1957), or when a tower crane swings across the land (*Anchor Brewhouse Developments Ltd v Berkeley House [Docklands Developments] Ltd* [1987]). It was argued in *Bernstein v Skyviews & General Ltd* (1978) that a private aircraft taking aerial photographs of land without permission was an invasion of airspace. In the course of the judgment Griffiths J stated that the passage of aircraft at a height which in no way interfered with the use of land was not in the same category as an overhanging structure. The judge said,

> The balance is in my judgment best struck in our present society
> by restricting the rights of an owner in the airspace above his
> land to such height as is necessary for the ordinary use and
> enjoyment of his land and the structures on it, and declaring that
> above that height he has no greater rights in the airspace than any
> other member of the public.

While aircraft appear to be safe from liability for trespass, it is suggested that 'if an aircraft, or anything from it, falls upon the land or comes into contact with a structure on it, that might be a trespass, no matter the height from which it fell'. (Winfield, p. 478.)

An apparently odd situation arises in relation to the highway. We all have a right to pass and re-pass along a highway and to use it for reasonable purposes, such as stopping to look into a shop window or resting on a seat provided for that purpose. Once the purpose is regarded as unreasonable, the person carrying on the unreasonable activity can be liable for trespass against the owner of the sub-soil on which the highway is built. (*Hickman v Maisey* [1900].)

> ### *Hickman v Maisey* (1900)
> Mr M was a racing tout, someone who made an income from watching race horses and selling information about likely winners. For about an hour-and-a-half on several occasions, he walked backwards and forwards along the highway next to Mr H's land watching the horses and taking photographs and making notes. *Held:* Mr M had abused the right of passage along the highway and was liable for trespass against the land of Mr H as Mr H owned the sub-soil under the highway.

An entry which is lawful can become unlawful if the purpose of the entry is abused. This is known as trespass *ab initio* and the abuse will make the original entry unlawful. Although it is an ancient doctrine dating back to the Middle Ages, it has its use in modern society particularly in respect of potential abuse by public authorities. In *Elias v Pasmore* (1934) it was held that the police were not liable for trespass *ab initio* when they wrongfully seized certain documents (although their other actions were lawful), but the court did not rule out the possibility that such abuse could make the entry unlawful.

Defences – lawful authority

As has been seen, a person who enters land with permission cannot be liable for trespass. Permission can generally be revoked but there are rules relating to contractual licences which in some circumstances are effectively irrevocable as revocation may lead to an action for breach of contract and prevent the person who remains on the land from becoming an unlawful entrant.

Many statutes confer rights for entry provided certain conditions are observed. Under the Police and Criminal Evidence Act 1984 a police officer may enter and search premises for a person where he has a power of arrest without warrant or where he has a warrant for this purpose. The Access to Neighbouring Land Act 1992 solves the problem of those whose buildings are so close to the boundary that 'trespass' is inevitable if repairs and decorations, etc., are to be carried out. In such circumstances, if the works are reasonably necessary for the preservation of the land, the court can permit access over neighbouring land imposing whatever conditions are appropriate.

Remedies

Re-entry and ejectment

A person who has been dispossessed by a trespasser may re-enter the land but may not use or threaten violence (Criminal Law Act 1977), although such force as is reasonable is permitted. The position is slightly different where the trespasser has made their home on the land. A landlord seeking possession from a residential occupier, or an owner seeking possession from residential squatters, must be careful to ensure that the necessary court orders have been granted or risk being found guilty under criminal law of unlawful eviction. (Protection from Eviction Act 1977.)

Rights of third parties

A person who has legal title can seek possession against a trespasser. What, however, is the position where the trespasser is ejected by someone else who does not have legal title? A person in actual possession of land may be regarded as having title, on the face of it, and can only be required to give it up to a person with a better legal right.

Mesne profits

This enables an owner to recover a sum which represents a reasonable payment for the period during which the trespasser has been in occupation, and damages for any deterioration and costs.

Trespass to land and privacy

Although many say that their privacy is a fundamental right, the law has not provided any direct protection of that right. The tort of trespass to land does provide indirect protection in that entry onto the land can be prevented but, as we have seen, only a person with an interest in the land can sue. This leaves others without any remedy. There is also little protection against the use of telephoto lenses to take photographs from a distance.

By Article 8 of the Convention on Human Rights people have a right to respect for their privacy and family life. It was thought that this would give extra protection to people who were at risk of losing their home. Unfortunately, Article 8 does not grant a right to a home; it merely requires a person to take proper legal steps to re-possess someone's home.

> ***London Borough of Harrow v Qazi*** (2003)
> Mr and Mrs Q were tenants of a council house. Mrs Q left and the tenancy was brought to an end by her action. Mr Q had no legal right to the house although he continued to live there as he had for more than seven years. The council got a court order for his eviction but Mr Q claimed that Article 8 meant that his right to privacy and family life extended to giving him a right to stay in his home. The House of Lords held that he was wrong. The council was entitled to possession as Article 8 could not be read in such a way as to give any right to a home as such.

Nuisance

The word 'nuisance' is defined by the Shorter Oxford Dictionary as

> Injury, hurt, harm, annoyance;
>
> Anything injurious or obnoxious to the community, or to the individual as a member of it, for which some legal remedy may be found;
>
> Anything obnoxious to the community or individual by offensiveness of smell or appearance, by causing obstruction or damage, etc;
>
> An obnoxious practice, institution, state of things, etc;
>
> A source of annoyance.

This definition gives the word several meanings. The tort has three parts to it:

- private nuisance,
- public nuisance, and
- statutory nuisance.

Each has different rules but as will be seen, each part falls within the meanings given by the dictionary.

> Make a list of things your neighbours do which annoy you. Can you identify the relevant part of the dictionary definition of 'nuisance' which fits each activity?

Private nuisance

Definition

An actionable nuisance occurs where a person's use or enjoyment of their own land is unlawfully interfered with by activities carried on by another person on their land. Usually the two pieces of land are close to each other. It is essential that it is something about the use of the second piece of land which interferes with the first; without interference any action may be lawful.

If the activity is authorised by law and the problem is the inevitable consequence, it cannot be unlawful. This is rarely the case and the courts are forced to try to balance the competing interests of neighbours to use their land as they choose. Case law sets out various matters which are relevant in deciding whether or not an activity is unlawful. The basic test is, 'Is the activity reasonable?' Over the years various cases have been decided from which relevant issues can be deduced. The list is not necessarily complete as each case must be decided on its own particular facts.

One of the most common forms of nuisance is the creation of noise. While playing music at full volume may well amount to unreasonable activity, noises which arise normally in the course of living in a property cannot be unreasonable even where it in reality causes interference with a neighbour's enjoyment of his property.

> ***Southwark LBC v Mills and Others, Baxter v Camden LBC***
> **(1999)**
> The cases were brought by tenants who lived in blocks of flats owned by the councils. The flats were badly soundproofed and the tenants complained that their lives were made miserable by the sound of ordinary everyday noises coming from next door. *Held*: as the noises complained of were part and parcel of everyday life, the behaviour of those causing the noise could not be unreasonable. It was not unreasonable activity which was the cause of the tenants' problems but the lack of proper soundproofing.

Locality

The place where an activity occurs is obviously of importance. As Lord Justice Thesiger said in *Sturges v Bridgman* (1879), 'What would be a nuisance in Belgravia Square would not necessarily be so in Bermondsey'. If your land is in the middle of an industrial estate, you

Figure 6.1

Nuisance

Something offensive, obstruction or cause of annoyance or disturbance

Private nuisance

Activity on D's land which interferes with C's use or enjoyment of C's land

Test: Is D's activity reasonable?

Action by individual with interest in affected land

Public nuisance

Activity on D's land which materially affects a class of people

Action by:

(a) attorney-general or local authority

(b) individual who suffers more than others

Statutory nuisance

Those matters stated by statute to be a statutory nuisance

Need not affect other land

Action by local authority

D = Defendant
C = Claimant

do not expect the same level of peace and quiet as you might get in a private residential area.

Where the nuisance has caused actual damage to property, the issue of locality is not relevant. If the nuisance causes inconvenience or interference with a person's comfort, peace or personal freedom, the issue of locality is important. (*St Helen's Smelting Co v Tipping* [1865].)

> ### *St Helen's Smelting Co v Tipping* (1965)
> Soon after Mr T moved into a large private estate a mile and a half away, the Smelting Co started very extensive copper smelting. The process produced toxic fumes which drifted to the estate causing damage to trees and shrubs as well as personal discomfort. *Held:* locality was irrelevant as physical damage had been caused.

Duration

Everyone has to put up with a certain amount of inconvenience and discomfort from time to time, and provided it does not go on for too long the activity which causes it is unlikely to be regarded as unreasonable and neither damages nor an injunction to stop it will be granted. If the activity amounted to a nuisance, were it not for its temporary nature, damages may be awarded.

> ### *Swaine v Great Northern Railway* (1864)
> Manure heaps generally caused no trouble but became a problem if removal was delayed and also because of the occasional presence in the heap of dead cats and dogs. *Held:* an injunction would be inappropriate as the problem was occasional but those who were inconvenienced were entitled to damages.

> ### *Andreae v Selfridge & Co Ltd* (1938)
> Demolition work created an excessive amount of noise and dust interfering with the business of an hotel. *Held:* although building work is not in itself an unreasonable activity, the extent in this case entitled the hotel owner to damages.

Duration is merely one factor. Building works which continue for twenty-four hours a day, seven days a week may well be stopped by injunction until more reasonable working hours are adopted.

> ### De Keyser's Royal Hotel Ltd v Spicer Bros Ltd (1914)
> A construction company was carrying out pile-driving at night interrupting the sleep of the owner of the hotel next door. *Held*: although it was a temporary activity, an injunction would be granted to stop the work at night.

Where building activity goes on for long periods of time, the outcome may be different. Each case will be decided on its own facts; case law merely gives some examples of activities which have been held to be unreasonable.

Problems arise where the damage is caused by a one-off escape which has resulted from some activity on the land, or some continuing state of affairs on that land. Where the activity creates the risk of escape, perhaps of a cricket ball from a cricket ground, there must be more than an isolated possibility that the escape will happen. (*Bolton v Stone* [1951] – for the details of this case see Chapter 3.)

A single incident may give rise to liability. In *Crown River Cruises Ltd v Kimbolton Fireworks Ltd* (1996) a firework display went on for between fifteen and twenty minutes, during which time the debris fell onto the claimant's property causing a fire; there was liability for nuisance.

Where a nuisance arises from a one-off incident arising from a natural state of affairs, there may be liability. In an Australian case, *Goldman v Hargrave* (1967) the Privy Council held a landowner liable in nuisance after his failure to put out a burning tree properly allowed the fire to spread to a neighbour's land. The original fire had been caused by a lightning strike. In *Leakey v National Trust etc.* (1980) the Court of Appeal held that there is a duty to abate a potential nuisance even where this arises from natural causes, if the danger is known. Failure to take reasonable steps to abate the nuisance may result in liability should damage to neighbouring land occur.

> ### Leakey v National Trust etc. (1980)
> A large mound of earth, known as Barrow Mump, was owned by the National Trust. From time to time there had been mud-slides and the slippage of trees, roots, etc., from the mound onto the land owned by the claimants. The

National Trust had been aware of the danger posed for at least eight years but had done nothing to abate it. Following a large fall, the claimants brought an action for nuisance which they won.

It was thought, after *Leakey*, that an occupier had a positive duty to deal with something which occurred naturally when the occupier knew of the likely problem which might arise. This view has since been considered in *Holbeck Hall Ltd v Scarborough Borough Council* (2000) when the Court of Appeal held that although a natural process was known to be occurring but the actual danger was unknown, the occupier was not liable.

> **Holbeck Hall Ltd v Scarborough Borough Council** (2000)
> Holbeck Hall was on the top of a cliff which was owned and occupied by the Council. It was known that the cliff was gradually being eroded by natural causes and was inherently unstable. A massive landslip happened which meant that the Hall fell off the cliff into the sea. *Held*: the Council was not liable in nuisance as the Council had not adopted nor continued the nuisance. The defect was not obvious nor was the landslip foreseeable.

Malice and motive

As a general rule, the motive for an action will not affect whether or not it is regarded as a tort. An evil or wrongful purpose cannot make an act unlawful which is otherwise lawful.

In *Bradford Corporation v Pickles* (1895) Lord Halsbury said,

> If it was a lawful act, however ill the motive might be, he had a right to do it. If it was an unlawful act, however good his motive might be, he would have no right to do it.

> **Bradford Corporation v Pickles** (1895)
> Mr P owned land near to the Corporation's land. The Corporation drew water from its own land. Mr P wanted the Corporation to buy his land and tried to force it to do so by extracting mineral deposits under his land which reduced the water flow under the Corporation's land and

> caused the water to discolour. The Corporation wanted an injunction to prevent Mr P from continuing his activities. *Held*: no matter what his motive, Mr P as landowner had the right to abstract and use water flowing under his own land. The Corporation had no rights in the water until it reached its land. No injunction was ordered.

Motive may be relevant in some cases where the court is deciding whether or not an activity is reasonable. Malice, or a bad motive, can have the effect of making what would otherwise be a reasonable and lawful activity, and therefore not a nuisance, into an unreasonable activity and therefore unlawful and a nuisance. This has been particularly relevant in cases involving noise nuisance.

> ### *Christie v Davey* (1893)
> The parties lived next door to each other in semi-detached houses. The claimant was a piano teacher and had a musical family so that the defendant was frequently able to hear music coming from next door. It got on his nerves and he retaliated by making his own noise – beating trays and banging on walls – to an extent that was excessive and unreasonable. *Held*: 'the noises which were made in the defendant's house were not of a legitimate kind ... they were made deliberately and maliciously for the purpose of annoying the plaintiffs [claimants]. If what has taken place had occurred between two sets of person, both perfectly innocent, I should have taken an entirely different view of the case. What was done by the defendant was done only for the purpose of annoyance, and in my opinion it was not a legitimate use of the defendant's house to use it for the purpose of vexing and annoying his neighbours.' (*per* North J)
>
> ### *Hollywood Silver Fox Farm Ltd v Emmett* (1936)
> The claimant ran a fox farm on land next to Mr E's farm. Mr E wanted to sell his farm for building and believed that a fox farm next door would diminish its value. He arranged for shots to be fired, on his land but close to the fox farm. He knew that vixens were particularly sensitive to loud noises during the mating season and if upset, they would eat their cubs. *Held*: Mr E's malice was enough to make the intentional firing of the guns to disturb the foxes an unreasonable activity.

Abnormal sensitivity

A person who is unusually sensitive or who carries out an activity which is unusually sensitive may find that even though inconvenience is caused by activities on nearby land, no nuisance has been committed. This rule can apply both where physical damage is caused on the claimant's land or where there is interference with health or comfort.

> **Robinson v Kilvert (1889)**
> The defendant ran a manufacturing process which raised the temperature in the premises above. The claimant used the upstairs premises to store a certain type of brown paper which was damaged by the heat. As ordinary paper would not have been affected, no nuisance had been committed.

Where the activity would damage something which is not unusually sensitive, a nuisance can be committed where something sensitive is harmed.

> **McKinnon Industries Ltd v Walker (1951)**
> Where fumes would damage ordinary flowers such as roses, the defendant will be responsible for damage to delicate flowers such as orchids.

> As the number of people suffering asthma and other illnesses caused by pollution are increasing, is a person with such an illness likely to be regarded as 'abnormally sensitive' if the illness is triggered by pollution arising from the defendant's use of their land?

This rule has given rise to some interesting cases concerning the reception of television programmes. In *Bridlington Relay Ltd v Yorkshire Electricity Board* (1965) it was held that the reception of television signals was not an ordinary use of property. It seemed that this might change when a Canadian case (*Nor-Video Services Ltd v Ontario Hydro* [1978]) held that television reception was an important part of the normal enjoyment of property and should be protected. In *Hunter v Canary Wharf Ltd* (1997), the House of Lords held that by merely erecting a building which had the unfortunate effect of causing interference, no nuisance was committed. The judges were in part motivated by a fear that to reach any other conclusion would open the floodgates to huge numbers of claims against developers but left open the possibility that malicious interference might lead to a different conclusion. It is perhaps difficult to see how a building could be erected maliciously.

> Do you agree with the judges that the ability to watch television without interference is an extraordinary use of land?

Defences

Prescription

It is no defence that the claimant moved to be near to the nuisance nor that the nuisance was known about before the victim moved in. However, where the nuisance has existed as an actionable nuisance (someone could have brought a legal action for the tort but did not do so) for the previous twenty years, no action can be brought. This problem occurs from time to time in rural communities. A church on the outskirts of a village may have rung its bells without complaint for hundreds of years but the villagers were some distance from the church and no actionable nuisance occurred. Once new properties are built closer to the church, the noise of the bells may be regarded as unreasonable for the first time. If this is the case, the actionable nuisance has started only from the time the new properties were first occupied and the calculation of the twenty-year period starts from that date.

> ### *Sturges v Bridgman* (1879)
> A doctor ran a practice from his house adjoining Wimpole Street in London. Some time after he moved in, he built a new consulting room at the bottom of his garden which adjoined premises owned by the defendants. The defendants had been carrying on business as confectioners for at least the past twenty-six years. The process included the grinding of sugar which was not a problem until the consulting-room was built adjoining the factory. The noise of the machinery meant that the new consulting-room was unable to be used. *Held*: the fact that the business had been carried on for twenty-six years was not relevant. It was only once the noise produced became an actionable nuisance, when the consulting room was built and used, that the matter was actionable and the twenty years must be counted from that time.

> Do you think that the rule that moving to a nuisance is no defence
> is fair? Look back at the Introduction and try to work out what
> ethical principles can justify this view.

Statutory authority

An Act of Parliament may specifically permit certain activities, which
cause problems for the neighbours, to be carried out. Whether or not this
activity amounts to an actionable nuisance will depend on the precise
wording of the statute. Where the nuisance is an inevitable consequence
of the activity, the Act can be used as a defence. If the nuisance is not an
inevitable result, the position will depend on the wording of the Act.
When the Act specifically states that no one affected by the nuisance
shall have a claim, the defence of statutory authority applies. If the statute
is silent and the nuisance could in fact have been prevented, the neighbours
may well succeed in a claim for nuisance. (See Chapter 10, pp. 214–217
on breach of statutory duty.)

Planning permission

A local planning authority has the responsibility under the relevant
legislation to decide what developments and changes of use of land
are appropriate for the area. This might lead a person to believe, not
unreasonably, that the permitted activity cannot amount to an
actionable nuisance. The position is not so simple:

- In *Gillingham Borough Council v Medway (Chatham) Dock Ltd*
  (1993) the planning permission which was granted
  inevitably had the effect of changing the character of the
  neighbourhood. The planning permission could be used as
  a defence having particular relevance to the issue of the
  nature of the locality.

- *In Wheeler v J.J. Saunders* (1995) it was held that the
  granting of planning consent for the erection of two
  pigsties did not have a similar effect. The sties resulted in a
  nuisance because of the smell which affected the
  claimant's property. It was held that the effect of the
  planning permission did not alter the character of the
  neighbourhood and could not be used as a defence.

The position appears to be that the grant of planning consent will
only be a defence where a change in the character of the neighbourhood is an inevitable consequence of the consent.

Usefulness

The fact that an activity is of benefit to other people does not mean that it cannot amount to a nuisance nor that an injunction cannot be granted to stop the activity.

> ### *Adams v Ursell* (1913)
> A fish and chip shop was in business in a nice residential street. It was extremely useful to the residents of a poorer area nearby and its closure would cause great hardship to the owner. Even so it interfered with the nearby residents in their occupation of their homes. *Held*: the business was a nuisance and an injunction was granted.

Usefulness may be relevant when the court is deciding the appropriate remedy.

Remedies

The granting of an injunction

This is the usual remedy for nuisance as payment of damages would in one sense enable someone, in a position to do so, to pay to break the law. The granting of an injunction should be the first option but in *Miller v Jackson* (1977) the Court of Appeal held that public interest had a role to play. The court may be persuaded to consider the extent to which the use amounts to a public benefit.

> ### *Miller v Jackson* (1977)
> A housing estate had been built next to a cricket ground which had been used for more than twenty years. The new houses were so close to the ground that balls regularly came into the gardens and this meant that using the garden during a cricket match was unsafe. The court agreed that there was a real risk that someone could be injured or property damaged. *Held*: the use of the cricket ground amounted to a nuisance but when considering the appropriate remedy, the Court of Appeal held that the public interest of the community was enough to outweigh the interests of the new residents. An injunction was refused and damages awarded.

The need to consider the granting of an injunction as the first option was reconsidered in *Kennaway v Thompson* (1981) when the court held that *Miller v Jackson* was probably wrongly decided. The court restated the principles set out in *Shelfer v City of London Electric Lighting Co* (1895), which held that where a serious interference with the claimant's rights occurs, damages should only be awarded in lieu of an injunction where the injury suffered by the claimant is trivial or very temporary in nature.

> ### *Kennaway v Thompson* (1981)
> Ms K moved to a house next to a lake. She had known when she moved in that the lake was used for water-sports and had been for the past ten years. When she moved in the noise and disturbance caused were acceptable to her but over the years this increased as the lake became a centre for world-wide competition. The court found that the level of noise had gone beyond what Ms K was reasonably entitled to expect, or indeed to put up with, and that a nuisance was being committed. *Held*: despite the benefits to those taking part, Ms K was entitled to an injunction which restricted the times at which the lake could be used. Her injury was not small and damages would not be an appropriate remedy. The court imposed restrictions on the number of occasions on which club, national and international events could take place; the number of boats which could be used for water-skiing and the power of power-boats or towing-boats was limited.

Public nuisance

Definition

> A public nuisance is one which materially affects the reasonable comfort and convenience of a class of Her Majesty's subjects who come within the sphere or neighbourhood of its operation. (Winfield, p. 492)

A public nuisance affects the community at large. This might be the demolition of a factory which causes dust over a wide area, or the use of a factory which affects many people. If a number of people have been affected, the law makes provision for an action to be brought in the criminal courts by the Attorney General as it would be unreasonable to expect any one individual to act. In *Att. Gen (on the relation of Glamorgan County Council and Pontardawe Rural District Council)* (1957) the issue of what number of people constituted a class was considered. Lord Denning's judgment stated an accepted definition when he said that,

> a public nuisance is a nuisance which is so widespread in its range or so indiscriminate in its effect that it would not be reasonable to expect one person to take proceedings on his own responsibility to put a stop to it, but that it should be taken on the responsibility of the community at large.

A person or persons who are affected have the right to seek a remedy, by way of injunction, by means of what is known as a 'relator' action brought by the Attorney General on behalf of the class.

Affected individuals

Although an individual cannot bring an action for public nuisance, there is provision for someone who is affected more than most to do so. A person seeking a remedy for public nuisance must show that they have suffered damage above and beyond that suffered by others.

> *Tate & Lyle Industries Ltd v Greater London Council* (1983)
> The GLC constructed ferry terminals in the Thames which caused the river bed to become clogged with mud obstructing access to the claimants' wharves. The claimants had to spend a lot of money to have the river bed dredged. There was no actionable private nuisance as the wharves themselves were unaffected and the claimants did not own the river bed. *Held*: the silting had interfered with a public right of free navigation, a public nuisance, and the claimants had suffered much more than the public generally. The additional suffering allowed the claimants to bring a successful action for damages for public nuisance.

As *Tate & Lyle Industries Ltd v GLC* shows, the usual rule that there must be interference with the claimant's land is modified by public nuisance. No action for private nuisance could be brought as the silting did not affect the wharves themselves but the use of the wharves was interfered with indirectly.

A case which illustrates the difference between public and private nuisance is *Halsey v Esso Petroleum Co Ltd* (1961).

Halsey v Esso Petroleum Co Ltd (1961)
The claimant lived on the Fulham Road in London, a busy area, near to a depot owned and operated by the defendants. As a result of the defendants' activities, Mr H found that when his washing was hung out to dry it was damaged by smuts from the depot, his car was damaged by acid smuts when it was parked on the road outside his house, the smell was dreadful and he was unable to sleep at night because of the noise of lorries turning into and out of the depot. *Held*: the damage to his washing and the smell arose from private nuisance (interference with his use of his land), and the damage to his car (not parked on his land) and the noise arose from public nuisance. He had suffered more than most and was entitled to a remedy for the public nuisance as well as the private nuisance.

Statutory nuisance

It is not necessary in a general book about torts to include detailed information about statutory nuisances, but an outline knowledge and understanding is appropriate.

Statutory nuisances are those matters which an Act of Parliament declares to be a statutory nuisance. It is not usually necessary to show that the problem affects other land but generally it must be prejudicial to health (for example, a landlord who fails to carry out essential repairs to residential property may be liable), or amount to a nuisance (which has the same meaning as for private nuisance).

The law is enforced by local authorities by means of an abatement notice, requiring the creator of the nuisance to put matters right. If the notice is not obeyed, the matter can be taken to the magistrates' court which has power to order compliance and to impose penalties in the event of non-compliance.

Some statutes permit the local authority much wider powers to carry out necessary actions, and then to charge the creator for the cost. In the case of a noise nuisance, the local authority has power to seize the offending equipment.

Other solutions to 'nuisance' behaviour

Bringing a court action is costly and although an injunction can be granted swiftly in an urgent case, the final decision takes time. If the local authority can be persuaded to use its powers in relation to something which is also a statutory nuisance, the action is likely to be quickly and effectively dealt with and will cost the victim nothing; council tax payers will foot the bill through the tax.

Stories of 'neighbours from hell' are frequently heard. Court action will often have the effect of making a bad situation worse in terms of enmity between neighbours. Some local authorities have introduced mediation schemes to try to bring peace, to try to find an effective solution and to save money. Further schemes are likely to be introduced as the Access to Justice Act 1999 comes fully into effect. The Act emphasises the importance of the role which 'Alternative Dispute Resolution' can play in cutting down the number of court cases and consequently saving costs. The Lord Chancellor's Department, which is implementing the reforms, has said that additional funding will be available for mediation and conciliation schemes.

Problems between neighbours can have a great effect on both individuals and the community. People are not always reasonable nor are they always prepared to accept that their behaviour is causing problems for others. The law of nuisance does not provide a remedy for situations where, for example, children are running riot or where abusive and aggressive behaviour regularly occurs. In such cases, the criminal law may sometimes provide a remedy; for example, vandalism will often amount to criminal damage, but this is not often a very effective remedy.

A new remedy was introduced by the Crime and Disorder Act 1998 which provides that an anti-social behaviour order can be made by the magistrate's court on the application of the police or a local authority. The order can take many forms, including imposing a curfew, or excluding a person from a particular area, or forbidding contact with named individuals. It can apply to anyone aged ten years or more who has been found guilty of behaving in such a way as to cause or be likely to cause harassment, alarm or distress to one or more persons. Anti-social behaviour is not defined by the Act but the Consultation Paper on Probationary Tenancies (Department of the Environment 1995) gives examples:

> Such behaviour manifests itself in many different ways and at varying levels of intensity. This can include vandalism, noise, verbal and physical abuse, threats of violence, racial harassment, damage to property, trespass, nuisance from dogs, car repairs on the street, joyriding, domestic violence, drugs and other criminal activities such as burglary.

Although the anti-social behaviour order is a relatively new remedy, it does seem that it will be a useful tool to deal with matters which affect a person's right to non-interference with their comfort and convenience. Orders have been obtained against teenagers who were prevented from entering a particular area following disturbances (*R v Manchester Crown Court ex p McCann* [2001]) and against tenants using their home for the purposes of drug dealing and prostitution (*Leicester CC v Lewis* [2000]).

The law relating to anti-social behaviour has been amended by the Anti-social Behaviour Act 2003, which extends the power to apply for an anti-social behaviour order in relation to housing matters to county councils and housing associations. It also deals, after a long campaign, with the problem of high hedges. Once Part 8 of the Act comes into effect, a person who is adversely affected by a hedge of two or more evergreen plants which grows to more than two metres high and which affects light or access to the victim's property will have a remedy. Complaint will need to be made to the local authority, which can make an abatement order. If all else fails, the order will be enforceable by the magistrates' court.

It was hoped that the European Convention on Human Rights could be used to deal with nuisance behaviour where the common law failed to do so. In *Hatton v UK* (2001), such hope appeared to be justified as the European Court of Human Rights held that night flights into Heathrow Airport were a breach of Article 8 (the right to privacy and family life). However, the UK government appealed and it was held that the economic well-being of the country meant that the inter–ference with Article 8 rights was justified (*Hatton v UK* [2003]). It is possible, but perhaps unlikely, that the European Convention will have some effect in relation to activities by the state which create a nuisance.

The Protection from Harassment Act 1997, discussed in detail in Chapter 1 page 22, may also provide an effective remedy for behaviour which is in reality a nuisance but which the law would not recognise as such.

Rylands v Fletcher

The tort of *Rylands v Fletcher* has its origins in the law of nuisance but has developed as a separate tort with its own rules. The tort imposes liability for the escape of something from land which causes damage. As we shall see, this part of the law, like nuisance, can be useful in dealing with cases of environmental damage.

Definition

The tort was originally defined by Blackburn J giving judgment at first instance in the case of *Rylands v Fletcher* (1865). His definition was approved by the House of Lords when the matter was heard on appeal and has not been improved on in any case since. Blackburn J said

> We think that the true rule of law is that the person who, for his own purposes, brings on his land and collects and keeps there anything likely to do mischief if it escapes, must keep it in at his peril, and, if he does not do so, is *prima facie* [on the face of it] answerable for all the damage which is the natural consequence of its escape.

In the House of Lords, Lord Cairns drew a distinction between what he described as 'natural use' such as the natural accumulation of rain water, and 'non-natural use', such as the storage of water in a purpose-built reservoir. In the case of natural use, there would be no liability for damage caused by its escape, whereas in the case of non-natural use, the law was as stated by Blackburn J.

Rylands v Fletcher (1865)
The defendants used reputable engineers to construct a reservoir to supply water to their mill. During the construction the engineers came across old mine shafts which were not properly sealed. Once the reservoir was in use, water poured down the mine shafts and into the claimant's mine which was nearby. The court found on the law at that time that there was no negligence on the part of the defendants. *Held*: the claimant was entitled to damages on the basis of what has become known as the tort of *Rylands v Fletcher*.

The elements of the tort

Dangerous things

The original case was about water. Most people would not think of water as being 'dangerous' in itself but would be aware that the escape of water can cause a lot of damage. The definition does not state that the thing accumulated must be dangerous in itself, but that it must be likely to cause damage ('do mischief') if it escapes. Over the years many things have been held to fall into this category, some of which are intrinsically dangerous, others which are not:

Figure 6.2

Rylands v Fletcher: questions to be decided by the court

(i)   Has there been an accumulation of something dangerous?

(ii) Has the thing escaped?

(iii) Was the accumulation a natural or non-natural use of the land?

(iv) Has the thing caused damage when it escaped?

(v)   Was the possibility of damage if the thing escaped foreseeable
      at the time it was accumulated?

- in *Hillier v Air Ministry* (1962) electricity escaped from
  high-voltage cables laid under the claimant's land and
  electrocuted his cows;

- in *Crowhurst v Amersham Burial Board* (1878) yew trees
  spread across a boundary and poisoned animals pastured
  in the adjoining field;

- in *Hale v Jenning Bros* (1938) a 'chair-o-plane' in a
  fairground caused damage when one of the chairs flew off
  and damaged adjoining land.

It might seem that anything kept on land has the potential for doing
damage if it escapes. But, in fact, the position is not quite so simple.

For many years the courts refused to define characteristics which
would make something dangerous, preferring to decide on a case-by-
case basis. It is now clear that the possibility of the thing causing
damage should it escape must be reasonably foreseeable at the time
the thing is accumulated. This was first decided in *Cambridge Water Co
v Eastern Counties Leather plc* (1994) when the claimant lost the case
because the damage caused by escaping chemicals could not have
been foreseen at the time they were brought onto the defendant's
land.

Cambridge Water Co v Eastern Counties Leather plc (1994)
The defendants had for years operated a tannery in what
was described as 'an industrial village'. The claimants drew
water from a nearby bore-hole which was fed by an aquifer
running under the defendants' land. The claimants
discovered that the water had been contaminated by
chemicals which it was found had come from the

> defendants' land. Over the years the chemical, which is not dangerous to health, had seeped into the aquifer from small spillages on the defendants' premises. The pollution was only a problem once new European Community Directives on the purity of drinking water came into effect, when the claimant was forced to use an alternative water supply. At the time of the accumulation, the 'danger' was not known. *Held*: defendants not liable.

The issue of foreseeability has been considered more recently in *Transco plc v Stockport Metropolitan Council* (2003) when Lord Bingham said:

> It must be shown that the defendant has done something which he recognised ... or ought reasonably to have recognised, as giving rise to an exceptionally high risk of damage ... if there should be an escape, however unlikely an escape may be thought to be.

***Transco plc v Stockport Metropolitan Council* (2003)**
The defendants built a block of flats. A large pipe from the water main led to tanks in the bottom of the building to meet the needs of 66 households. The large pipe broke and water escaped over a period of time. No one was negligent in relation to either the break or the length of time it took for the leak to be discovered. It was eventually discovered, by which time the escaping water had caused an embankment under the claimant's gas mains pipe to collapse. This meant that there was serious danger. The claimants took immediate action and then claimed the cost from the defendants on the basis of *Rylands v Fletcher*. The court held that on the facts the accumulation of water for domestic use and not under pressure did not give rise to an exceptionally high risk of danger.

For some time there has been confusion as to whether 'damage' can include personal injury. In *Hale v Jennings* (1938) damages were awarded for personal injury but this was disputed in *Read v Lyons* (1947) when Lord Macmillan said 'It [*Rylands v Fletcher*] has nothing to do with personal injury'. In *Transco v Stockport* (2003) two of the judges, Lord Bingham and Lord Hoffmann, made it clear that the tort cannot extend to a claim for personal injury. Although their comments are *obiter*, the point is probably now settled and a claim can relate only to damage to land in which the claimant has an interest.

Escape

As the definition makes clear, the defendant is liable for the damage caused by an 'escape'. In simple terms the thing must move from the defendant's land to cause damage elsewhere. If there is no escape, there will be no liability, as was held in the case of *Read v J Lyons & Co Ltd* (1947).

> **Read v J Lyons & Co Ltd (1947)**
> Mrs R was an inspector of munitions working in the defendant's munitions factory. She was injured by the explosion of a shell while she was in the factory and sued for damages. There had been no negligence by the defendant. *Held*: Mrs R could not succeed in *Rylands v Fletcher* as there had been no escape. Escape means 'escape from a place where the defendant has occupation or control over land to a place which is outside his occupation or control'.

Non-natural use

As we have seen, Lord Cairns in *Rylands v Fletcher* made a distinction between natural and non-natural use. This is a refinement of the principle stated by Blackburn J that there would be liability for things brought onto the land and accumulated by the defendant.

The problem has been that the courts were undecided as to what was natural and what was non-natural. In *Rickards v Lothian* (1913), Lord Moulton explained the meaning of non-natural by saying:

> It is not every use ... that brings into play that principle of [*Rylands v Fletcher*]. It must be some special use bringing with it increased danger to others and must not merely be the ordinary use of the land or such a use as is proper for the general benefit of the community.

In *Read v J Lyons & Co Ltd* (1947) Viscount Simons suggested that making munitions at a time of war was a natural use as it was intended to defeat the enemy. In the same case, Lord Porter held that what was natural or non-natural needed to be decided according to the circumstances at the time. It seems clear that the judges regarded the making of munitions as being of benefit to the general community.

The question of benefit to the community was influential in *British Celanese Ltd v A H Hunt (Capacitors) Ltd* (1969).

> **British Celanese Ltd v A H Hunt (Capacitors) Ltd** (1969)
> The defendants had a lot of metal strips on their land as part of their business. The strips were blown about by the wind and landed on an electricity sub-station causing a blackout. It was known from previous experience that this could happen. *Held*: the defendants were not liable under *Rylands v Fletcher*.

Giving judgment in *British Celanese*, Lawton J held that

- the use of land on an industrial estate for industrial purposes was an ordinary use of that land

- the metal strips were needed for the manufacture of goods of a common type 'for the general benefit of the community'.

The issue of natural use was also considered by Lord Goff in *Cambridge Water* when he said, *obiter*:

> If the words are extended to embrace the wider interests of the local community or the general benefit of the community at large, it is difficult to see how the exception can be kept within reasonable bounds ... [T]he storage of substantial quantities of chemicals on industrial premises should be regarded as an almost classic case of non-natural use.

It is clear that following *Cambridge Water* it would be even more difficult to decide when liability under *Rylands v Fletcher* would be imposed. The problem has been settled by *Transco v Stockport* when the judges unanimously found that storage of water not under pressure for domestic use did not amount to non-natural use. In Transco Lord Bingham said:

> ... ordinary user is a preferable test to natural user, making it clear that the rule in *Rylands v Fletcher* [applies] only where the defendant's use is shown to be extraordinary and unusual.

No doubt there will be argument about what activities should be seen as 'extraordinary and unusual' but it seems to be clear that the issue of benefit to the community will no longer be enough to excuse a defendant.

> The government has recently licensed the use of genetically modified maize, a decision which is very controversial. Do you think that this will be seen as an ordinary or extraordinary use of land?

Strict liability?

Traditionally the tort has been regarded as one of strict liability, which means that it is not generally necessary to prove fault by the defendant. It can be argued that in reality this has not been the case for many years. We have seen that the judges have used the concepts of natural and non-natural use to allow a defendant to avoid liability for the escape of something which on the face of it clearly falls within the rule.

The concept of fault was introduced by *Cambridge Water*. It was made clear that the potential for the thing accumulated to cause damage if it were to escape must be reasonably foreseeable at the time of the accumulation. The requirement of reasonable foresight has been confirmed in *Transco v Stockport* but the judges appear to be reluctant to abandon the idea that tort is one of strict liability. Lord Hobhouse explained that once a recognisable risk has been created then 'the liability for the foreseeable consequences of failure to control and confine it is strict'.

Although Lord Hobhouse was trying to clarify the issue, at first sight it seems that all he has done is to create confusion. On second thoughts, however, it is clear that there is indeed a requirement to prove fault by the defendant. Defendants will be liable if they fail reasonably to foresee the potential dangers of an escape. While this appears to create a duty of care, the court in *Transco v Stockport* expressly refused to decide that matters dealt with by *Rylands v Fletcher* could in fact be dealt with using the tort of negligence. In an Australian case, *Burnie Port Authority v General Jones Pty Ltd* (1994), the Australian court abolished *Rylands v Fletcher*, holding that it was no longer needed. The torts of negligence and nuisance were enough to give a claimant protection from things escaping and causing damage. The House of Lords in *Transco v Stockport* discussed what had been done in Australia but declined to follow the same course. The judges were unanimous in deciding that *Rylands v Fletcher* still has a role to play.

> Still with the agricultural theme: a debate is raging about the potential damage which may be caused to the environment with the introduction of genetically modified crops. Do you think that *Rylands v Fletcher* might help farmers whose land is 'contaminated' by GM crops grown on adjoining land to obtain compensation?

Defences

Consent

If a person has consented to the accumulation, complaint cannot be made if there is an escape and damage is caused. The position would be different if the escape had been caused through negligence in which case liability under that tort might be possible. A common example of implied consent occurs in buildings where different tenants occupy different floors. Each is taken to have consented to the ordinary use of water on the other floors.

Act of a stranger

If the escape is caused by the unforeseeable act of a stranger, there is no liability in *Rylands v Fletcher*. In *Perry v Kendricks Transport Ltd* (1956) Lord Jenkins explained that the essence of the defence is the absence of any control by the defendant over the acts of a stranger on his land.

> **Perry v Kendricks Transport Ltd (1956)**
> The defendants stored a motor coach on land. The petrol tank was empty. Three children were playing, one of whom removed the cap of the petrol tank and threw in a lighted match. The claimant was burned in the resulting explosion. *Held*: the acts which led to the explosion were the acts of a stranger over whom the defendants had no control. The actions were unforeseeable. There was no liability in *Rylands v Fletcher*.

If the act of a stranger could reasonably have been anticipated or its consequences prevented, the defendant will be liable.

Statutory authority

Liability in *Rylands v Fletcher* may be expressly excluded by statute but more often the Act is silent and the courts have to use the rules of interpretation to decide whether or not there can be liability for the escape of a dangerous thing. If the accumulation which is authorised may inevitably have the consequence of causing damage in the event of an escape, there will be no liability.

- *Charing Cross Electricity Co v Hydraulic Power Co* (1914) involved the escape of water under high pressure from the defendants' mains. The defendants had permissive power to provide water for industrial purposes which did not include a duty to maintain high pressure. Escape was not inevitable and the defendants were liable for the damage caused.

- By contrast, in *Green v Chelsea Waterworks Co* (1894) the water company had a statutory duty to maintain pressure in its water mains. Inevitably damage would be caused by the occasional burst main but, in the absence of negligence, the defendants would not be liable for any damage.

Act of God

An Act of God is an unforeseeable natural phenomenon. In the context of *Rylands v Fletcher*, the escape must occur as a result of some natural occurrence which could not be anticipated and which no person could guard against. The defence was used successfully in *Nichols v Marsland* (1876) when a series of ornamental lakes overflowed and washed away four bridges. The flood had been caused by heavy rain which was described as 'greater and more violent than any within the memory of witnesses'. In the later case of *Greenock Corporation v Caledonian Railway* (1917), in which the facts were similar to those in *Nichols v Marsland*, the House of Lords held that rainfall, even if exceptionally heavy, was not an Act of God.

It seems that Act of God is confined to natural occurrences which cannot be anticipated. In the United Kingdom this would not include high winds or extraordinarily high tides, but would probably include lightning, earthquakes and tornadoes.

Default of the claimant

A person who causes the damage cannot complain and cannot hold the defendant liable. An example of this is found in *Ponting v Noakes* (1894) when the claimant's horse died after reaching across a boundary fence to reach and eat from a poisonous tree. It was held that the damage was due to the horse's intrusion into the defendant's land and in any case there had been no escape. The claimant did not succeed in his claim.

Environmental protection

Over the past years, public awareness of the effect of environmental damage has increased, ranging from concern about global warming and the destruction of the rainforests to a greater awareness of personal responsibility, evidenced by the growing consciousness of the need to recycle household waste.

On the face of it, it would seem that the torts of nuisance and *Rylands v Fletcher* have a potentially important role to play in dealing with matters of pollution. When the torts are looked at in depth, it is apparent that their effectiveness in dealing with anything other than an individual problem is questionable. Both torts protect interests in land from actions on other land which causes damage or interference. The torts are concerned with rights in land rather than with the environment generally. It is true that in some cases, the activity complained of has an effect on the environment but this is not necessarily the case and the fact that there may be environmental damage does not of itself give rise to liability for the torts.

The courts are aware of the potential for the torts to be used to protect the environment. Some idea of the way in which the judges view the issue is given by the judgment of Lord Goff in *Cambridge Water* when he says:

> The protection and preservation of the environment is now perceived as being of crucial importance to the future of mankind; and public bodies, both national and international, are taking significant steps towards the establishment of legislation which will promote the protection of the environment, and make the polluter pay for damage to the environment for which he is responsible ... But it does not follow from these developments that a common law principle, such as the rule in *Rylands v Fletcher*, should be developed or rendered more strict to provide for liability in respect of such pollution. On the contrary, given that so much well-informed and carefully structured legislation is now being put in place for this purpose, there is less need for the courts to develop a common law principle to achieve the same end, and indeed it may well be undesirable that they should do so.

Much of the legislation referred to by Lord Goff stems from the law of the European Union. Two of the basic principles underpinning EU law are

- the promotion of sustainable development
- the polluter should pay.

The EU acts by means of Directives, allowing each Member State to implement the requirements in a way appropriate to the individual State. In the United Kingdom this has largely been done by means of primary enabling legislation, the Environmental Protection Act 1990 and the Environment Act 1995, and by statutory instruments creating enforceable Regulations. Enforcement is the responsibility of the Environmental Protection Agency and the Local Authorities. Among other things, the regulations deal with liability for water pollution, waste management and air pollution.

Other areas of law and policy also work to protect the environment. The law relating to Town and Country planning requires a developer to carry out an 'environmental impact assessment' before planning permission can be granted. Transport policies are designed to decrease the problem of traffic pollution.

Ultra-hazardous activities have for many years been regulated by specific statutes dealing with the particular industry. Examples include the Nuclear Installations Act 1965 which is concerned with liability for damage caused by ionising radiations and the Merchant Shipping Act 1995 which imposes civil liability for oil pollution damage caused by ships. Both Acts, although providing for specific defences, impose strict liability. It is likely that for the foreseeable future, the law in relation to ultra-hazardous activities will continue to develop piecemeal, the Law Commission having rejected the idea of a general theory of strict liability for such activities ('Civil Liability for Dangerous Things and Activities' Law Com No 32 1970).

The law of torts may still evolve to give greater protection from hazardous activities. Although Lord Goff in *Cambridge Water* took the view that 'it is more appropriate for strict liability in respect of operations of high risk to be imposed by Parliament', the judges in *Transco v Stockport* took a different view. Lord Hobhouse said:

> The area of regulation is not exhaustive; it does not necessarily give the third party ... an adequate or ... any say ... it will not normally deal with civil liability for damage to property; it does not provide adequate knowledge and control to [enable a person] to evaluate and protect himself from the consequent risk.

It seems therefore possible that the torts of nuisance and *Rylands v Fletcher* will continue to develop in connection with what can be termed 'individual' or 'local' problems, but liability for wider problems will continue to be viewed as an issue for Parliament.

The environment is of concern to many people. Make a list of environmental matters which are important in your area. Do you think that the present law is adequate to deal with these?

SUMMARY

Trespass to land

- occurs when person without lawful authority enters or remains on someone else's land or puts anything under, on or over it

- defence of particular relevance – lawful authority, e.g. Police and Criminal Evidence Act 1984, Access to Neighbouring Land Act 1992

Remedies

- re-entry and ejectment using reasonable force if necessary – restricted by Protection from Eviction Act 1977 in case of residential squatters

- rights of third parties – allow trespasser to take legal action against anyone who commits trespass against them except someone with better title, e.g. the legal owner

- mesne profits; reasonable payment for the period of the trespass plus damages for any deterioration

Private nuisance

- interference with a person's use or enjoyment of their own land by the activity of another on the other's land

- activity on the other's land must be unreasonable

- relevant matters taken into account by the court
    locality: unless physical damage has been caused in which case locality is irrelevant – *St Helen's Smelting Co v Tipping* (1865), *Sturges v Bridgman* (1879)
    duration: generally the activity must be continuous or regular – *Swaine v Great Northern Railway* (1864), *Andreae v Selfridge & Co Ltd* (1938) – or done at unreasonable time – *De Keyser's Royal Hotel Ltd v Spicer Bros Ltd* (1914) – single incident can be enough – *Crown River Cruises Ltd v Kimbolton Fireworks Ltd* (1996), *Goldman v Hargrave* (1967), *Leakey v National Trust* (1980)
    malice: can make otherwise reasonable act unreasonable and therefore unlawful – *Christie v Davey* (1893), *Hollywood Silver Fox Farm v Emmett* (1936)
    sensitivity: is person or property damaged unusually sensitive? If so, no nuisance unless persons and things of ordinary sensitivity are also damaged – *Robinson v Kilvert* (1889), *Hunter v Canary Wharf Ltd* (1997)

- Defences
    prescription: activity which has been an actionable nuisance for at least the past twenty years and no one able to bring an action has done so – *Sturges v Bridgman* (1879)

statutory authority: activity authorised by statute with creation of nuisance an inevitable consequence

planning permission: only if a change in the character of the neighbourhood is an inevitable consequence of the permitted development – *Gillingham BC v Medway (Chatham) Dock Ltd* (1993), *Wheeler v JJ Saunders* (1995)

usefulness: fact that the nuisance activity is of benefit to people is irrelevant – *Adams v Ursell* (1913); may be relevant to nature of remedy awarded

- Remedies
  injunction: first choice of remedy unless interference with claimant's land is trivial or very temporary – *Shelfer v City of London Electric Lighting Co* (1895), *Kennaway v Thompson* (1981) – usefulness of activity may help decide terms of injunction – *Kennaway v Thompson*

Public nuisance

- affects the community at large

- person who suffers above and beyond others may be able to sue – *Tate & Lyle Industries v GLC* (1983), *Halsey v Esso Petroleum* (1961)

- crime as well as tort

- legal action taken on behalf of those affected by Attorney General or local authority

Statutory nuisance

- those matters stated by statute to be a nuisance, e.g. failure to deal with dampness in a tenant's home

- enforced by local authority by service of abatement notice – failure to obey notice leads to prosecution and enforcement through the magistrates' court

Other solutions to nuisance behaviour

- mediation and conciliation schemes

- anti-social behaviour orders

- injunction under s.3 Protection from Harassment Act 1997

Rylands v Fletcher

Definition

- anyone who brings onto their land and keeps there anything which is likely to cause damage if it escapes is liable for all the consequences if it does escape

What is dangerous

- anything can be dangerous in this sense – water as held in *Rylands v Fletcher*, electricity as in *Hillier v Air Ministry* (1962), yew trees as in *Crowhurst v Amersham Burial Board* (1878)

- the possibility of damage should the thing escape must be reasonably foreseeable at the time it is accumulated – *Cambridge Water v Eastern Counties Leather* (1994), *Transco plc v Stockport Metropolitan Council* (2003)

The need for escape

- without an escape from the defendant's land onto another's land there can be no liability – *Read v J Lyons & Co Ltd* (1947)

Distinction between natural and non-natural use

- originally a simple test – does the thing naturally accumulate on the land or not – *Rylands v Fletcher*

- later cases said issue of public benefit is relevant – *Read v J Lyons & Co Ltd* (1947) – as is the nature of the area – industrial use of industrial premises on an industrial estate natural use – *British Celanese Ltd v A J Hunt* (Capacitors) Ltd (1969)

- issue now decided by *Transco plc v Stockport Metropolitan Council* (2003) – use must be extraordinary and unusual

Defences

- consent: a person who consents to the accumulation cannot complain if there is an escape

- act of a stranger: the defendant cannot be blamed for actions by others over whom the defendant has no control – *Perry v Kendricks Transport* (1956)

- statutory authority: if the thing which is authorised may inevitably cause damage if it escapes, the statutory duty to accumulate it provides a defence – *Charing Cross Electricity Co v Hydraulic Power Co* (1914), *Green v Chelsea Waterworks Co* (1894)

- Act of God: an unforeseeable natural phenomenon, e.g. earthquake, lightning or tornado

- default of the claimant: a person who causes the damage cannot complain – *Ponting v Noakes* (1894)

QUESTIONS

1. In the course of modernising his house in accordance with planning permission granted by the local authority, Jay has upset his neighbours, Ron and Ethel. He has been working all night at times, hammering and drilling so that Ron and Ethel have found it impossible to sleep. Jay disposes of old wood etc. by burning what he can, lighting a bonfire at least three times a week regardless of whether or not the wind is blowing the smoke and soot straight into the house next door. Ethel, made irritable by lack of sleep, is made more tired by having to clean up regularly after Jay has had a bonfire.

   Jay has received a letter from Ron and Ethel telling him that unless he stops work immediately, an injunction will be obtained to force him to do so and that they expect him to pay for redecorating their home where it has been damaged by the soot.

   Advise Jay. How, if at all, would your answer differ if, instead of writing a letter, Ron and Ethel had decided to get their own back and started to play loud music at all times of the day and night? (OCR 1998)

2. Chris and Helen have bought a cottage which requires much work doing to it. They do most of the work themselves during evenings and at weekends. Pete, who lives next door, did not complain at first but the work has gone on for several months and there is no sign that it will soon be finished. He is disturbed by the noise of drilling and hammering which goes on late most evenings and by the noisier work which goes on at weekends. Another source of annoyance is the noise created most weekends by Helen and Chris's friends who have come to help and who stay late into the night having a party in the garden whenever the weather is fine. The neighbours have now fallen out over the situation and Pete is threatening to take court action to stop the work and the parties.

   Advise Helen and Chris of the likely outcome of any action which Pete takes in the courts. (OCR January 2002)

3. Giles runs a business, in a city centre, recycling broken pottery. He uses chemicals to clean the pottery, but some of the chemicals can cause damage if they escape onto adjoining land. His neighbour, Pam, runs a small organic farm which is often visited by local school children.

   During a recent heavy storm, some of the bags of chemicals used by Giles have split and the contents have been washed onto Pam's farm, meaning that the contamination will prevent her from selling her crops. Giles blames the school children who have from time to time come onto his land from the farm and, according to Giles, have cut some of the bags open making it more likely that the rain would wash the contents out.

Advise Pam of any legal action which she can take to obtain compensation. (OCR January 2002)

4. Ross owns and operates a small coal mine employing 50 people. The waste from the mining operation is piled up on the boundary of the mine, which is next to a small residential estate. Ross also stores flammable liquid on the site in a wooden hut. Children are known to use the site as a short-cut to the local playground although Ross does all he can to chase them away and keep the fencing secure.

Last week the pile of waste slipped into Fatima's garden, damaging many of her plants. The slip appears to have been caused by exceptionally heavy rain which had washed away the supporting earth under the pile. A couple of days later, the wooden hut was set on fire, causing the barrels of flammable liquid to explode, breaking the windows in all of the houses backing onto the site. On investigation, it was discovered that the hut had been broken into and children had been seen running away just as the fire started.

Advise Ross as to his potential liability in the law of tort for the damage to Fatima's garden and for the broken windows. (OCR June 2003)

5. Critically consider whether the law relating to trespass to land is adequate to protect the privacy of occupiers of land. (Oxford 1997)

6. 'The tort of trespass to land to some extent acts to protect the occupier's privacy.'

Critically consider how adequate the law is to this purpose. (OCR 1999)

7. People are entitled to decide who, if anyone, may come onto their land and for what purpose. Discuss whether or not the law relating to trespass to land upholds this right. (OCR January 2002)

8. The protection of the environment is a matter of concern to many people. To what extent does the law relating to private nuisance contribute to such protection? (Oxford 1997)

9. To what extent does the tort of private nuisance succeed in balancing the competing interests of neighbours to use their premises as they choose? (OCR 1999)

10. How useful is the tort of *Rylands v Fletcher* in the control of environmental pollution? (OCR 1998)

11. Consider the elements of the tort created by *Rylands v Fletcher* (1868). Illustrate your answer with cases and/or examples of situations in which an action based on this principle may arise. (Oxford 1993)

7   Strict liability

The concept of strict liability

The words 'strict liability' can lead to some confusion. Most torts require an element of fault on the part of the alleged wrongdoer but in a tort of strict liability fault is largely irrelevant. If the wrong has occurred, the defendant will be liable, regardless of blame. This does not mean that there can be no defence, although the available defences may be limited. This part of the book looks at two areas of strict liability, liability for animals and liability for dangerous products. Both are statutory torts and both are subject to statutory defences which mean that the wrongdoer can escape liability.

Liability for animals

The law is found in the Animals Act 1971 and in the common law. The basic assumption is that because animals are by their nature unpredictable, a person who keeps an animal does so at his peril. Where, however, the animal is usually domesticated and regarded as harmless, strict liability does not apply unless the animal has given cause to fear that it might be dangerous. Perhaps this was the origin of the saying that 'every dog is allowed one bite!', although as we shall see this is not strictly true.

Who is liable?

The Animals Act 1971 imposes strict liability on the 'keeper' of an animal. By s.6(3)

> a person is a keeper of an animal if:
>
> (a) he owns the animal or has it in his possession; or
>
> (b) he is the head of a household of which a member under the age of sixteen owns the animal or has it in his possession.

If an animal strays the original keeper remains liable until another person fulfils the definition. If the animal is taken into safe-keeping to prevent it from causing damage or until it can be returned to the keeper, the temporary owner is not regarded as the keeper.

The Act does not define what is meant by 'head of a household', but it is likely that the parent or guardian of a child who owns an animal will be liable in respect of that animal.

The keeper of a dangerous species has strict liability if it causes damage; the keeper of an animal of a non-dangerous species will have liability if the animal is known to be unreliable.

Which animals are 'dangerous' and which 'non-dangerous'?

By s.6(2),

> A dangerous species is a species:–
>
> (a) which is not commonly domesticated in the British Isles; and
>
> (b) whose fully grown animals normally have such characteristics that they are likely, unless restrained, to cause severe damage or that any damage they may cause is likely to be severe.

All other animals are 'non-dangerous'.

If an animal falls within the definition, it is 'dangerous' even if the particular animal is unusually tame. This reflects the rule under the old law, as stated in the following case:

> ### Behrens v Bertram Mills Circus Ltd (1957)
> Mr and Mrs B ran a booth in a fun fair operated by the owners of a circus. The elephants passed the booth as they were taken into the ring for the performance. One, known as Bullu, was frightened by a small dog and in its fright trampled the booth, injuring Mr and Mrs B. *Held*: although Bullu was described as being 'no more dangerous than a cow', it was a dangerous animal and the circus owners had an absolute duty to control it and prevent damage.

When is the keeper liable?

By s.2(1), 'Where any damage is caused by an animal which belongs to a dangerous species, any person who is a keeper of the animal is liable for the damage.'

Various defences may be available as set out in the Act but the basic rule is that the keeper of a dangerous species has strict liability. This has recently been explained by Lord Nicholls in *Mirvahedy v Henley and Another* (2003) when he said

> If you choose to keep a dangerous animal ... you are liable for damage done by the animal ... Liability is independent of fault. Liability is independent of knowledge of the animal's dangerous characteristics.

By s.2(2),

> Where damage is caused by an animal which does not belong to a dangerous species, a keeper of the animal is liable for the damage if:
>
> (a) the damage is of a kind which the animal, unless restrained, was likely to cause or which, if caused by the animal, was likely to be severe; and
>
> (b) the likelihood of the damage or of its being severe was due to characteristics which are not normally found in animals of the same species or are not normally so found except at particular times or in particular circumstances; and
>
> (c) those circumstances were known to that keeper or were at any time known to a person who at that time had charge of the animal as that keeper's servant or where that keeper is the head of a household, were known to another keeper of the animal who is a member of that household and under the age of sixteen.

This section has caused a lot of difficulty because of the way in which it is drafted. It is rather confusing to say the least. The House of Lords has, for the first time, been able to consider s.2(2) in *Mirvahedy v Henley* (2003). The facts of the case are given here and reference will be made to specific parts of the judgment as they are relevant.

> ***Mirvahedy v Henley and Another*** (2003)
> Three horses were kept by Mr and Mrs H in a field next to their house. For some unknown reason, the horses were 'spooked' one night. They broke through an electric fence and a wooden fence round the field and bolted down a track. They eventually bolted onto a main road where one

of the horses collided with the car driven by Mr M. The horse was killed and Mr M was seriously injured. Mr M brought an action under the Animals Act.

The claimant lost in the High Court and won in the Court of Appeal. The defendants appealed to the House of Lords, which held by majority decision that the defendants were liable.

The House of Lords concentrated mainly on the meaning of s.2(2)(b) so that earlier judgments continue to provide some help in deciding the effect of the other sub-sections.

The question to be decided under s.2(2)(a) is whether the damage is of a kind which the particular animal, unless restrained, was likely to cause, or if caused was likely to be severe. Thus a bite by a large dog is likely to be severe and there may be liability.

Curtis v Betts (1990)

The claimant, aged eleven, was attacked and bitten by Max, a bull mastiff weighing nearly 140 lb (approximately 70 kg). The child knew the dog and as he cycled past he called to Max who was being put into a vehicle to go to the park. The dog leapt at the child and bit him on the face. It is a characteristic of bull mastiffs that they will defend their territory and it was thought that Max regarded the vehicle as his territory. The child was in no way to blame for what happened and it was found that there had been no negligence on the part of Max's owners. *Held*: s.2(2)(a) was satisfied, Lord Slade saying, 'Max was a dog of the bull mastiff breed. If he did bite anyone, the damage was likely to be severe.'

The words 'was likely' which are used twice in s.2(2)(a) have a wide meaning. It can include an event 'such as might well happen' or 'a material risk that it will happen' rather than 'more probable than not'.

Smith v Ainger (*The Times*, 5 June 1990)

Mr S was knocked over by Mr A's large mongrel dog when he tried to stop it attacking his dog. Mr S broke his leg. Mr A's dog was known to attack other dogs. The question the court had to decide was whether there was a difference

> between a dog bite and being given a buffet by a dog which knocked the victim over. *Held*: there was no distinction to be drawn between a bite and a buffet. If Mr A's dog attacked another dog there was a risk that the other dog's owner would intervene and would be bitten or buffeted as a result, so that Mr S's injury was damage of a kind which the dog was likely to cause.

S.2(2)(b) has been looked at in different ways over the years. It can be divided into two parts:

1   the damage was caused by characteristics 'which are not normally found' in that species – in other words, the animal is abnormal in some respects when compared with others of that species; or

2   the damage was caused by characteristics which are only present at 'particular times or in particular circumstances'.

The problem has been that some judges have taken the view that the two requirements should be read together. This would mean that whenever the second part of the sub-section could apply, it would be necessary for the claimant to show that the reaction was abnormal as required by the first part. The facts of *Mirvahedy* illustrate the potential problem. All horses are likely to bolt when frightened so that this cannot be an abnormal characteristic for the purpose of s.2(2)(b). If the two parts are read together, then the claimant must lose. Two of the judges in the House of Lords took this view. The majority held that the two parts were independent of each other. This means, for example, that the owner of a bitch which bites someone who seems to be a threat to her pups is liable under the second part. It is not necessary for the reaction to be abnormal, simply one that only occurs at certain times or in certain circumstances.

In *Mirvahedy* Lord Nicholls held that, although the horses were behaving normally for frightened horses, 'It was precisely because they were behaving in an unusual way caused by their panic that the road accident took place.' This means that the earlier cases are still helpful illustrations of how the judges are likely to interpret the second requirement. In *Curtis v Betts* (1990) it was found that bull mastiffs have a tendency to react fiercely at particular times and in particular circumstances, in other words when defending the boundaries of their territory. This was enough to satisfy s.2(2)(b).

The difficulty caused by s.2(2) was highlighted in a case involving a police dog (*Gloster v Chief Constable of Greater Manchester Police* [2000]). There was no doubt that the damage which such a dog could cause was likely to be severe but could it be argued that the likelihood of damage was caused by characteristics which were not normally found in a dog? The court found that the fact that the dog had been specially trained did not give it characteristics which were not normally found in a German shepherd dog. 'The dog did not cease to be normal as a result of its training as a police dog.' (*per* Pill LJ.)

> ### Gloster v Chief Constable of Greater Manchester Police (2000)
> Jack, a German shepherd dog, had been trained as a police dog and was rated as 'satisfactory' and 'not over-aggressive'. A police officer, Mr G, who had not heard a warning that Jack was to be sent to chase a car thief, was chased and bitten after the dog had been set loose when his handler tripped and fell enabling Jack to slip his collar. Jack assumed that this was his instruction to chase and, mistaking Mr G for the thief, bit him twice in the leg before he was called off. *Held*: the relevant characteristic was the breed's ability to respond to specific training and instruction – a characteristic which is normally found in German shepherd dogs and which is not a 'characteristic not normally found in animals of the same species'. Mr G was not entitled to damages under the Animals Act 1971.

The meaning of 'characteristics' is still unclear. One of the judges in *Mirvahedy* criticised the decision in *Gloster v Chief Constable of Greater Manchester Police* saying that 'the likelihood of being chased and bitten was due to a characteristic of the police dog not normally found in German shepherd dogs'. The other judges in *Mirvahedy* did not comment on *Gloster* so that the question of what amounts to a characteristic remains something of a problem.

In most cases the characteristic which has caused the damage will be a tendency to attack people, but this is not essential. In *Wallace v Newton* (1982) Mr W successfully claimed damages after he had been injured by a horse. The horse was known to be unreliable and unpredictable and suddenly became violent and uncontrollable when being loaded into a trailer, injuring Mr W.

By s.2(2)(c) the keeper must know about the relevant characteristics. Actual knowledge may be presumed in the case of a head of a household where the keeper is under sixteen. It is not necessary to show that the animal has actually caused damage in the past, but it is essential that it has shown a possibility that it will do so. In *Curtis v*

Betts it was held that the owners knew about Max's relevant characteristics, namely his tendency to attack fiercely when defending what he regarded as his own territory.

Defences

The defences are found in s.5 of the Act. In s.5(1) the Act states that the victim cannot succeed in a claim if the damage is entirely due to the victim's fault. In *Marlor v Ball* (1900) a person was injured when stroking a zebra; in *Sylvester v Chapman Ltd* (1935) the victim entered a leopard's pen to remove a lighted cigarette. In both cases the victim was held to be entirely to blame.

A keeper has no liability to a person who 'voluntarily accepted the risk' (s.5(2)). In *Cummings v Grainger* (1977) the claimant, who entered premises knowing about the guard dog which injured her, was held to have voluntarily accepted the risk. A similar decision was reached in *Dhesi v Chief Constable of West Midlands Police* (2000).

> ***Dhesi v Chief Constable of West Midlands Police*** (2000)
> Mr D and some other youths were involved in a confrontation with the police. Mr D was carrying a hockey stick which he was swinging from side to side; he was angry and aggressive. He ran off and hid among brambles in waste land. He was tracked by a police officer and a police dog. Having been warned that the dog would be set free if

Figure 7.1: Liability for animals

Is the animal dangerous?

Yes, if not usually domesticated in the UK

Strict liability for any damage except to trespasser

No, if usually domesticated in the UK

Keeper liable if animal causes, unless restrained, damage which it is likely to cause or which if caused is likely to be severe
and
likelihood of damage due to particular characteristics
and
characteristics were known to keeper

> he did not surrender, Mr D remained hidden. The dog was released after two further warnings had been given. In his struggle to get away from the dog, Mr D was bitten several times. *Held*: Mr D had voluntarily accepted the risk of being bitten and the resulting damage was wholly his own fault.

By s.5(3) if a trespasser is injured by an animal which is not being kept for protection, the keeper has no liability. Where, however, an animal is kept for the protection of persons or property, there will be liability to a trespasser if the court finds that it was unreasonable to keep the particular animal for that purpose.

> ### Cummings v Grainger (1977)
> Mr G ran a breaker's yard and at night allowed an Alsation (German shepherd) dog to run free for security purposes. Ms C knew about the dog when she entered at night with a friend. Ms C was a trespasser. As the dog was kept for security purposes the court had to decide whether or not this was reasonable. *Held*: 'The only reasonable way of protecting the place was to have a guard dog. True it was a fierce dog. But why not? A gentle dog would be no good. The thieves would soon make friends with him. It seems to me that it was very reasonable – or, at any rate, not unreasonable – for the defendant to keep this dog there' (Lord Denning). Lord Denning also stated in relation to the defence referred to in s.5(2) that 'any burglar or thief who goes on to premises knowing there is a guard dog there' must be taken to have voluntarily taken the risk. 'If he is bitten or injured, he cannot recover [damages].'

It should be noted that the Guard Dogs Act 1975, passed after the incident which gave rise to Ms Cumming's claim, makes it a criminal offence to allow a guard dog to run free unless it is under the control of a handler.

> Many people keep a dog as a pet, partly because the dog will act as a deterrent to burglars and for reasons of personal protection. Will the keeper be liable if the dog bites an invited visitor whom the dog has mistaken for a burglar?

While Act of God and act of a third party are not defences which can be used in relation to the Animals Act, the Court of Appeal found a way round this in *Jandrill v Gillett* (1996). Horses were maliciously released onto a road at night. They panicked and galloped into a car driven by the claimant. The court held that the real cause of the accident was the release of the animals onto the road and not any particular abnormal characteristic of the horses. The keeper, in the circumstances, was not liable.

Whether *Jandrill v Gillett* would be decided in the same way following *Mirvahedy* is not clear but it is likely that if the case were to come before a court today, the defendants would be found liable.

Liability for straying livestock

'Livestock' means cattle, horses, asses, mules, hinnies, sheep, pigs, goats, poultry and deer not in the wild state.

The key provisions dealing with livestock are as follows:

- An owner of livestock which strays onto land owned or occupied by someone else and causes damage to the land itself or any property on it, is liable for the damage.

  Note that the section does not give a remedy for personal injuries which might have been caused.

- s.7. An occupier onto whose land the livestock strays has a right to detain the livestock and to sell it to recoup the cost of damage done to his property although there are rules which must be followed before this can be done.

- s.5(4).The owner of land is generally under no duty to fence land to keep livestock out. In those cases where such a duty does exist and the land is unfenced, the owner of livestock is not liable if it strays onto the land.

- s.5(5). An owner of livestock lawfully present on a highway, for example in areas like the national parks where local people have a right to graze their livestock on the highway, is not liable if the animals stray from the highway and cause damage.

Dogs – the farmer's friend or foe?

Although there is no general liability for damage caused by straying dogs, s.3 of the Act gives a right of action against any person who is the keeper of a dog which kills or injures livestock. Liability is strict. It is no defence that the keeper has no knowledge of the dog's tendency to worry livestock nor to show that the dog has abnormal characteristics.

An owner of livestock may kill the dog if they act for the protection of livestock which is owned, or on land owned or occupied, by them. The owner of the livestock must have no other reasonable means of ending or preventing the worrying. When a dog has been worrying livestock, has not left the vicinity and is not under the control of any person or there is no practicable means of ascertaining to whom it belongs, the owner of the livestock has a similar right to kill the dog (s.9(3)). The owner of the livestock must have a reasonable belief that the dog is worrying or about to worry the livestock and in the other matters set out in the sub-section. The killing must be notified to the police within 48 hours.

Would it be right to make the keeper of a dog strictly liable for any damage that it causes if it escapes? Think about the ethical principles which support the arguments for and against such a rule.

What about animals which stray onto the highway?

The old common law rule that an owner of land adjoining the highway was under no duty to prevent tame domestic animals from straying onto the highway was abolished by s.8(1). The sub-section imposes a duty to take such care as is reasonable to see that animals do not stray onto a highway and cause damage. This means that failure to fence could be the basis of a claim in negligence. *Birch v Mills* (1995) is an example of such a case.

> ### *Birch v Mills* (1995)
> Mr M kept a herd of cows in an unfenced field which ran alongside a public road. He knew that the cows were frisky and prone to chase dogs. As Mr B was walking past with his dogs, which were on leads, the cows chased the dogs. As a result Mr B was hurt. *Held*: Mr M was liable. It was reasonably foreseeable that a person leading a dog past that field would be hurt.

Liability extends to any animal, not just livestock, and damage includes personal injuries.

A person who has a right to place animals on common land or on land in an area where fencing is not customary or on a town or village green is not liable for breach of any duty of care if they stray onto the highway (s.8(2)).

The common law

Liability for damage caused by animals is possible in relation to many torts. Setting a dog to attack a person could give rise to liability for assault and battery. The escape of a dangerous animal may come within the rules of *Rylands v Fletcher*. The mere keeping of animals on land could be the basis of an action for nuisance. It is even suggested that a parrot could be taught to say something which amounts to defamation.

The most likely action to arise under common law as a result of animals is in negligence. The normal principles apply. In *Fardon v Harcourt-Rivington* (1932) the House of Lords held that liability may be founded on a person's negligent treatment of an animal which was not normally dangerous.

> ### *Fardon v Harcourt-Rivington* (1932)
> A dog had been left in a car in very hot weather. In trying to escape the dog broke a window and a splinter of glass injured Mr F's eye. *Held*: Mr H-R was not liable as he was not required to guard against a 'fantastic possibility' but in principle the court acknowledged that an action in negligence for the handling of an animal could be established.

It is clear that while there is no liability under the Animals Act for damage caused by a non-dangerous animal which has previously shown no violent propensities, liability in negligence may not be excluded.

> ### *Aldham v United Dairies (London) Ltd* (1940)
> A milkman, the employee of the defendants, left a pony attached to a milk cart for half an hour while he made deliveries to a block of flats. The pony became restive and injured a passer-by. The animal was known to have become restive in the past and some persons had been alarmed by its behaviour. *Held*: while there was no knowledge on anyone's part that the pony was likely to attack humans, the employers were, in view of the pony's character, liable for the milkman having left it without attendance.

163

> ***Draper v Hodder*** (1972)
> A pack of Jack Russell terriers owned by H ran into the
> next door garden and savaged the child playing there. It
> was impossible to identify which dog or dogs had actually
> injured the child and knowledge by H of violent propensities
> could not be proved. *Held*: H was liable in negligence on
> the basis that a pack of terriers was liable to attack any
> moving target and H, as an experienced dog-breeder, knew
> this.

The Animals Act 1971 was designed in part to deal with the
difficulties encountered by people trying to obtain a remedy for injuries
and damage caused by animals. The Act provides what is probably
an effective means of ensuring the availability of a remedy when the
animal involved is a member of a dangerous species. Where, however,
the damage is caused by a non-dangerous species, the extent of liability
is in reality limited by reason of the available defences, thus
dependance on the common law will in many cases provide the only
hope for the claimant to obtain compensation.

Liability for products

A person who is injured in some way by defective goods which that
person has bought will have substantial protection under the law of
contract, particularly under the provisions of the Sale of Goods Act
1979 and under the Supply of Goods and Services Act 1982. Consult
a textbook on consumer or business law for details of the statutory
protection. A person who did not buy the defective goods faces much
more difficulty. At common law such a person can only be helped if a
case can be established using the tort of negligence. This means that
the injured person has to establish who was actually in breach of the
duty of care and may find that the only party at fault was the
manufacturer based in the Far East. The common law is not in such
cases of much practical help.

In the 1970s a number of babies were born in the United Kingdom
who were seriously damaged by a drug taken by their mothers in the
early stages of pregnancy for severe morning sickness. The drug,
Thalidomide, was suspected of causing birth defects (which was later
proved to be true) and was banned in many countries, including the

United States of America. The parents of the British children brought an action against the drugs company concerned but were forced to settle as it was thought to be unlikely that negligence by the drugs company could be proved.

The European Union, partly prompted by the scandal of the Thalidomide tragedy, issued a Directive which was intended to give anyone injured by a defective product a right to compensation without the need to prove fault. This resulted in the creation of the Consumer Protection Act 1987 which imposes strict liability for damage caused by defective products. The common law is still relevant in some cases and will be discussed later.

Who is liable?

By the Consumer Protection Act 1987 s.2(2) the following may be liable:

(a) the producer of the product;

(b) any person who, by putting his name on the product or using a trade mark or other distinguishing mark in relation to the product, has held himself out to be the producer of the product;

(c) any person who has imported the product into [the European Union] from a place outside the Member States in order, in the course of any business of his, to supply it to another.

S.2(2)(b) includes an 'own-brander' who gives the impression that the product has in fact been manufactured by him.

For the purposes of the Act the word 'producer' means any person who manufactured the product or who abstracts raw materials, for example oil or coal, or, when a product does not fit either of the classes already mentioned, a person who produces a product the essential characteristics of which are due to an industrial or other process having been carried out. The word 'product' means goods or electricity or a product which is part of another product.

The producer of the defective product may not be known to a claimant. By s.2(3) the person who supplied the product will have liability unless details of the producer are given when requested by the consumer. This, combined with the liability of importers imposed by s.2(2)(c), means that the consumer has a right of action against an identifiable party.

The extent of liability

By s.2(3) there is liability for any damage caused wholly or partly by a defect in a product. The defect must have caused the damage. There is full liability for death and/or personal injury but in respect of damage to property there is no liability for loss and damage to the product itself nor where the amount of the loss does not exceed £275. (s.5(4))

The Act does not apply to products which are not usually supplied for private use and which are not intended to be used for private purposes. (s.5(3))

There is liability only if the product is 'defective'. By s.3(2) 'there is a defect in a product ... if the safety of the product is not such as persons generally are entitled to expect'.

When deciding what can generally be expected, the court must have regard to all relevant circumstances and in particular to the way in which the product has been marketed, any instructions or warnings which come with it, what it would normally be used for and the time when the product was supplied. (s.3(2))

By s.7 any attempt to limit or exclude liability is void.

> ### *Abouzaid v Mothercare (UK) Ltd* (2000)
> Mr A was injured when he was trying to fasten elastic straps to secure a sleeping bag to a pushchair. As he was attempting to fasten the buckle, the elastic slipped through his fingers and the buckle hit him in the eye. The defendants were held to be liable under the Consumer Protection Act. Adequate instructions had not been given to make sure a user of the pushchair knew how to fasten the straps safely. The product was defective.

Defences

The defences are set out in s.4. The first are straightforward:

(a) that the defect was caused by compliance with a legal requirement; or

(b) that the defendant did not supply the product; or

(c) that it was not supplied in the course of business nor with a view to profit; or

(d) that the defect did not exist in the product when it was put into circulation.

The defence given by s.4(1)(e) is controversial, although the Directive does allow its inclusion. The sub-section provides what is known as 'the state of the art' defence. In other words, given the state of scientific and technical knowledge at the time, the producer could not be expected to have discovered the defect. The Directive allows a defence based on the scientific knowledge available at the time but the inclusion of what the producer could have been expected to discover, a concept introduced by the United Kingdom, appears to have something in common with the fault principle in negligence. The law in the United Kingdom could mean that another Thalidomide-type tragedy could slip through the safety net, leaving victims with no remedy. S.4(1)(e) was challenged in *EC Commission v UK (Case C-30/95)*, but the European Court of Justice held that there was nothing to suggest that the British courts would not achieve the result the Directive intended. A case heard in 2001 shows that the European Court of Justice was right.

> ### *A v National Blood Authority* (2001)
> The claimants had been infected with hepatitis C after receiving blood transfusions from products supplied by the defendants. The risk of such infection was known about from 1988 but a screening test was not available until 1991. The claimants were infected after 1988. The defendants attempted to use the 'state of the art' defence arguing that because there was no screening test, they should not be liable. The judge disagreed. The defendants knew about the danger and yet chose to supply blood products in spite of the risk. The defendants must take the consequences when injury did result.

The final defence provides that where goods are supplied to be incorporated into another product, the designer of the final product or the person responsible for the specifications will be liable for the defect in the final product if this arises from inappropriate use of the goods or a wrong specification.

The common law defence of contributory negligence is incorporated by s.6(4).

The common law

Liability for injuries caused by a defective product can be established using the tort of negligence. In the case of *Donoghue v Stevenson* (1932) (the case of the snail in the bottle of ginger beer) it was settled that a manufacturer owes a duty of care to the ultimate consumer if the goods reach the consumer in substantially the same condition as they left the manufacturer. This might appear to make the tort an effective remedy, but other problems can arise. In order to establish a successful claim for negligence, the victim has firstly to prove a duty of care was owed to them. This is dealt with by *Donoghue v Stevenson* and by the general rules which apply to this issue. The second requirement is that there must have been a breach of the duty of care. The victim may well find that this causes difficulty. A manufacturer or supplier who has taken reasonable care to avoid acts or omissions which it is reasonably foreseeable may cause injury will not be liable. This is the 'fault' element of negligence and can make the outcome of a case uncertain and, in some cases, deprive a victim of a remedy.

In addition, it may be difficult to sue a potential defendant whose business is outside the United Kingdom and the European Union although theoretically it would be possible in some cases.

The Consumer Protection Act 1987, by introducing strict liability for damage caused by a defective product and by dealing with the problem of overseas defendants, has dealt with some of the common law problems, but it will still be necessary to rely on the tort in some cases, for example where the product has not been supplied in the course of business.

SUMMARY

Animals Act 1971

- liability imposed on 'keeper': person who owns or possesses or is head of household in which child owns or possesses an animal – s.6(3)

- 'dangerous animals': those which are not domesticated in the UK and which are likely to cause severe damage when fully grown if not restrained – s.6(2); all other animals are 'non-dangerous'

- keeper strictly liable for all damage caused by dangerous animal – s.2(1)

- keeper strictly liable for damage caused by non-dangerous animal if
  (a) such damage is likely to be caused by the animal unless restrained and is likely to be severe

  (b) the animal had unusual characteristics for its species and these characteristics caused the likelihood of damage

  (c) the keeper knew about the characteristics

- defences
  (a) default of victim – s.5(1)

  (b) voluntary assumption of risk by victim – s.5(2)

  (c) victim was unlawful visitor

- livestock – cattle, horses, asses, mules, hinnies, sheep, pigs, goats, poultry and deer not in the wild state

- owner liable for property damage caused by straying livestock – s.4

- owner of livestock may kill dog worrying the stock – s.9

- keeper of dog which worries livestock is strictly liable for damage caused – s.3

- animals which stray: keeper liable for damage caused if in breach of the duty to take reasonable care to prevent straying – s.8(1)

Consumer Protection Act 1987

- imposes liability for any damage caused by a defect in a product – s.2(3)

- full liability for death and/or personal injury, liability for damage to property only where the sum involved exceeds £275, no liability for damage to the product itself – s.2(3)

- person liable will be
  (a) producer

  (b) own-brander

  (c) importer into the EU from outside EU – s.2(2)

- defences
  (a) compliance with legal requirement

  (b) defendant did not supply product

  (c) product not supplied in the course of business or for profit

  (d) defect did not exist when product put into circulation

  (e) defect could not be discovered at the time of production due to the state of scientific/technical knowledge at that time – s.4

QUESTIONS

1. Albert bought a soft toy from Bryants, a toy-shop, which he gave to his three-year-old niece Celia. As a result of a defect in the toy, Celia was injured while playing with it and her parents intend to sue on her

behalf for compensation. The toys were made in the Far East. They were then imported into France by Frere Jacques who later exported the toys to the UK.

Advise Celia's parents as to any action they may be able to take under the Consumer Protection Act to obtain compensation. (OCR Law for Business – Consumer Law 1999)

2. Ahmed is twelve. His parents allow him to have a pet dog on the condition that he takes full responsibility for it. The dog, Buster, is large and very strong. Despite Ahmed's attempts to train the dog, Buster still goes for smaller dogs and attacks anyone who comes to its home.

    Last week while Ahmed was walking the dog, Buster attacked a small dog being exercised by Belinda. In trying to protect her dog, Belinda was knocked to the ground by Buster and broke her leg. That evening Belinda's partner, Darren, came to Ahmed's home to tell Ahmed's parents that Belinda would take legal action. Darren was invited in but as he was standing in the hall he started shouting loudly and aggressively at Ahmed and his parents. Buster escaped from the room where he was shut up and bit Darren.

    Consider whether Belinda and/or Darren has a right of action under the Animals Act 1971 and against whom any such action would be taken. (OCR June 2002)

3. To what extent is it true to describe the Animals Act 1971 as imposing strict liability for damage caused by an animal which does not belong to a dangerous species? (OCR Specimen Paper)

4. In what circumstances does the law of tort impose strict liability? Are these instances of importance in the modern law of tort? (Oxford 1992)

8 Vicarious liability for the acts of others

Employees

For centuries employers have been liable for the wrongdoing of employees. Among the reasons given for this rule is the undoubted fact that the purpose of employment is to allow the employer to profit from the employee's work. The ethical principle of justice would support the argument that as employers take the profit, so the risk should belong to them. In theory at least, the employers are in a better position to bear the risk especially as insurance is available, the costs being included in the calculation of prices and therefore paid ultimately by the customers, whereas an individual might find personal liability insurance only available at a prohibitive cost.

It can also be argued that even without insurance, employers are in a better financial position than their employees to meet claims. A claimant might find that although an action against an employee is successful, the employee is a 'man of straw' – in other words, the employee has no resources from which a judgment can be met except a salary which would generally mean payment by small instalments.

Another reason for employers bearing liability is that the employer has the responsibility for choosing and appointing the employee. It is up to the employer to make sure that the employee has relevant qualifications, is competent and carries out the job in a satisfactory manner. Employers have the right to tell an employee not only what is to be done, but also how it is to be done and to take disciplinary measures against an employee who breaks the rules. The doctrine of vicarious liability reinforces the employers' obligation to ensure that employees work in a lawful way.

As will be seen, the doctrine gives rise to what employers would certainly think of as injustice. An employer can be liable for an employee's act even though the employee has broken an express rule of the business and the employer has taken all possible steps to guard against such occurrence.

Who is an employee?

The answer to this question might seem obvious – anyone who has a job for which the employer pays a wage. In reality it is not so simple and over the years the courts have struggled to find an appropriate definition.

The 'control test'

A simple test, dating from early days, is to ask whether the alleged employee is under the control of the employer. Does the employer have the right to dictate not only what must be done but how it is to be done? Historically this test was probably satisfactory but as life has got more complicated, employers have been forced to employ people who are expert in a field where the employer has no competence and therefore in reality cannot tell the employee how to do the job even though technically the right exists.

The 'organisation' or 'integration test'

As the control test became obviously unsatisfactory, the courts were forced to develop another test. This led to the organisation or integration test – explained by Lord Denning in *Stevenson Jordan & Harrison Ltd v Macdonald & Evans* (1952), when he said,

> It is often easy to recognise a contract of service when you see it, but difficult to say wherein the difference lies [between a contract of service and a contract for service]. A ship's master, a chauffeur, and a reporter on the staff of a newspaper are all employed under a contract of service; but a ship's pilot, a taxi-man and a newspaper contributor are employed under a contract for service. One feature which seems to run through the instances is that, under a contract of service, a man is employed as part of the business, and his work is done as an integral part of the business; whereas, under a contract for services, his work, although done for the business, is not integrated into it but is only accessory to it.

This test has never been widely used.

The 'multiple' test

The test most commonly used over recent years is the multiple test which acknowledges that there is no simple answer to the original question of 'Who is an employee?' The test takes into account all relevant terms of the agreement between the alleged employer and the alleged employee and decides whether, on balance, the agreement has more characteristics of employment or self-employment. Among the factors to be taken into consideration are:

(a) are wages paid net of tax and national insurance contributions?

(b) who provides the tools for the job?

(c) does the employee have to obey orders?

(d) how is payment calculated – a weekly or monthly sum or a lump sum for the total job?

No one factor is conclusive; for example there are some trades in which by tradition the workers supply their own tools. In his judgment in *Ready Mixed Concrete (South East) Ltd v MPNI* (1968), from which the multiple test is derived, Mckenna J said that for there to be employment as opposed to self-employment, there were three conditions:

(1) that the employee agrees to provide skill in return for a wage;

(2) that the employer exercises a degree of control;

(3) that the terms of the agreement are consistent with a contract of service or employment.

It is clear that the decision will largely be based on the third condition which may involve the court in considering the terms of the agreement one by one.

The parties to the agreement may have tried to decide the issue for themselves, describing the contract as one 'of service' (employment) or one 'for service' (self-employment) but this is not necessarily conclusive. The description given by the parties will certainly be an important factor in the court's decision as to the status of the worker but is not the only relevant factor. There may be other reasons for describing the agreement in a particular way; for example employees are liable to have income tax deducted from their wages by employers under the PAYE tax system, and the level of national insurance contributions is different for the self-employed.

In *Ferguson v John Dawson Ltd* (1976) Mr F was employed on a building site as a self-employed labourer which meant that he paid less income tax. He fell from the roof because no guard rail had been provided by the defendants. The defendants owed a duty to make sure that a guard rail was in place but the duty was owed only to employees. The court looked at the reality of the situation – the employers exercised control over what Mr F did, how and when he did it. The court had no difficulty in finding that Mr F was in reality an employee, not someone who was self-employed despite the terms of the agreement between the parties.

An employer may sometimes 'lend' an employee to another person for a specified purpose. In such a case, if during the period of lending the employee commits a tort, the question arises, 'Who is liable – the"owner" of the employee or the person to whom he has been lent?' This issue was considered in *Mersey Docks & Harbour Board v Coggins & Griffith (Liverpool) Ltd* (1947).

Mersey Docks & Harbour Board v Coggins & Griffith (Liverpool) Ltd (1947)

B was a driver of a mobile crane and was employed by A. The crane and driver were hired from A by C. The contract said that B was to be regarded as C's servant but B continued to be paid by A and only A had the power to dismiss B. When someone working on a ship was injured by B's negligence, it had to be decided who was B's employer? *Held*: A as the permanent or general employer of B was liable.

It may be that where a person alone is 'lent', the 'borrower' will be liable but where the person is 'lent' with machinery which only they can operate, the 'lender' will remain liable.

Most students have paid employment of some kind while they are at college. Many register with an employment agency and obtain a variety of temporary posts. Were a student to commit a tort while doing the temporary job, who would have vicarious liability as the employer?

The employee who is 'on a frolic of his own'. Is the employer liable?

The general and basic rule is that an employer is liable for the wrongful acts of the employee committed in the course of the employment. The obvious question raised is, 'What is the course of employment?' Can it include acts done by the employee in disobedience to the rules set by the employer? It is necessary to turn to case law for help in deciding the answer to these basic questions.

The course of employment includes not only activities carried out during the hours of work but also activities which are closely connected to it. Cases which illustrate this are *Whatman v Pearson* (1868) and *Ruddiman & Co v Smith* (1889).

Whatman v Pearson (1868)

An employee was allowed an hour's break for lunch but was not supposed to take a detour and was forbidden to leave his horse and cart unattended. He went home for lunch, travelling about a quarter of a mile off his direct route to do so, and left the horse and cart unattended outside his home. The horse bolted and damaged some railings. *Held*: per Byles J. 'When the servant left the horse at his own door without any person in charge of it, he was clearly acting within the general scope of his authority to conduct the horse and cart during the day.'

Ruddiman & Co v Smith (1889)

An employee went to wash his hands a few minutes after his working day came to an end. He left the tap running and the resulting overflow caused damage to the claimant's premises below those belonging to the employer. *Held*: the negligent act was an act which was incidental to his employment and therefore his employers had vicarious liability.

Each case will be decided on the particular facts which are relevant to it but the court will look to see if the torts were so closely connected with the employment that it would be fair and just to hold the employer vicariously liable. (*Lister v Hesley Hall Ltd* [2001])

Lister v Hesley Hall Ltd (2001)

The defendants were the employers of a warden whose responsibilities included the day-to-day running of a home for children with emotional and behavioural difficulties. The warden had, over a period of three years, sexually abused boys aged between 12 and 15 living at the home. The warden was convicted of criminal offences and jailed for seven years. The issue which now had to be decided was whether or not his employers had vicarious liability for his torts of trespass to the person. *Held*: the fact that the employee was acting for his own benefit does not of itself mean that the employer cannot have vicarious liability. The question to be asked is whether there was a close connection between the employment and the torts. In this case the torts were committed in the time and on the premises of the employers while the warden was also caring for the children. The torts were so closely connected with the employment that it was in the circumstances fair and just to hold the employers vicariously liable to the victims.

When the employee can be described as having gone off on a 'frolic of his own' the employer may not be liable. Case law illustrates the kind of thing which may be regarded as a 'frolic'.

Storey v Ashton (1869)
A driver delivered some casks as required. As he was driving back to the employer's premises, he was persuaded by the clerk who was with him to divert to the clerk's home to pick up a cask which belonged to the clerk. This took him away from the direct route. An accident was caused by the driver's negligence. *Held*: in this case the driver had been about business which was nothing to do with the employer; he had been on a frolic of his own.

General Engineering Services Ltd v Kingston & Saint Andrew Corporation (1988)
Firemen were working a 'go-slow' in support of a pay claim. As a result they took 17 minutes to complete a journey which would normally have taken three and a half minutes. By the time the fire-engine arrived, the premises had been completely destroyed by the fire. *Held*: the firemen were not doing an authorised act in an unauthorised way; they were not in fact doing the authorised work at all. They were on a frolic of their own.

Travelling to and from work – is this in the course of employment?

Generally, as common sense would suggest, an employer will not have liability for the wrongs committed by employees on their journeys to and from work. There are exceptions to this rule when the employee can be described as being about the employer's business.

An employer who requires an employee to use a particular mode of transport or to travel from place to place in order to do the job, for example a travelling salesperson, will have liability for the employee's negligence during the travelling.

> ### Smith v Stages (1989)
> Mr M and Mr S were employed as laggers by an engineering construction company. In an emergency they could be sent to various power stations throughout the country. On the day in question, a Tuesday, they had been sent to Pembroke power station with instructions to return to work at the main site on the Wednesday. They were paid wages to cover the journey time in both directions and a sum to cover a return rail-fare. They worked without a break for 24 hours to get the job finished, having travelled in Mr M's car. Despite their lack of sleep, they decided to drive straight back. On the way, due to Mr S's negligent driving, Mr M was injured. *Held*: 'An employee travelling in the employer's time ... to a workplace other than his regular workplace or in the course of a peripatetic occupation or to the scene of an emergency will be acting in the course of his employment.' (Lord Lowry) The employers were vicariously liable for Mr S's negligence and had to pay damages to Mr M.

> The employers in *Smith v Stages* clearly expected that the men would use public transport to travel to their destination – the employers paid them a sum equivalent to a return rail-fare. What ethical principles can you think of which explain the apparent injustice of the outcome of the case?

The over-enthusiastic employee

An employer can sometimes find that there is liability for an act which the employer would never have authorised but where the employee has caused damage in the mistaken belief that the employer's interests required action.

> *Poland v Parr & Sons* (1926)
> Alf, a carter employed by the defendants, honestly and
> reasonably believed that the claimant, a lad aged 12 years,
> was stealing or about to steal sugar from one of the
> defendants' wagons. Alf hit the lad on the back of the neck,
> knocking him under one of the wheels of the wagon injuring
> the lad's foot. The boy later had to have his leg amputated.
> *Held*: Alf had acted reasonably and honestly to protect the
> defendants' property. The defendants had vicarious liability
> for the lad's injuries. 'Any servant is, as a general rule,
> authorised to do acts which are for the protection of his
> master's property' – *per* Lord Atkin.

The careless employee

An employer can be liable for any authorised act which is done
carelessly and results in damage. This can apply even if the act of the
employee is extremely foolish and would have been specifically
forbidden had it crossed the employer's mind that it was a possibility.
Century Insurance Co Ltd v N. Ireland Road Transport Board (1942) provides
a good example. A petrol-tanker driver, employed by the defendants,
decided to light a cigarette while petrol was being transferred from
the tanker into underground storage. He lit the cigarette and threw
the match to the ground. There was an explosion and fire which caused
extensive damage. It was held that the defendants were liable, the act
of the driver being done in the course of his employment.

The disobedient employee – is the employer still liable?

Employers will normally try to anticipate the kind of things that can
go wrong and expressly forbid actions by employees which might
lead to an accident. If the prohibition merely restricts the employee
in the way in which the job is to be done, the employer may well find
that there is still liability.

> *LCC v Cattermoles (Garages) Ltd* (1953)
> A garage-hand was required to move cars as part of his
> employment but had to do so by hand; he was not allowed
> to drive the cars. He disobeyed the clear instruction of the
> employer and, driving negligently, caused damage. *Held*:

he was doing the job he was authorised to do in an unauthorised way. His employers were liable for the damage caused by his negligence.

Limpus v London General Omnibus Co (1862)

The defendants' bus drivers were expressly forbidden to race with the drivers of buses belonging to rival bus companies. A driver disobeyed the instruction and negligently caused damage. *Held*: the prohibition merely limited how the job was to be done. The driver was doing the job he was employed to do even though in a way which was forbidden. His employers were vicariously liable.

If the prohibition forbids the employee to do certain acts, the employer may escape liability when the employee disobeys. The prohibition must have the effect of limiting the sphere of employment by excluding specific matters.

Iqbal v London Transport Executive (1973)

A bus conductor, trying to be helpful, drove a bus, although he was specifically forbidden to do so. His negligent driving caused damage. *Held*: the prohibition excluded a certain activity and therefore limited the sphere of the conductor's employment. The employers were not vicariously liable.

The case law in this area is somewhat confused. In *Rose v Plenty* (1976) a milkman employed a boy aged 13 to help on the round even though he was expressly forbidden to allow a child to ride on the milk-float. When the boy was injured by the milkman's negligence, it was held that the prohibition merely extended to the way in which the job was to be done and did not limit the sphere of the work. The employers had vicarious liability.

In the earlier case of *Twine v Bean's Express Ltd* (1946) the driver of a van gave a lift to a hitch-hiker in spite of the fact that he was expressly forbidden to do so. The hitch-hiker was injured by the driver's negligence. In this case the Court of Appeal held that the prohibition against giving a lift was a limitation on the sphere of employment and that by giving a lift the driver had not performed an act in an unauthorised way, but performed an act which he was simply not employed to do. The employers were not vicariously liable.

Is the employer liable for the criminal acts of the employee?

As it is an essential element of criminal liability that the criminal should have intended to break the law, it is surprising that the answer to the question is that an employer may be liable for the criminal activities of an employee. The fact that the employee intended to benefit personally from the crime rather than promote the employer's interests may not be relevant. In *Lloyd v Grace Smith & Co* (1912) a firm of solicitors was held to have vicarious liability for the dishonest acts of a clerk, and in *Morris v C W Martin & Sons Ltd* (1966) employers had liability for the theft of property by an employee. Both cases illustrate the point that employers are expected to take care to appoint honest people to carry on the employer's business. In both cases the employee committed the crime while doing the work they had been employed to do.

Lloyd v Grace Smith & Co (1912)
A clerk was employed by solicitors to carry out conveyancing business. He was not under supervision. Mrs L sought advice about some of her property and was persuaded by the clerk to sell the property. She signed two documents which she understood were intended to lead to the sale but which were in reality a conveyance to the clerk. The property was later sold by the clerk for his own dishonest benefit. *Held*: the criminal act was committed in the course of the clerk doing what he had been employed to do and the solicitors were vicariously liable to Mrs L.

Morris v C W Martin & Sons Ltd (1966)
Mrs M sent her fur coat to be professionally cleaned. The coat was stolen by the employee who had been given the task of doing the work. *Held*: defendants had vicarious liability as the employee had done what he was required to do but in an unauthorised way.

Employees, like other people, sometimes lose their tempers and act in a way which most certainly would not be permitted or condoned by their employers. In *Warren v Henly's Ltd* (1948) it was held that an employee who had assaulted a customer had acted so excessively that he could not be said to be doing an unauthorised act. A more recent case, *Fennelly v Connex South Eastern Ltd* (2000), states that the test is one of fact – was the act complained of so closely linked with an authorised act that it could be viewed as part and parcel of the authorised act? If this were the case, the employer would be liable even for the criminal acts of an employee.

> **Fennelly v Connex South Eastern Ltd** (2000)
> Mr F was a passenger on the railway run by the defendants when he was stopped by Mr S who was employed by the defendants as a ticket inspector. Mr S wrongly accused Mr F of not having paid his fare. There was an argument between the two men but eventually Mr F went on his way. He was immediately followed by Mr S who pulled him back and put him into a headlock, dragging him down some steps. *Held*: Mr S had acted within his authority to check tickets and to block the onward movement of passengers. What he did was an unauthorised mode of doing what he was employed to do and as a result his employers were vicariously liable.

Following the decision in *Fennelly v Connex South Eastern Ltd* (2000) and *Lister v Helsey Hall Ltd* (2001) it seems that *Warren v Henley's Ltd* (1948) would probably not be decided in the same way if it came before the courts today. It seems that employers will have vicarious liability for the acts of their employees not only when the criminal activity has been facilitated by the employer, as in *Lloyd v Grace Smith & Co* (1912), but also when the act is closely linked to an authorised act, as in the more recent cases.

Can the employer get the compensation back from the employee?

Under the Civil Liability (Contribution) Act 1978, a person held liable to pay compensation has the right to seek a contribution towards the sum paid from any other person who is also liable. As has been seen, the employee in each of the situations which have been discussed has liability as the primary cause of the damage. On the face of it, the employer has the right to seek repayment.

The employer also has a right in common law to recover damages from the employee of the amount which the employer has had to pay. In *Lister v Romford Ice & Cold Storage Co* (1957) it was held that employers were entitled to be reimbursed damages they had to pay as a result of the employee's negligent driving. The negligence was held to be a breach of the employee's duty to perform his duties with reasonable care and skill.

It was thought that the ruling in *Lister* was not fair and an inquiry was set up. As a result, the insurance companies which provide employers' indemnity insurance agreed that repayment by an employee would only be sought where the employee had been wilfully or grossly negligent.

Figure 8.1: Vicarious liability

Employer is liable for torts of employment if:

Employee is doing authorised job
even if in unauthorised way

Employer can recover cost from employee
if employee grossly or wilfully negilgent

> Try to think of ways in which an employer could protect the interests of the business against vicarious liability, for example by close supervision, which would of course increase costs and therefore reduce profits.

Independent contractors

By the action of using an independent contractor to carry out a task, a person is unlikely to have vicarious liability as employer. As we have seen, there may be vicarious liability for the acts of employees but not for the acts of the self-employed. Independent contractors fall within the grouping of the self-employed.

There may be liability when the employer has been negligent in the selection and appointment of the contractor. The employer is expected to use reasonable care to select a contractor who is competent to undertake the task, to ensure that it is carried out with reasonable care and skill and to ensure that it has been properly completed.

> ### *Bottomley v Todmordon Cricket Club* (2003)
> Mr B was injured when a firework exploded in his face. He had been asked by independent contractors to help with a display for the defendants. The defendants had employed the independent contractors on earlier occasions which had been successful. On this occasion, the independent contractors were staging the display on a voluntary basis. The independent contractors were not insured and had not prepared a safety plan so that Mr B sued the defendants on the basis that they had failed to ensure that the contractors employed by them were competent. He also claimed against the contractors. He won his case in the High Court and the defendants, but not the contractors, then appealed to the Court of Appeal. *Held*: 'On the facts ... the club ought to have taken reasonable care in its selection of a suitable "contractor" to conduct the dangerous pyrotechnics display ... the club allowed the event to take place with no public liability insurance and no written safety plan because it neglected to take ... ordinary precautions.' (per Brooke LJ) The defendants were held liable as the injuries suffered by Mr B were foreseeable as there was no safety plan, there was sufficient proximity between Mr B and the defendants and it was fair, just and reasonable to impose a duty of care on the defendants for failure to take reasonable steps to ensure the competence of the independent contractor.

Certain duties are described as being 'non-delegable'. In other words if the duty is specifically imposed, the employer cannot escape liability. Examples of 'non-delegable' duties include an employer's obligation to fence dangerous machinery and to ensure the safety of the employees.

Activities which are particularly hazardous may also impose a non-delegable duty on an employer. An example of this is seen in *Balfour v Barty-King* (1957) when the defendant was held liable for a fire which spread to the claimant's premises. The fire had been started by an independent contractor who had used a blow-lamp to thaw frozen pipes! Work which involves the risk of fire imposes a non-delegable duty to keep the fire safe.

Drivers

When a person is employed as a driver, for example as a bus driver or as a chauffeur, the usual rules of vicarious liability for the acts of employees apply. The situation is not so clear when the owner of a car arranges for someone else to drive it. The issue is important because of the statutory requirements of road vehicle insurance.

> Where A, the owner of a vehicle, expressly or impliedly requests or instructs B to drive the vehicle in performance of some task or duty carried out for A, A will be vicariously liable for B's negligence in the operation of the vehicle. (Winfield, p. 717)

It is clear that if A simply gives permission for B to drive the vehicle, this is not enough to make A vicariously liable if B drives negligently.

In *Morgans v Launchbury* (1973) Lord Wilberforce said 'in order to fix vicarious liability on the owner of a car, it must be shown that the driver was using it for the owner's own purposes'.

Morgans v Launchbury (1973)

A husband who was using his wife's car with her agreement, asked a friend to drive the vehicle after the husband had too much to drink. The friend drove negligently and caused an accident. Was the wife vicariously liable for the negligence? *Held*: the friend could not in any way be said to be acting on behalf of the wife. She did not have vicarious liability.

The fact that B benefits from the driving will not necessarily mean that A is not liable if B is at the same time benefiting A.

Ormrod v Crosville Motor Services Ltd (1953)

The owner of a car asked a friend to drive it from England to Monte Carlo. The owner would arrive in Monte Carlo later and the two friends would have a holiday together. The friend drove negligently. *Held*: although the friend was also benefiting and serving his own purposes by driving the car, he was carrying out a task for the benefit of the owner. The owner was vicariously liable for the negligence.

Can the doctrine of vicarious liability be justified?

At the beginning of this chapter we saw that a number of reasons are given to justify the doctrine that an employer can have liability for the acts of an employee even though the employer is not at fault. These reasons can be summarised as:

(a) the employer gets the profits from the employee's work and should therefore bear the losses if the employee commits a tort;

(b) the employer is often in a better position to meet a claim than an employee would be and may well have insurance;

(c) the costs to the employer can be shared among all the customers of the business;

(d) if an employee is negligent, the employer was also negligent in appointing an incompetent person or in failing to make sure the work was done properly and safely.

It can be argued that it is unfair that the employer can do little to prevent vicarious liability from arising. We have seen that an employer may be liable even though the employee has done something which is forbidden or which could not have been anticipated and guarded against by the employer.

The doctrine does serve a useful purpose in that it contributes to the maintenance of safety standards and also that it enables the victim of negligence by an employee to be reasonably certain that someone will be in a position to pay compensation.

It is difficult to argue that there are any very clear principles justifying the doctrine which Lord Pearce has said 'has grown from social convenience and rough justice'. (*ICI Ltd v Shatwell* [1965])

Joint wrongdoers

Vicarious liability is not the only time that at least two people have legal responsibility to pay compensation for the tort which has been committed and the victim can choose whom to sue. There may be joint liability in other situations, for example where one person encourages another to commit a tort, or where the combined actions of two or more people contribute to the damage.

Where more than one person has contributed to the damage suffered by the claimant, the wrongdoers are known as either *joint tortfeasors* or *several concurrent tortfeasors.*

- In the case of joint tortfeasors, each has been involved in the same incident, for example the instigator and the perpetrator of the tort, employer and employee by virtue of vicarious liability and those involved in a joint enterprise.

- Where separate actions have contributed to the damage, the wrongdoers are several concurrent tortfeasors. An example of this kind of incident occurs when two negligent drivers have an accident in which a pedestrian is injured. Both drivers are liable to the pedestrian.

Does the difference matter as the claimant can bring an action for full compensation against any one of the wrongdoers and will get no more by way of damages by suing all of them rather than only one? In most cases the answer is no, as the claimant will sue all potential defendants but the situation can be more complicated if a settlement is reached. Settlement with one joint tortfeasor means that the others are released from their obligation to the claimant, who could end up with less than their entitlement for the injury. This is simply avoided by making sure that any agreement to settle with one joint tortfeasor expressly states that rights are reserved against the others.

In such cases, both wrongdoers are liable to the victim for the full value of the claim but, by the Civil Liability (Contribution) Act 1978 s.1(1), the court can order payment of a contribution by one wrongdoer to another. The amount of the contribution is the proportion of the total damages which fairly reflects the extent of the contributor's liability. The principles which apply to decide the amount to be paid are basically the same as those which guide the courts in deciding the extent of contributory negligence under the provisions of the Law Reform (Contributory Negligence) Act 1945. (See Chapter 5, pp. 100–103)

In a case involving vicarious liability on the part of the employer, the same rules apply (*Lister v Romford Ice & Cold Storage Co* [1957]), but as was seen earlier in this chapter (pp. 181–182), a contribution will not usually be claimed from an employee unless the action was wilfully or grossly negligent.

SUMMARY

Liability for employees

Who is an employee?

- anyone with a contract of service

- tests for employment
  (a) control test

  (b) integration test – *Stevenson Jordan & Harrison v Macdonald & Evans* (1952)

  (c) multiple factor test – *Ready Mixed Concrete v MPNI* (1968)

Acts which are not directly part of the employment (frolics)

- employer liable only for acts committed in the course of employment for acts closely connected with the employment – *Whatman v Pearson* (1868), *Ruddiman & Co v Smith* (1889), *Lister v Hesley Hall Ltd* (2000)

- employer not liable where employee is 'doing his own thing' – *Storey v Ashton* (1869), *General Engineering Services v Kingston & St Andrew Corp.* (1988)

- employer generally not liable for torts committed while travelling to and from work but liable for torts committed while travelling as required by the employment – *Smith v Stages* (1989)

Over-enthusiasm and carelessness

- employer liable for acts done in fit of enthusiasm or acts of extreme carelessness or foolishness within the general scope of the employment – *Poland v Parr & Sons* (1926), *Warren v Henly's Ltd* (1948), *Century Insurance v N Ireland RTB* (1942)

Disobedience

- if prohibition merely restricts the way the job is done, employer liable if it is done in another way which causes damage – *LCC v Cattermoles (Garages) Ltd* (1953), *Limpus v London General Omnibus Co* (1862), *Rose v Plenty* (1976)

- if prohibition has effect of limiting the sphere of employment, employer not liable – *Iqbal v London Transport Exec.* (1973), *Twine v Bean's Express* (1946)

Criminal activities

- employer liable if the criminal act was facilitated by the employment – *Lloyd v Grace Smith & Co* (1912), *Morris v C W Martin & Sons Ltd* (1966), *Lister v Hesley Hall Ltd* (2000)

Reimbursement by employee

- at common law and by Civil Liability (Contribution) Act 1978, employer is entitled to be reimbursed what the employee has cost the employer

- right will generally only be exercised where employee's behaviour is grossly or wilfully negligent – *Lister v Romford Ice & Cold Storage* (1957)

Independent contractors

- provided reasonable care taken to select contractor and to check work properly done, the employer will not be liable

- exception in case of non-delegable duties – e.g. employer's duty to fence dangerous machinery

Drivers

- person employed as a driver is employee if usual tests for employment are satisfied

- owner of vehicle not liable for torts by driver unless owner also benefits from the journey – *Morgans v Launchbury* (1973), *Ormrod v Crosville Motor Services* (1953)

Can the doctrine be justified?

- arguments in favour
  (a) employer gets profit and should bear losses

  (b) employer probably insured

  (c) cost of insurance can be shared among clients/customers as part of the general cost of the business

  (d) employer should be more careful to ensure employee was working competently

- arguments against
  (a) in reality employer cannot have total control over activities by employee

  (b) employment protection legislation has made it more difficult to discipline/dismiss an incompetent employee

(c) it's not fair – employer is being blamed for something for which often the employer has no actual or moral responsibility.

Joint wrongdoers

- joint tortfeasors – each contributes to the damage/injury caused

- several concurrent tortfeasors – the combination of separate actions causes the damage/injury

- each tortfeasor is fully liable to victim but can seek contribution from the others

QUESTIONS

1. Mike is employed by Reliable Garages Ltd to repair motor vehicles. His duties also include ensuring that the work has been properly carried out by test driving the vehicles. During test drives he is expressly forbidden under Reliable's rules from giving lifts to anyone.

   Recently while test driving a Porsche he gave a lift to one of his friends, Bill, as it was raining. Mike drove too fast, showing off, and negligently skidded the car into a ditch, injuring Bill.

   Some days later, while test driving another car, Mike stopped to do some shopping and took it home before driving back to the garage. His negligent driving caused another accident in which Julie, a pedestrian, was injured.

   As Mike has now disappeared, advise Bill and Julie as to the possibility of successful claims against Reliable Garages Ltd. (Oxford 1997)

2. Andy owns a small photography business. For a small fee he retains Bob, another photographer, to help out at extra busy times and on an hourly rate when Bob actually works.

   Last week Bob was helping by taking wedding photographs. At the reception Bob drank so much that he became drunk and aggressive. He got into an argument with Chris and threw a glass of wine over her, ruining her wedding dress, and when Dave, the groom, tried to throw Bob out, Bob hit him.

   Andy has now received a claim for damages from both Chris and Dave. He is very angry as he specifically told Bob that under no circumstances was he to drink alcohol while working. Bob has now disappeared so that Andy is faced with payment of compensation for the torts which Bob committed.

Advise Andy whether or not Chris and Dave are likely to be successful in their claims against him. (You do not need to discuss the torts committed by Bob in detail.) (OCR January 2002)

3. In some circumstances a person may incur liability as a result of the acts of another when he is not himself at fault. Can this apparently unfair situation of vicarious liability be justified? (Oxford 1996)

4. Critically consider whether recent developments in the law relating to vicarious liability can be said to have made the doctrine fairer from the point of view of an employer. (OCR Jan 2004)

9　Protecting reputation

Defamation

Definitions

This part of the law attempts to protect a person's reputation by allowing a remedy if unpleasant and damaging statements are made about them. By the end of the chapter, you should be able to decide whether or not the law is successful.

The tort of defamation is divided into two parts – libel and slander – but once the appropriate definition is met, the two branches have many matters in common. We will first define the two branches and then look at the other important issues common to both.

Defamation

The Shorter Oxford Dictionary defines defamation as

1. The bringing of ill fame upon anyone; disgrace;

2. The uttering of reproachful speeches, or contumelious language of any one, with an intent of raising an ill fame of the party thus reproached; and this extends to writing …

For once, the dictionary does not really help us to understand what the word means.

A more helpful definition is provided by Winfield:

> Defamation is the publication of a statement which reflects on a person's reputation and tends to lower him in the estimation of right-thinking members of society generally or tends to make them shun or avoid him.
>
> (Winfield, p. 391)

Libel

Libel is generally thought of as a statement in permanent form, the obvious example being something which is written. Other statements which have been held to amount to libel include paintings and cartoons, statues, waxworks and effigies.

The common view is that libel is more serious than slander because the statement tends to be spread more widely – a newspaper is read by many people. It is therefore not surprising that statute has made specific provision for other forms of statements, which are transitory, to be treated as libel. Thus radio and television broadcasts are capable of being a libel by virtue of the Broadcasting Act 1990; theatrical performances by virtue of the Theatres Act 1968.

An important point is that libel is actionable *per se* (without proof of damage), and in some very limited circumstances it can also be treated as a criminal offence.

Slander

A simple definition is that slander is a defamatory statement in a transitory form, usually the spoken word. A slander can also be committed using sign language, mimicry and gesture.

Generally it is necessary for the claimant to prove that damage has occurred as a result of the slander but there are some cases, where the allegation is regarded as more serious, when slander, like libel, is actionable *per se*.

It is a slander actionable *per se* to suggest or imply that a person is guilty of a criminal offence for which punishment for a first offence could be imprisonment.

A suggestion or implication that a person is suffering from an infectious or contagious disease which makes others avoid them is also actionable *per se*. The diseases which have been held to fall into this category include venereal disease, leprosy and plague. It is not clear whether or not an imputation that a person is a victim of AIDS would be actionable.

The Slander of Women Act 1891 states that a woman or girl who is alleged to be unchaste or to have committed adultery does not have to prove damage. The law has proved to be sufficiently flexible so that the moral beliefs of the nineteenth century are not likely to be applied without modification in the twenty-first!

Slander is also actionable *per se*, by virtue of the Defamation Act 1952 s.2, when the statement is calculated to imply that a person is unfit, dishonest or incompetent in connection with an office, for example unfit to hold office as local mayor, or in connection with a profession, trade or business or in connection with a calling.

> In the twenty-first century, do you think that the distinction between libel and slander continues to be appropriate?

Figure 9.1

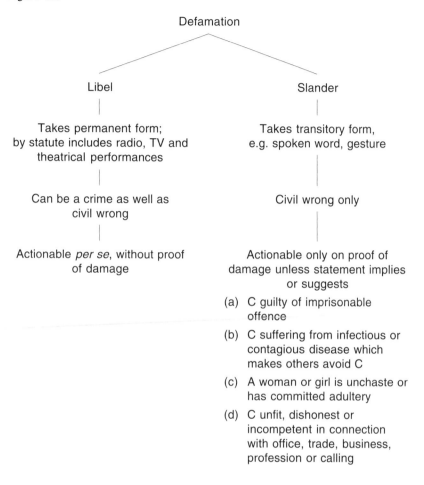

Defamation

Libel — Takes permanent form; by statute includes radio, TV and theatrical performances → Can be a crime as well as civil wrong → Actionable *per se*, without proof of damage

Slander — Takes transitory form, e.g. spoken word, gesture → Civil wrong only → Actionable only on proof of damage unless statement implies or suggests

(a) C guilty of imprisonable offence

(b) C suffering from infectious or contagious disease which makes others avoid C

(c) A woman or girl is unchaste or has committed adultery

(d) C unfit, dishonest or incompetent in connection with office, trade, business, profession or calling

The elements

The general meaning of 'defamatory'

The essence of defamation is that the statement is untrue or conveys an untrue implication as a result of which the claimant's reputation suffers. The initial question to be asked in a trial is, 'Are the words used capable of being defamatory?' – a question to be answered by the judge; the second question is, 'Were the words in fact defamatory of the claimant?' – a question to be decided by the jury if one is hearing the case, otherwise by the judge.

In many cases, the statement will clearly be defamatory if untrue, for example calling a person a thief. In other cases it is not so clear. A statement can be made about a named person which on the face of it is nothing to their discredit. Those who hear or read the statement may be led to read into it a meaning which is defamatory because of their own personal knowledge of the claimant, which would lead a reasonable person to draw a similar adverse conclusion (an innuendo).

> ### *Cassidy v Daily Mirror Newspapers Ltd* (1929)
> A picture was published in the newspaper which showed Mr C and a young lady under a heading which stated that she and Mr C had just announced their engagement to be married. Mrs C, who was generally known to be Mr C's wife, although the two mainly led separate lives, was able to prove that several people who knew her believed as a result of the article that she had been 'living in sin' with Mr C, a serious social problem for her in the 1930s. *Held*: the words were capable of the defamatory meaning alleged. The jury found in favour of Mrs C.
>
> ### *Tolley v Fry & Sons Ltd* (1931)
> Mr T was a well-known amateur golfer in the days when amateur status was regarded as having great importance. The defendant published an advertisement for 'Fry's Chocolate Cream' which showed a sketch of Mr T in golfing gear with a packet of chocolate creams protruding from a pocket. The sketch was accompanied by a piece of verse which read:
>
> > The caddie to Tolley said: 'Oh, Sir!
> > Good shot, Sir! That ball, see it go, Sir.
> > My word, how it flies,
> > Like a Cartet of Fry's.
> > They're handy, they're good, and priced low, Sir.'
>
> Mr T alleged, successfully, that the words, while not defamatory in themselves, had a defamatory meaning by innuendo as they implied that he had been paid to let his name be used for the advertisement. This was a serious matter which would potentially have prevented him from further participation in golf as an amateur.

Each case will have to be decided on its own particular facts. Are the words capable of being defamatory or not? What would a reasonable person believe? In *Lewis v Associated Newspapers Ltd* (1963) a newspaper article was published which stated that Mr L's company was being investigated by the Fraud Squad. Mr L alleged that the words meant that both he and his company were suspected by the police of being guilty of fraud. It was in fact true that the police were investigating the company at the relevant time but did this mean that a statement to this effect implied that Mr L or the company were in fact guilty? The House of Lords held that a statement of fact, i.e of the investigation, does not impute guilt, even though some readers may say, 'There's no smoke without fire'. This was not, on the facts, a reasonable assumption by such readers.

The definition given at the beginning of this chapter states that the statement must 'tend to lower [the claimant] in the estimation of right-thinking members of society generally'. The problem here is to decide who are the 'right-thinking members of society' whose views are decisive. As Mr Byrne found out, in *Byrne v Deane* (1937), it is possible to lose friends and suffer a loss of reputation because of an untrue statement but to find oneself without a remedy.

Byrne v Deane (1937)

Mr B was a member of a golf club. In the club house there were a number of illegal gambling machines, known as 'diddlers'. Someone informed the police who promptly removed the machines. The next day a piece of verse appeared on the club notice board:

> For many years upon this spot
> You heard the sound of a merry bell
> Those who were rash and those who were not
> Lost and made a spot of cash.
> But he who gave the game away
> May he byrnne in hell and rue the day.
> (Diddleramus)

Mr B alleged that the words referred to him and that he had been accused of informing the police about the machines. *Held*: 'to allege of a man that he has reported certain acts, wrongful in law, to the police, cannot possibly be said to be defamatory of him in the minds of the general public. We have to consider the view which would be taken by the ordinary good and worthy subject of the King [who] would not consider such an allegation in itself to be defamatory' (Lord Slesser). The fact that Mr B had lost his friends and become unpopular because of the false allegation was irrelevant.

Another way in which a statement can be defamatory is if it 'tends to make [other people] shun or avoid [the claimant]'. This can be the effect of words which are not defamatory in the first sense of the definition but which mean that ordinary people do not continue normal social contact with the claimant.

> **Youssopoff v Metro-Goldwyn-Mayer Pictures Ltd** (1934)
> Ms Y, a Russian princess, alleged that she had been defamed by a story-line in a film in which she was said to have been raped by the so-called 'mad monk' Rasputin, a figure of great and allegedly evil influence in pre-revolutionary Russia. *Held*: the allegation of rape tended 'to make the plaintiff [claimant] to [be] shunned or avoided without any moral discredit on her behalf'. (Slesser LJ)

It is easy to upset people by making comments about them but it will not be defamation unless the statement affects reputation. If the words used simply cause hurt feelings or annoy the person concerned this will not be enough. In *Berkoff v Burchill* (1996) Lord Justice Millett said '... mere chaff and banter are not defamatory, and even serious imputations are not actionable if no one would take them to be meant seriously'. However, if the words used are capable of being perceived as capable of lowering the claimant's standing in the estimation of the public, then the fact that they were not intended to be taken seriously may well be irrelevant.

> **Berkoff v Burchill** (1996)
> An actor was described as 'hideously ugly' by a journalist. The actor claimed that this would expose him to ridicule or cause other people to shun or avoid him. *Held*: in the particular situation the actor was in the public eye and the words were capable of being defamatory.

The context in which the words are used is also relevant in deciding whether or not the words are capable of being defamatory. An article or other work in which the words appear must be read as a whole.

> ### *Norman v Future Publishing* (1999)
> Jessye Norman, a famous opera singer, complained that a passage in an article which said that she had told a joke using an African-American dialect was defamatory because it appeared to show that she had used ungrammatical language and used a derogatory stereotype or that she had mocked people of African-American heritage. *Held*: in the context of the article as a whole, a reasonable reader could not have understood the words in the way alleged by Ms Norman.

> All our 'best friends' from time to time make comments which we do not like. Make a list of comments which you know or believe may have been made about you and decide whether or not the comments are defamatory.

The statement must refer to the claimant

A person who is clearly named in the statement generally has no difficulty with this element, it being a simple matter to show that the statement referred to them. It is possible for a person who is not named to bring an action provided they can show that reasonable people believed that the statement referred to them. Very often there will be some fact or phrase in the statement which those who hear or read it will connect with the claimant making it clear in their minds that the allegation is about that person.

> ### *Morgan v Odhams Press Ltd* (1971)
> The *Sun* newspaper contained an article in which it described how a Miss Murray, likely to be a major witness in a dog-doping trial, had gone into hiding, having been kidnapped a week earlier by members of the dog-doping gang. She had in fact been staying with Mr M a week earlier. Mr M said that ordinary people would assume that he was a member of the kidnap/dog-doping gang and witnesses who had seen the two together gave evidence that this was in fact what they had believed. *Held*: the question to be decided was, 'Would readers having knowledge of the circumstances reasonably have understood that the article referred to Mr M?' The answer was obviously 'yes',

> therefore the article was capable of being defamatory of Mr M even though at no time had he personally been named.

It is possible for a person to be defamed 'by accident' if they happen to have the same or a similar name to a person referred to in a statement. The facts may be true of the other person but not of the person alleging defamation.

> ### *Hulton v Jones* (1910)
> A Sunday newspaper published a fictitious article about 'Artemus Jones, a churchwarden from Peckham' who had spent a weekend in Dieppe with a lady who was not his wife. The real Artemus Jones was a barrister, single and did not live in Peckham but he was able to bring witnesses who said that on reading the article they had believed that it referred to him. *Held*: it is not necessary to show that the claimant was intentionally referred to; it is enough that those reading the article reasonably think that the claimant is the person referred to.
>
> ### *Newstead v London Express Newspaper Ltd* (1939)
> The newspaper carried a report of a case before the local court in which it stated that Harold Newstead, a 30-year old man from Camberwell, had been convicted of bigamy. This was true but there was another Harold Newstead of about the same age, a hairdresser who came from Camberwell, of whom it was not true. *Held*: reasonable persons would have understood that the description referred to the second Harold Newstead and the article was defamatory of him. Sir Wilfrid Greene MR said, 'If the words used, when read in the light of the relevant circumstances, are understood by reasonable persons to refer to the plaintiff (claimant), then refer to him they do for all relevant purposes. Their meaning cannot be affected by the ... honesty of the writer.'

It is obvious that the media may take substantial risks of being sued for defamation as 'accidental' or unintentional defamation can easily occur. For this reason, the Defamation Act 1996 (replacing and amending the Defamation Act 1952) allows for the making of an offer of amends which can be effective as a defence in certain circumstances (see p. 207).

It is generally not possible to defame a class of people who have not been individually identified. A member of a group or class of people must show that they were referred to. This means that the group about which the statement is made must be small enough for each member reasonably to believe that they are the one referred to. Alternatively there must be some other statement which points in some way to the claimant. In *Eastwood v Holmes* (1858) Willes J pointed out that 'if a man wrote that all lawyers were thieves, no particular lawyer could sue unless there was something to point to the particular individual'.

Although it is generally no defence that a person has accidentally been defamed, a recent case has provided some assistance to the media. In *O'Shea v MGN Ltd and Another* (2001) it was held that the restrictions which limit the right to freedom of expression under Article 10 Convention on Human Rights could not be used where an intolerable burden would be placed on the publisher. It is likely that the case will have fairly limited effect but it provides a useful and interesting insight of how the European Convention on Human Rights may affect the common law.

O'Shea v MGN Ltd and Another (2001)
The *Sunday Mirror* newspaper published an advertisement which included a picture of a well-known glamour model. The claimant claimed that as the photograph closely resembled her (she was a 'look-alike') it would be believed to be a photograph of her. *Held*: although at common law she was entitled to bring an action for libel, the effect of the right to freedom of expression under Article 10 of the Convention on Human Rights meant that the common law went beyond what was reasonably necessary to protect a person's reputation. It would put an intolerable burden on a publisher if every photograph had to be checked to make sure that it did not accidentally resemble a person other than the person actually in the photograph.

The statement must be published

No action can be brought where the statement, no matter how untrue or offensive, is made only to the person about whom the allegation is being made. At least one other person must hear or read the statement which must be understood by that person – a deaf person who cannot lip read would not 'hear' a slander, a foreigner who cannot read English would not have the necessary understanding of a libel without a translation.

Newspapers and books are published so any defamatory matter which they contain is published at the same time. A letter is published when it is dictated to a secretary (if this is the process it goes through) and also, if it is not marked 'Confidential', when it is opened by anyone other than the person referred to. Postcards are published when they are sent through the post.

A husband cannot publish information to his wife, nor a wife to her husband. To hold otherwise 'might lead to disastrous results to social life' (*Wennhak v Morgan* [1888]). These points are illustrated by the case of *Huth v Huth* (1914).

> ### Huth v Huth (1914)
> Mr H sent his wife a letter in an unsealed envelope alleging that they were not in fact married and that their children were illegitimate. Mrs H could not sue her husband but the children brought an action for libel. The evidence of publication was given by the family butler who said that he had read the letter before handing it to Mrs H. *Held*: as it is no part of a butler's duties to open letters addressed to his employers and Mr H had no reason to suppose that the butler would in fact do so, there was no publication to him. Mr H won the case on the basis that there had been no publication.

Defences

Justification

As it is an essential requirement that the statement is untrue, the publication of a true statement can never amount to defamation.

This seemingly straightforward statement has led to some difficulty; what if the statement is almost true but contains some error? The answer to the problem is the concept of justification. By s.5 Defamation Act 1952

> justification shall not fail by reason only that the truth of every [allegation] is not proved if the words not proved to be true do not materially injure the [claimant's] reputation having regard to the truth of the remaining [allegations].

A statement which is substantially true but which contains some error will not be regarded as an untrue statement unless the error in some way adds to the 'sting' of the defamation.

> ### *Alexander v N.E. Railway Co* (1865)
> The defendants published a notice in which it was stated that Mr A had recently been convicted of not paying his fare. He had been fined with an order that failure to pay would mean a sentence of three weeks' imprisonment. In reality he had been sentenced to fourteen days in default. *Held*: justification was a good defence. The essence of the allegation was true and had not been distorted by the mistake.

Consent

A person who consents to a publication cannot later complain that it is defamatory. 'Someone who telephones a newspaper with false information about himself will not be able to sue in defamation when the newspaper publishes it.' (Street, p. 457) Consent may be express or implied.

Innocent publication

In theory a book or newspaper can be published many times over – by the author to the editor, by the editor to the printer, by the printer to the wholesaler, by the wholesaler to the retailer and by the retailer to the buyer. The law provides a defence in such circumstances which is now to be found in s.1 Defamation Act 1996, which states that it is a defence for the defendant to show that they were not the author nor the editor or publisher, in a commercial sense, of the material; that all reasonable care was taken; and that they did not know and had no reason to believe that the material contained a defamatory statement.

This defence extends to those who provide access to information on the internet, provided the information is provided by a person over whom there is no effective control, and to those responsible for a live broadcast where there is no effective control over the maker of the statement. Despite the defence, an internet service provider will be liable for failure to remove material from one of the websites hosted by the provider once the provider has been informed of the defamatory nature of the material. (*Godfrey v Demon* [1999])

The matters which may be relevant in deciding whether or not publication was innocent were described by Lord Romer in *Vizetelly v*

Mudie's Select Library Ltd (1900) when he said that the defendant must show

(1) that he was innocent of any knowledge of the libel in the work disseminated by him;

(2) that there was nothing in the work or the circumstances under which it came to him or was disseminated by him which ought to have led him to suppose that it contained a libel, and

(3) that, when the work was disseminated by him, it was not by any negligence on his part that he did not know that it contained the libel.

> **Vizetelly v Mudie's Select Library Ltd (1900)**
> The owners of the library subscribed to a publication in which the publishers had placed a notice asking for the return of copies of a book which contained a libellous statement so that the matter could be put right. They ignored the notice and no member of staff had been employed to read the book. *Held*: the owners of the library had failed to satisfy the requirements of innocent dissemination and were liable as publishers of the libel.

Honest comment on a matter of public interest

The defence applies where a statement is an honest comment on a matter of public interest. (This defence was previously known as 'fair comment'.)

Most people have opinions and will make comments, not all of them reasonable, about many things. So-called 'experts' and commentators, journalists, critics and others are no exception but their opinions are likely to have a wide circulation. An opinion can have as damaging an effect on a reputation as an untrue allegation of fact.

If the defence is used, the defendant must show that the matter commented on is a matter of public interest. There is no definition as to what will amount to such a matter but case law makes it clear that it can extend to anything in which the public is interested as well as to matters with which the public is concerned.

The statement must be an opinion but this is not always easy to recognise. Winfield suggests that 'calling a man a fornicator or a swindler looks like a statement of fact, but what is calling him immoral or a sinner? Are immorality and sins facts or matters of opinion?' (Winfield, p. 423) In most cases the issue will depend on the context and on other supporting material. Where a clear statement of fact is made and then a comment on those facts there will be no difficulty. The meaning of public interest is perhaps now of more importance given the protection afforded to a person's privacy by Article 8 of the Convention on Human Rights. A useful explanation was given by Lord Denning in *London Artists Ltd v Littler* (1969) when he said,

> Whenever a matter is such as to affect people at large, so that they may be legitimately interested in, or concerned at, what is going on or what may happen to them or others, then it is a matter of public interest on which everyone is entitled to make fair comment.

The comment must be based on true facts in existence at the time the statement is made. It is not enough to publish some adverse comment and then to go and try to find facts to support it.

The comment must be fair in the sense that it is an opinion which is honestly formed and held even if others would think it unreasonable. Lord Denning explained this concept (in *Slim v Daily Telegraph,* 1968) when he said,

> If [the defendant] was an honest man expressing his genuine opinion on a matter of public interest, then no matter that his words conveyed derogatory imputations; no matter that his opinion was wrong or exaggerated or prejudiced; and no matter that it was badly expressed so that other people read all sorts of innuendoes into it; nevertheless he has a good defence of fair comment. His honesty is the cardinal test.

Diplock J emphasised the importance of the defence to protect freedom of speech. In *Silkin v Beaverbrook Newspapers* (1958) he said,

> The basis of our public life is that the crank, the enthusiast, may say what he honestly thinks just as much as the reasonable man or woman who sits on a jury, and it would be a sad day for freedom of speech in this country if a jury were to apply the test of whether it agrees with the comment instead of applying the true test: was this an opinion, however exaggerated, obstinate or prejudiced, which was honestly held by the writer?

If the comment is made maliciously by the defendant, the defence cannot be successful. The claimant will try to persuade the court that the opinion was not honestly held nor believed by the defendant who wanted to damage the claimant's reputation.

> **Thomas v Bradbury Agnew & Co Ltd** (1906)
> *Punch* magazine published a review of a book which was extremely hostile. The claimant was able to show that the reviewer was motivated by malice, using the words of the review itself and also the way in which the reviewer behaved in the witness box. *Held*: the defence failed.

> Do you believe that 'public interest' unfairly allows the media to publish details of a person's private life? How should we decide where private life ends and public interest begins?

Absolute privilege

There are circumstances in which a person needs to be free to say whatever they wish or whatever is necessary without fear of being sued for defamation. The law recognises this and in limited circumstances will give the necessary protection by finding that the statement has absolute privilege, in other words the statement cannot be used as the basis for legal action.

Statements made in either House of Parliament have absolute privilege (Bill of Rights 1688, Art.9). This privilege extends to papers and reports published by the authority of either House, including *Hansard* (Parliamentary Papers Act 1840). In *Church of Scientology of California v Johnson-Smith* (1972), the court held that statements made in the House of Commons and reported in *Hansard* could not be used to establish malice.

The Defamation Act 1996 s.13 gives a member of Parliament the right to waive (to give up) parliamentary privilege for the purpose of legal proceedings.

Statements made in the course of judicial proceedings have absolute privilege. The statement may be in writing or made orally, it may be clearly malicious and it may be made by anyone from the judge down to the witnesses. Judicial privilege covers not only things said in a court but also extends to things said in other places with a judicial or quasi-judicial function, such as an administrative tribunal.

Judicial privilege extends to other matters relevant to the proceedings, such as the witness statement prepared by a solicitor or the report prepared by an expert witness. Legal professional privilege ensures that anything said between a person and their solicitor and/ or barrister has absolute privilege provided it is about an actual or potential case.

State business might grind to a halt were there to be a risk of action for defamation. As a result communications between officers of state have absolute privilege, as was established in *Chatterton v Secretary of State for India* (1895–9).

> **Chatterton v Secretary of State for India (1895–9)**
> An official had written a letter to the Under-Secretary for State which contained an allegedly libellous statement about Mr C. In the Court of Appeal, Lord Esher, in his judgment dismissing the claim on the ground that the statement had absolute privilege, explained the reasoning behind the principle. He said:
>
> [The law] does not exist for the benefit of the official ... An inquiry would take away from the public official his freedom of action in a matter concerning the public welfare.

In *Fayad v Al-Tajir* (1988) the court held that an internal memorandum of a foreign embassy in London was also protected by absolute privilege.

By the Defamation Act 1996, fair, accurate and contemporaneous reports of court proceedings have absolute privilege in whatever part of the media they appear.

Qualified privilege

The law recognises that there are other circumstances when a person needs to be free to tell the truth as they believe it to be, even though in reality it may not be the truth. The protection which can apply in some circumstances is found in the doctrine of qualified privilege. This can have the same effect as absolute privilege in that a statement cannot be the basis of a claim for defamation.

At common law, a statement has qualified privilege if it is made by a person who has a legal, moral or social duty to make it to a person who has a similar duty to receive it. This was explained by Baron Parke in *Toogood v Spyring* (1834) when he said:

> In general, an action lies for the publication of statements which are false in fact, and injurious to the character of another unless it is made by a person in the discharge of some public or private duty whether legal or moral, or in matters where his interest is concerned. In such cases the occasion affords a qualified defence depending on the absence of actual malice. If fairly warranted by any reasonable occasion, and honestly made, such communications are protected for the common convenience and welfare of society.

It is difficult to see how the media can use this defence unless it can be accepted that there is a duty to inform the public generally. In *Reynolds v Times Newspapers Ltd* (1999) (a case concerning an article in a newspaper) the House of Lords held that when the defence is raised the question for the court is essentially, 'Is it in the public interest that the publication should be protected in the absence of malice?' In some circumstances, particularly concerning people in political life, the general public can be said to have an interest in receiving the information. The issue of what is in the public interest is a difficult one. The courts will take all relevant circumstances into account including the need for freedom of expression for the media and the very serious consequences to a person in public life if they are defamed by the media.

A common situation where the defence may be used is in connection with a reference for employment. An employer very rarely has a contractual obligation to provide a reference for an employee and is free to refuse, though most are prepared to do so. If the reference is to be any use to a potential employer, it must give an honest picture of the employee's competence and character. The person giving the reference, although mistaken in believing things to be true which are in fact untrue, will not be liable for defamation. In such circumstances there may be liability for negligence if the person has failed to take reasonable steps to ensure the accuracy of what is said. (*Spring v Guardian Assurance plc* [1994])

The defence may also apply where the statement is made by a person who has an interest to protect to a person who has a corresponding interest or a duty to protect the interest of the other. Generally this will apply to business or commercial interests. It may, for example, be a communication about the quality of work done or the behaviour of fellow employees or the wrongful way in which a business is conducted. This defence has been available to employees who 'blow the whistle', but such employees have sometimes been treated, quite legally, as in breach of a confidentiality clause in their contract of employment and been subjected to disciplinary action, including dismissal. The Public Interest Disclosure Act 1998 protects an employee from disciplinary action provided the disclosure is made to an appropriate person, and provided the employee has an honest and reasonable belief in the truth of the allegations.

The defence of qualified privilege has been expanded by statute. Most recently the Defamation Act 1996 has made changes of detail and expanded the lists of reports which are protected by qualified privilege. Protection is given for the publication in any part of the media of any matter of public concern or public benefit. Once this is established, then Schedule 1 Part I of the Act sets out reports which are privileged 'without explanation or contradiction'. These include fair and accurate reports of the public proceedings of any parliament or court anywhere in the world and fair and accurate reports of proceedings at a public inquiry anywhere in the world.

Schedule 1 Part II lists matters which are privileged 'subject to explanation or contradiction'. These include fair and accurate copies or extracts from documents produced by any parliament of a state which is a member of the European Union, the European Parliament or the European Court of Justice. It also includes fair and accurate reports of proceedings at a general meeting of a United Kingdom public company and of the findings or decision of various associations such as an association formed for the purpose of promoting sport, art, science, religion or learning.

Qualified privilege under Schedule 1 Part II will be lost if the defendant is shown to have refused or failed to publish in a suitable manner a reasonable letter or other document by way of the claimant's explanation or contradiction of the report. The defendant may also be required to give a claimant a 'right to reply'. The rules already discussed as to fairness and substantial accuracy apply.

A person who acts with malice cannot use the defence of qualified privilege. In this context the term 'malice' means that the person making the statement either had no honest belief in its truth or that it was made for some improper motive, for example with an intention to harm the claimant.

> If you failed to get a job because your former employer honestly and without negligence stated something to your discredit, would you feel that the law had let you down? Think about the ethical principles which are relevant to this problem.

Offer of amends

This is not strictly speaking a defence but can have a similar effect. By s.4 Defamation Act 1996 the defendant, having admitted that the statement was wrong at least in part, can offer to publish a suitable correction and a sufficient apology. The proposed form of publication must be appropriate and suitable. The defendant must also offer payment of compensation and costs. The claimant is free to accept or reject the offer but if it is rejected and the case goes to court, the defendant can use the offer as a defence.

Remedies

Injunction

If the claimant becomes aware that defamatory material is about to be published or more widely disseminated, they can apply to the court for an injunction to prevent publication. In this way the tort can be an effective way to protect privacy but it will rarely be of practical use.

It is very difficult to obtain an interim injunction to prevent publication unless the claimant can establish that it is clear that the statement is untrue. If the defendant may be able to use any of the defences, no injunction can be granted. (Human Rights Act 1998 s.12.) Once there has been a full trial, a full injunction may be granted in an appropriate case.

Damages

If a jury is used in a defamation trial, the level of damages is often very high. This in part marks the jury's disapproval of newspapers which have apparently published defamatory matter in order to boost sales, although this is not always the true picture.

A jury can be used unless the trial requires detailed consideration of documents or scientific matters which the jury is unlikely to be able to cope with. A recent example of this has been the trial of the libel action brought by David Irving against Penguin Books and Deborah Lipstadt concerning Mr Irving's views of the Holocaust; all parties agreed that it was not a suitable case for a jury as it involved consideration of numerous historical and other documents published over the past half century or longer.

In many cases where a jury is used, the level of damages is regarded as excessive. The Court of Appeal, under s.8 Courts and Legal Services Act 1990, was given power to substitute a more reasonable figure. Prior to the Act the court had power to set aside a jury award but had to order a re-trial. The court has shown willingness to exercise the new and simpler power. In *Rantzen v Mirror Group Newspapers* (1986) Ltd (1994) an award of £250,000 to a television presenter was set aside and an award of £110,000 substituted in its place. In *John v Mirror Group Newspapers* (1997) the singer Elton John had an award of £75,000 in respect of general damages reduced to £25,000.

Malicious falsehood

A false statement, even though it is not defamatory, can have a profound influence on the way others view the 'victim'. This is especially true of the effect on a business where, for example, a newspaper prints a statement that the business has ceased operations. There is often no remedy in defamation because the statement, although untrue, does not 'tend to lower [the claimant] in the estimation of right-thinking members of society generally', but the effect can nonetheless be devastating for the claimant.

The tort of malicious falsehood provides a remedy if it can be shown that a false statement was made maliciously to some person other than the claimant as a result of which the claimant has suffered damage. The statement can take any form – written, oral or conduct – which relates to the claimant or their activities and which the claimant can prove to be false. The claimant must also prove that the defendant acted maliciously, for example that the defendant published, even though it was known that the statement was false or if the defendant can be shown to have been reckless; in other words that the defendant did not care one way or another about the truth.

The claimant must prove special damage. In these cases, the usual way is for the claimant to show that business profits have fallen since the publication which was likely, if not intended, to have that result.

By the Defamation Act 1952 s.3(1) the claimant need not prove special damage if the statement is in writing or other permanent form or if the words are calculated to cause pecuniary damage to the claimant's business.

The court action

Actions for defamation in many cases attract substantial publicity which of course only serves to make even more people aware of the defamatory matter. Until the Defamation Act 1996, all defamation actions had to be heard in the High Court, a slow and costly exercise, and no legal aid was or is now available. There is some element of truth in the allegation that only the rich have reputations worth protecting, the cost of court proceedings being well beyond the reach of ordinary people. In the case of *McDonald's Corp. v Steel* (1997), the award to McDonald's was only £60,000 (a sum which was excessive bearing in mind that the defendants had a joint annual income of less than £7,500), but the costs exceeded £1 million.

The contingency fee system of funding a civil case introduced by the Courts and Legal Services Act 1990 may go some way to allowing an ordinary person to bring an action for defamation but depends on a solicitor being willing to take on the case and in any event offers no protection against liability for the other side's costs should the case be lost.

The Defamation Act 1996 has introduced a new 'fast track' procedure in the county court (the judge sitting without a jury) to allow summary judgment in cases where the claimant's case is either extraordinarily weak or extraordinarily strong. This may reduce the amount of costs. The level of compensation cannot exceed £10,000 but the order can include provision for a declaration that the statement was defamatory and for publication of an apology.

Protection of privacy and freedom of information

It is sometimes argued that the tort of defamation protects an individual's right to privacy. As has been seen, this is not an accurate statement. Most victims of defamation only find out they have been defamed once friends and others react to the publication. In such cases the damage is done and any court action, by the publicity it may attract, only makes a bad situation worse. In other cases, the victim finds that something has been published which is detrimental to reputation but true. In such a case there is no remedy.

There is no legal action under common law which can be taken specifically to protect privacy although other actions may indirectly have this effect. Actions for trespass to land, for example, may lead to an injunction excluding specific persons from the land and an injunction may be granted to prevent the publication of a libel. In some limited circumstances the courts have shown themselves ready to grant an injunction to restrain the publication of confidential material, but this again depends on prior knowledge being available to the victim to enable action to be taken in time. The obligation of confidentiality will in most cases arise from the terms of a contract between the claimant and the defendant. A confidentiality clause is common in contracts of employment.

The Human Rights Act 1998 makes the European Convention for the Protection of Human Rights and Fundamental Freedoms part of the law of the United Kingdom to the extent set out in the Act. By Article 8 of the Convention:

(1) Everyone has the right to respect for his private and family life, his home and his correspondence.

(2) There shall be no interference by a public authority with the exercise of this right except such as is in accordance with the law and is necessary in a democratic society in the interests of national security, public safety or the economic well-being of the country, for the prevention of disorder and crime, for the protection of health or morals, or for the protection of the rights and freedoms of others.

It was thought that the Convention would provide fertile ground for the development of a tort of privacy. To date this has not materialised, the courts taking the view that a right to respect for privacy is an underpinning principle and that no separate right of action is needed as other parts of the law will suffice. It may be that this is an area where developments can be anticipated but whatever happens the right to freedom of speech (Article 10 of the Convention) is likely to be regarded as having equal importance. A right to privacy also has to be balanced against the right to freedom of information which is granted by the Freedom of Information Act 2000, due to come into effect in 2005.

The debate on these issues is ongoing and may lead to some important and substantial changes to the existing law protecting reputation in the not too distant future. For further discussion of these issues see Chapter 12 'Tort law in context'.

SUMMARY

Defamation

- libel – a defamatory statement in a permanent form; usually written but by statute including radio and TV broadcasts and theatrical performances; actionable *per se*; can also be a crime

- slander – a defamatory statement in a transitory form; the spoken word or gesture; actionable only on proof of damage unless statement suggests that claimant is guilty of imprisonable offence, claimant suffering from contagious or infectious disease, a woman or girl is unchaste or has committed adultery, claimant is unfit, dishonest or incompetent in connection with office, trade, profession, business or calling

- meaning of defamatory – a statement which tends to lower the person referred to in the eyes of right-thinking persons generally or makes them shun or avoid him

- claimant must prove
  (a) statement is defamatory – *Byrne v Dean* (1937)

  (b) statement referred directly or indirectly to the claimant – *Hulton v Jones* (1910), *Newstead v London Express Newspaper* (1939)

  (c) statement was published

- Defences
  (a) statement is wholly or substantially true – s.5 Defamation Act 1952

  (b) claimant consented to the publication

  (c) innocent publication – s.1 Defamation Act 1996

  (d) honest comment on a matter of public interest – something in which the public are interested

  (e) absolute privilege

  (f) qualified privilege

- remedies of particular relevance – injunction, damages

Malicious falsehood

- publication of a false statement made maliciously as a result of which claimant has suffered damage

QUESTIONS

1. Sally and Dan, who are solicitors, are both candidates standing for election to Parliament. During a debate at a recent public meeting, Sally lost her temper and shouted at Dan alleging that he had accepted bribes and was unfit to be a solicitor or a Member of Parliament. Dan responded by slapping Sally on her face, saying that she was hysterical.

   Yesterday Dan appeared in the local magistrates' court where he was found not guilty of assault. The *Trumpeter*, a local newspaper, has today reported the court case under the headline 'Local Candidate Punches Rival' with a prominent photograph of Dan. In the small print it was made clear that Dan had in fact been acquitted.

   Dan believes that his professional standing has been damaged and that his chances of success in the election have been ruined by Sally and the *Trumpeter*.

   Discuss whether Dan is likely to be successful in an action against Sally and the *Trumpeter* for defamation. (OCR 1999)

2. It has been argued that 'there is no need for a law to protect privacy; the existing law of defamation achieves this'. Does the law of defamation successfully protect privacy? (Oxford 1995)

3.   'The tort of defamation protects interests in reputation.' (Hepple and Matthews.)

Does the tort of defamation operate in a logical and effective way? (Oxford 1993)

10   Breach of statutory duty

Many Acts of Parliament create a duty to do something. The question then arises whether a person who is injured or suffers damage because the duty has not been carried out can sue in tort for damages for breach of statutory duty. Some statutes expressly grant a right to claim damages, for example the Nuclear Installations Act 1965, while others expressly exclude any right to damages, for example the Medicines Act 1968. The Health and Safety at Work etc. Act 1974 now provides an example of a statute which both gives a right to obtain damages and excludes any such right! By the Management of Health & Safety at Work and Fire Precautions (Workplace) (Amendment) Regulations 2003 employees are given the right to bring an action against an employer for the employer's breach of the statutory duty to ensure the safety of employees. The new rules only apply to employees; independent contractors or anyone else who is injured by a breach of the statutory duty are still prevented from using breach of the Act or the Regulations made under it as the basis of a claim. A third category of statutes causes problems as a person can be subject to punishment for a breach but the Act is silent about the question of civil liability. It is the last category that we are concerned with.

In those cases when the statute does not clearly state the answer one way or the other, the courts are forced to decide what Parliament intended in relation to each statute, reading the statute as a whole. There are many difficulties is deciding what Parliament intended.

> I'm the Parliamentary Draftsman,
> I compose the country's laws,
> And of half the litigation
> I'm undoubtedly the cause.
> (J.P.C., 'Poetic Justice' cited in Hepple, p. 536.)

As we shall see, the courts will ask:

- was the Act passed for the benefit of a specific class of people or individuals or for the benefit of the public at large;

- is the harm suffered by the individual the kind of 'mischief' that the Act was designed to deal with;

- is the remedy provided by the Act adequate?

The rules of statutory interpretation help the courts to decide whether or not Parliament intended to give a civil remedy as well as to impose a criminal punishment. Where the courts use the mischief rule or the purposive approach and give effect to the principle of the Act rather than to its literal meaning, it is perhaps easier for the answer to be reached.

It should be remembered that although the statute may not give a remedy for breach of statutory duty, it may still be possible for a victim to succeed in an action for damages for negligence provided the usual rules can be satisfied.

What did Parliament intend?

If the Act was passed to benefit the public generally, there is unlikely to be liability for damage suffered by an individual. This is prompted in part by the fear of opening the floodgates to a stream of litigation if an unlimited class of people was able to sue for breach. In *Atkinson v Newcastle Waterworks Co* (1874–80) Lord Cairns, when referring to a statute which imposed penalties for failure to maintain water-pressure, said:

> The proposition ... appears to be somewhat startling that a company supplying a town with water – although they are willing to be put under obligation to keep up the pressure, and to be subject to penalties if they fail to do so – should further be willing to assume, or that Parliament should think it necessary to subject them to liability to any householder who could make out a case. In the one case they are merely under liability to penalties if they neglect to perform their duty, in the other case they are practically insurers.

Atkinson v Newcastle Waterworks Co (1874–80)
The water company had a statutory duty to maintain a certain pressure in the mains pipes for the purposes of fighting fires. Mr A's premises caught fire and because water pressure was low, the premises were seriously damaged. Mr A's claim for damages for breach of statutory duty failed.

The purpose of the Act is also relevant: is the harm suffered by the victim of a type or kind that the Act was intended to prevent? In *Gorrie v Scott* (1874) a number of sheep were washed overboard from a ship. The Contagious Diseases (Animals) Act 1869 required sheep to be penned when in transit and this had not happened. It was held that the farmer who had lost the sheep could not claim damages for breach of statutory duty as,

> looking at the Act, it is perfectly clear that its provisions had no purpose, direct or indirect, to protect against such dangers [as the sheep being washed overboard]; but, as is cited in the preamble, the Act is directed against the possibility of sheep being exposed to disease. (Lord Kelly)

The nature of any penalty imposed for breach will be relevant when deciding whether it is adequate. In *Groves v Lord Wimborne* (1895–99) an employee had suffered injury as a result of the employer's failure to fence dangerous machinery as required by statute. The statute provided that breach should carry a maximum penalty of £100. In considering the employee's claim for damages for breach of statutory duty, Lord Rigby said that in the light of the fact that the maximum penalty applied regardless of whether a workman had merely been slightly injured or killed,

> The legislature could not seriously have intended that whether the workman suffered death or mutilation the liability of the master should never exceed £100. Moreover, whatever the fine may amount to, there is no provision in the Act that the injured person or his relatives shall be benefited by it. The employer was held to be liable for breach of statutory duty. The penalty was inadequate to recognise the damage.

In *Ex parte Island Records Ltd* (1978), it appeared that the courts were moving towards a less restrictive view. The case was about pirated copies of copyright material in respect of which the relevant Act imposed a small fine. The victims sought damages for breach of statutory duty. In his judgment, Lord Denning said that 'whenever a lawful business carried on by one individual in fact suffers damage as the consequence of a contravention by another individual of any statutory prohibition the former has a civil right of action against the latter for such damage'.

The issue was considered more recently in *X (Minors) v Bedfordshire County Council* (1995) when the House of Lords held that children who alleged breach of statutory duty in connection with decisions made about their welfare which had, with hindsight, been shown to be wrong had no claim for compensation. The judges acknowledged that the children were clearly members of the class that the legislation was designed to protect but that it would be wrong to impose liability on a public authority for decisions which later investigation showed to be erroneous. The Act was intended to benefit society in general and not particular individuals. The case, now *Z and Others v UK* (2001), was taken to the European Court of Human Rights on appeal and the decision of that court has indicated another way in which such claimants might be able to get compensation. The ECHR held that the children had been subjected to 'torture or to inhuman or degrading treatment' which is prohibited by Article 3 of the Convention and that they had been refused an effective remedy for that breach as required by Article 13. Now that the Human Rights Act 1998 has come into effect, English courts would be able to reach a similar decision and it is possible that this will mean that more people are able to obtain a remedy for breach of statutory duty than has previously been the case. (For a discussion of this case in the context of negligence, see Chapter 2, pp. 35–37.)

The House of Lords has recently considered the issue of breach of statutory duty in a case which started with a claim for nuisance and breach of ECHR Article 8 but which ended with a useful consideration of remedies for breach of statutory duty.

Marcic v Thames Water Utilities Ltd (2003)
From 1992 Mr M's front garden and occasionally his house were flooded with untreated sewage. Mr M complained in 1992 but nothing was done. Mr M brought an action claiming an order that Thames Water should take steps to remedy the situation, alleging common law nuisance and breach of Art. 8. In the High Court, the judge decided that there was no nuisance but that Art. 8 rights had been infringed. In the Court of Appeal, it was held that Mr M's claim for nuisance and for breach of Art. 8 should succeed. When the case reached the House of Lords an unexpected twist occurred. The judges considered the extent of the duty imposed on Thames Water by the Water Act 1991 and the remedies given by that Act for breach of duty. *Held*: the Water Act 1991 provided for enforcement by the Director-General of Water Services. Lord Nicholls explained, '... one important purpose of the enforcement scheme ... is that individual householders should not be able to launch proceedings in respect of failure to build sewers'. Mr M lost the case but the work was in fact completed in 2003 before he started his action.

The issue of causation

A victim of alleged breach of statutory duty has further hurdles to cross once the fact that he is intended to have a civil claim is established. It must also be established that the defendant was in breach of the duty and that the breach caused the damage.

It is technically possible for a person to suffer from a breach of duty for which another bears statutory responsibility, but at the same time the only person actually to blame for the injuries is the victim themselves. An employer has a duty to comply with health and safety legislation, but what happens when an employee is injured solely or partly as a result of ignoring the rules?

In *Ginty v Belmont Building Supplies & Another* (1959) a roofing contractor knew that statute required him to use boards when working on an asbestos roof. There was an ample supply of boards but he chose not to use them and fell through the roof. His employers were in breach of their statutory duty to use the boards. The question was – could the employee claim against the employers? It was held by the court that the only question to be asked, accepting that the employers had a statutory duty, was 'Whose fault was the accident?' Its answer was as follows: 'If the answer to the question is that in substance and reality the accident was solely due to the fault of the plaintiff [claimant] so that he was the sole author of his own wrong, he is disentitled to recover.'

It is not as difficult for an employee to prove breach of statutory duty as it is for others injured as a result of breach. But the reasons for the injury must always be looked at carefully. In *Boyle v Kodak Ltd* (1969) a painter was required to paint a large tank. Statutory regulations required that ladders should be secured at top and bottom – an absolute duty on both employer and employee. The painter, instead of using a staircase, decided to climb a ladder which he intended to tie at the top, as he had seen other employees doing. As he was climbing, he fell. The issue for the courts was, was the employer liable to the painter for failing to have done all that could reasonably be done to ensure that the regulations were complied with? It was held that although the defence of contributory negligence is available to a claim for breach of statutory duty, there may be full liability where a person under the duty has failed to take all reasonable steps to prevent others committing breaches. In the case, the employer and the employee were held to be equally to blame. The issue of causation was also considered in *Caswell v Powell Duffryn Associated Collieries Ltd* (1939) in which it was held,

The person who is injured must show not only a breach of duty
but that his hurt was due to the breach. If his action is entirely due
to his own wilful act no cause of action arises as, for instance, if
out of bravado he puts his hand into moving machinery. (Lord
Atkin)

The future

Membership of the European Union has brought with it the possibility
for further rights of action arising from breach of statutory duty. Where
a European Directive is involved, the national government has a duty
to give effect to that Directive in national law which will be enforced
by the national courts. A victim of failure to implement a Directive
may have a claim against the government (*Francovich v Italy* [1992])
and can rely on the Directive to support a claim for damage in the
British courts against another party arising from breach of a duty
imposed by European law (*Garden Cottage Foods Ltd v Milk Marketing
Board* [1984]).

It is obvious that life would be much simpler were Parliament to
state quite clearly what its intentions were whenever a statutory duty
is imposed. This was recommended by the Law Commission in its
report, *The Interpretation of Statutes* (Law Comm. No/21 1969) when it
suggested that a statutory presumption should apply which would
decide the issue. The suggested wording of the proposed Bill on
Statutory Interpretation states:

1   Where any Act passed after this Act imposes or authorises
    the imposition of a duty, whether positive or negative and
    whether with or without a special remedy for its enforcement,
    it shall be presumed, unless express provision to the contrary
    is made, that a breach of the duty is intended to be actionable
    (subject to the defences and other incidents applying to actions
    for breach of statutory duty) at the suit of any person who
    sustains damage in consequence of the breach.

There is no sign as yet that Parliament has heeded the advice of the
Law Commission which means that for the foreseeable future, the
courts will continue to be faced with difficult decisions as to whether
or not a victim of a statutory breach of duty has a right to claim damages
for that breach.

SUMMARY

- if an Act of Parliament specifically states that compensation is payable – no problem

- if the Act is silent the questions are:
    was the Act to benefit a particular class of people?
    is the problem suffered by the individual covered by the Act?
    how adequate is the remedy provided by the Act?

- decision based on rules of statutory interpretation

- once breach established, causation becomes an issue – *Caswell v Powell Duffryn Ass. Collieries* (1939)

QUESTION

1. Explain the principles upon which the courts provide a remedy for breach of statutory duty. In your opinion, does the law provide an adequate remedy for a victim of such a breach?

11   Defences and remedies generally

Defences

As the various torts have been described, we have looked at defences which are particularly relevant to the individual torts. It is useful to draw the rules together as a reminder that although a particular defence might be more often used in relation to a particular tort, nonetheless many are of general application. This chapter begins, however, by looking at defences which have not previously been considered.

Limitation periods

If a court action could be started at any time after the event giving rise to the alleged claim various problems would arise; memories become blurred with time and the ability of witnesses to give an accurate and detailed account of events diminishes. Witnesses might also disappear, moving to another part of the country or even emigrating. A person against whom there is a potential action needs to know as soon as possible whether or not the case will be pursued. With these and others reasons in mind, Parliament has acted to impose limitation periods which mean that generally an action must be started within a specified period of time from the event that gives rise to the claim. The present law is found in the Limitation Act 1980 as amended by the Latent Damage Act 1986 and the Defamation Act 1996.

Torts actions which do not involve any claim for personal injury must generally be brought within six years from the date on which the cause of action accrued, personal injury claims within three years and defamation and malicious prosecution cases within one year. A cause of action accrues on the date on which events occur, which means that an action could be brought on the date of the accident. As we shall see, the Act makes provision for the court to grant leave for an action to be started after the specified time has expired.

One of the problems caused by strict application of the rules relating to the date of accrual is that a claimant may not know that damage has been suffered until some time after the event. This is not a problem in the case of torts actionable *per se*, such as trespass and libel, but raises difficulty in some cases where damage has to be proved. In such cases the cause of action accrues on the date that damage occurs. If the damage does not become apparent for some time after the event, as with certain industrial diseases like asbestosis which cannot always be diagnosed until many years after exposure to asbestos dust, injustice would occur were the victim unable to bring a claim.

Where the claim does not include a claim for personal injury, the Latent Damage Act 1986 can be of assistance. Although the basic six-year period usually applies, the Act allows a period of three years from the earliest date on which the claimant knew or ought reasonably to have known that there was a right to sue. An overall absolute limit of fifteen years from the negligent action itself applies.

Where the claim is for damages for personal injuries or death, the limitation period is three years from the accrual of the cause of action or from the date the claimant had the necessary knowledge. Section 11 Limitation Act 1980 states that a person is deemed to have the necessary knowledge when the following facts are known:

- that the injury was significant;
- that the injury was caused at least in part by an act or omission which allegedly amounts to negligence;
- the identity of the defendant;
- if the act or omission of another person is the alleged cause of the injury, the identity of that person and the reasons why the defendant should be liable.

In essence time begins to run when the claimant knows that there is a real possibility that the defendant's act or omission caused the injury, sufficient to start preliminary steps to begin preparation of the case. 'Knows' does not necessarily mean actual knowledge but the knowledge that might be reasonably deduced from known facts either by the claimant or by experts whom it would have been reasonable to consult, such as a doctor.

By s.33 of the Act the court has power to override the statutory time limits if it would be equitable to do so having regard to the prejudice caused to the claimant by the strict rules and having regard also to any prejudice which might be caused to the defendant were the power to be used. The court must take into account

- the length of the delay and why it occurred;
- the effect of the delay on the evidence;
- the conduct of the defendant including any response to a request for information;

- the duration of any legal disability (unsoundness of mind or infancy) of the claimant;

- the promptness with which the claimant acted once the necessary knowledge was available;

- the steps taken by the claimant to obtain expert advice and the nature of such advice.

The Law Commission has produced a preliminary consultation paper (LCCP no. 151 1997) in which it is suggested that this area of the law needs reform. The proposal is that a limitation period of three years should apply to most claims running from the date when the existence of a claim was discoverable by the claimant, with an absolute limit of ten years (thirty years in the case of personal injuries).

Necessity

A person is entitled to take action which is urgently necessary in order to prevent damage to people or property. The defence can be used to an action for trespass to land, for example, where a neighbour enters adjoining land to put out a fire which is threatening to spread to their property. Any steps taken must be reasonable and proportionate to the danger. Although it may become clear later that the action was not in fact needed, the defence will apply so long as it was justified when the danger was perceived. The following cases provide good examples of how this defence can work.

> ### *Kirk v Gregory* (1876)
> After a man had died (from excessive alcohol) his servants had a feast. The man's sister-in-law moved his jewellery to a safe place from which it was actually stolen! *Held*: her interference was not shown to be necessary and she was liable.
>
> ### *Cope v Sharpe* (1912)
> A fire broke out on A's land and threatened to spread to an area over which C had shooting rights. While A's servants were trying to put the fire out, C's gamekeeper set fire to a strip of heather to protect C's nesting birds. A's servants succeeded in putting out the fire before it reached C's area. A sued C for trespass to land. *Held*: at the time of the interference, the action was reasonable. C was not liable.

The doctrine can also be used in cases where a person cannot consent to medical treatment or other forms of care. See *Re F (Adult: Court's Jurisdiction)* (2000) in Chapter 1, p. 19.

Statutory authority

If an Act of Parliament authorises an activity which inevitably involves committing a tort, the defendant can use the provisions of the Act as a defence. As we have seen, this defence has particular relevance to the torts of nuisance and *Rylands v Fletcher*. It must be remembered that an Act may provide for compensation to be paid in specific cases. In other cases, the Act may be interpreted in such a way as to allow a person aggrieved by the activity to seek compensation for breach of statutory duty. (See Chapter 10, pp. 214–217.)

Act of God

This defence is only available to the tort of *Rylands v Fletcher*. An Act of God is something which cannot reasonably be anticipated and guarded against by the defendant. (For further details, see Chapter 6, p. 145.)

Other general defences

These have been considered in detail in Chapter 5, namely

- contributory negligence
- voluntary assumption of risk (*volenti*)
- participation in an unlawful act (*ex turpi*).

Remedies

Injunctions

An injunction as we have seen is an order of the court restraining the defendant from doing or continuing a wrongful act or omission. Failure to obey an injunction is a contempt of court and can be punished by a period of imprisonment. In the law of torts, injunctions are most commonly sought in actions for nuisance or trespass but the order could be granted where appropriate in relation to any tort.

An injunction is an equitable remedy which means that the court has no duty to grant the order. It must be satisfied that in all the circumstances it is right to grant the order. The court will take into account all the relevant circumstances, including the claimant's own behaviour, asking among other things 'Did the claimant provoke the defendant?'

The court has power to order damages in lieu of an injunction but this is limited to those cases where damages will be an adequate remedy. We have seen that there has been consideration of this in relation to nuisance. The basic rule, found in *Shelfer v City of London Electric Lighting Co* (1895), is that damages should only be awarded in lieu of an injunction if

- to grant an injunction would be oppressive to the defendant;

- the injury to the claimant's rights is small and capable of being estimated in money;

- monetary compensation is adequate.

Damages

This is probably the most important remedy in torts. In this section we shall look at the purpose for which damages are awarded and other relevant matters.

The main purpose of damages is to compensate the claimant, not to punish the defendant, and, so far as it is possible to do so by means of money, to put the claimant into the same position as before the cause of action arose.

The first point to note is that only one award of damages can be made. If damage turns out to be more serious than was anticipated at the time of the award, there is no further action available to the claimant. This can cause hardship in personal injury cases and by the Supreme Court Act 1981 s.32A the court has power to make a provisional award which allows the claimant to return to the court should further anticipated serious deterioration occur. This power is not commonly used.

Although most awards are of sums which reflect the actual loss suffered by the claimant, not all awards have quite the same effect.

Contemptuous damages

Contemptuous damages are awarded where the claimant can establish a cause of action but the court takes the view that the claim should not have been brought or that in some ways the claimant 'deserved what he got'. Such awards are not uncommon in libel actions.

Nominal damages

Nominal damages are used when no actual damage has occurred but the claimant's right has been infringed. Such an award is not unusual in an action for trespass to land or nuisance when the main purpose of the action has been to obtain an injunction.

Exemplary damages

Exemplary damages, designed to punish the defendant and to deter future similar behaviour, are awarded where there has been arbitrary, oppressive or unconstitutional behaviour by a government servant. Such matters may in the future be dealt with by an action for breach of rights under the Human Rights Act 1998. Exemplary damages may also be awarded where the defendant has calculated that the amount of any damages which would normally be payable will be less than the profit which the tortious action would bring. Such awards are sometimes given in libel cases.

Self-help

We have several times come across the phrase 'reasonable force' which may be used to achieve a particular purpose. In torts this is particularly relevant in connection with trespass to the person (reasonable force may be used in self-defence) and in connection with trespass to land (reasonable force may generally be used to eject a trespasser). The problem will always be to decide what degree of force will be regarded as 'reasonable'. All that can be said by way of a general rule is that each case will depend upon its own particular facts and that any force must be proportionate to the threat.

SUMMARY

Defences

- limitation period has expired – generally six years for claim unless personal injury is part of claim in which case three years

- necessity – defendant's response to risk was proportionate to the perceived danger

- statutory authority – a statute authorises the action the inevitable consequence of which is the commission of a tort

- Act of God: natural phenomenon – available only in *Rylands v Fletcher*

Remedies

- injunction: order, in relation to torts, to cease something which is tortious; equitable remedy – not granted if damages would be adequate compensation

- damages: designed to put claimant back to position they were in before tort committed – can be general, nominal or aggravated

- self-help – reasonable and proportionate action to resist or prevent damage to persons or property

12   Tort law in context

What is tort?

In the Introduction to this book, we saw that Winfield states that tort is a breach of a duty fixed by law while Martin and Gibbins talk about a wrong which entitles an injured person to seek compensation. The duty situation is seen clearly in connection with negligence and in connection with breach of statutory duty. Negligence arises when a duty is breached and a person suffers resulting damage. An Act of Parliament may give rise to a right to sue for breach of duty in similar circumstances. In relation to other torts, the duty is not always so obvious but it can be found. Nuisance imposes a duty to use our land reasonably so as not to cause interference with the use of another's land; trespass to the person reinforces a duty to respect another person's autonomy; defamation imposes a duty to tell only the truth about someone else.

It seems that both definitions can be shown to be correct but neither is particularly helpful in explaining exactly what a tort is in a way which is readily understood. It is perhaps easier to suggest a principle which underlies the development of this part of the law.

The issue of fault

All of the torts discussed in this book have one thing in common – each in effect sets a standard of behaviour. Failure to meet the standard which causes injury to someone else allows the victim to seek a remedy from the courts for the defendant's failure; in other words because the defendant was at fault, the defendant must pay.

Lord Atkin, in *Donoghue v Stevenson* (1932), acknowledged that the law of tort is:

> based upon a general public sentiment of moral wrongdoing for which the offender must pay.

This reflects the old legal adage, 'There can be no liability without fault'. Case law demonstrates that this is now accepted as a principle in relation to all torts with the exception of those which are actionable *per se*, for example trespass to the person or to the land.

The tort of negligence provides a number of examples of the development of the concept of fault, for example in respect of the duty of care itself and in respect of negligent misstatement and liability for nervous shock. With the judgment in *Anns v Merton LBC* (1978), it began to appear that a claimant who could simply prove fault in the sense of blameworthiness would be able to obtain damages. As the consequences of the judgment became apparent, the courts acted to limit potential claims by defining more precisely what needed to be proved in order to establish fault and *Anns v Merton LBC* was overruled by *Murphy v Brentwood DC* (1991). (See Chapter 2, p. 39.)

It can be said that the prospect of being held to have been at fault, with its concurrent liability to provide a remedy, will help to ensure that standards of behaviour will be maintained and that potential tortfeasors will be deterred. It is difficult to see how the tort of negligence can have a deterrent effect as the defendant will not have intended to cause the damage. The issue of the increasing use of insurance also reduces the deterrent effect, certainly on the part of business and commercial enterprises when the cost of insurance, even if the premium is increased, is simply met by treating the cost as part of the price for the goods or service. A private person might be deterred, or at least persuaded to act more carefully. Most private drivers are concerned that if they have an accident, the insurance premium will increase and they may well lose their no-claims bonus.

The concept of fault can also cause injustice in that the amount of compensation may be out of all proportion to the degree of blame. This can be seen in the very large awards of damages which are sometimes made for personal injury. The level of blame does not change whether the injury is serious or trivial but the level of damage changes according to the effect on the claimant.

Law, ethics and morality

The law sets a standard and draws a balance between individual rights but where does this come from? What is it that says that one course of action is acceptable while another is not? As we saw in the Introduction to this book, we all have moral and ethical beliefs which come from our culture, our religion and our environment. It is one of the purposes of law to ensure that a balance is drawn between our right to hold our particular views or values and the right of others to hold different views. If the balance is achieved, then justice is done.

The judges acknowledge the importance of taking modern social views and customs into account as well as the need to enforce clear legal rules. In *McLoughlin v O'Brian* (1982) Lord Scarman had this to say:

> The real risk to the common law is not its movement to cover
> new situations and new knowledge but lest it should stand still,
> halted by a conservative judicial approach. If that should happen
> there would be a danger of the law becoming irrelevant to the
> consideration, and inept in its treatment, of modern social
> problems. Justice would be defeated. Flexibility carries with it, of
> course, certain risks, notably a degree of uncertainty in the law
> and the 'floodgates' risk.

The principle of justice states that one acts justly towards a person
when that person has been given what they deserve whether by way
of reward or punishment. This was particularly acknowledged by Lord
Atkin in *Donoghue v Stevenson* (1932) when he said that the tort of
negligence was 'based upon a general public sentiment of moral
wrongdoing for which the offender must pay'. Lord Atkin also
acknowledged the need to maintain a balance when he stated the
practical view that 'acts or omissions which any moral code would
censure cannot in a practical world be treated so as to give a right to
every person injured by them to demand relief'.

The development of the law of torts throughout the twentieth
century shows how the judges have attempted to achieve a balance
between competing interests and with it justice. In the tort of negligence
there is Lord Atkin's 'neighbour principle' which can be used to decide
when a duty of care is owed. Development of the principle can be
seen in relation to the need for compensation for nervous shock which
also shows how the judges have been aware of other pressures which
perhaps mean that the quest for justice has to be compromised. The
limitations put on potential claims by secondary victims may cause
some injustice, but create an approach which takes account of the
need for a scheme which society can afford – the influence of economic
policy.

Parliament also plays its part in trying to ensure justice. The
Consumer Protection Act 1987 can be said to achieve a balance
between the interests of commercial and business organisations and
those of consumers by ensuring that a consumer has an effective
remedy if injured by a defective product. Parliament also acts to reflect
changing views. The law relating to an occupier's liability to trespassers
is an example of this. The original rules developed at a time when the
rights of a landowner were generally regarded as paramount and
anyone who infringed such rights was taken to 'deserve whatever
happened – he should not have been there in the first place'. The
Occupiers' Liability Act 1984 reflects the modern view that a minimum
level of care must be taken to protect even trespassers.

The way the English legal system itself operates also helps to achieve
a balance. The doctrine of precedent creates certainty in that legal

principles are clear but it also provides flexibility by the way in which earlier cases can in appropriate circumstances be distinguished from the present case, allowing the law to develop. The introduction of the Practice Statement in 1966, allowing the House of Lords to overrule its own earlier decisions, contributes to the maintenance of the balance. An example of this is provided by *BRB v Herrington* (1972) in which the House of Lords overruled its earlier decision and held that a 'duty of common humanity' was owed to trespassers to protect them from known dangers.

When judges are faced with a new situation, they will need to struggle in some cases to deal with precedents which effectively 'tie their hands' on the decision. An example of this is to be found in relation to the concept of public benefit/utility in private nuisance. In his judgment in *Miller v Jackson* (1977), in the Court of Appeal, Lord Denning stated his reasons for not following the precedent set by *Sturges v Bridgman* (1879): this states that a claim for nuisance cannot be defeated by the fact that the claimant moved to the nuisance. Lord Denning took into account the fact that the claimant bought the house next to the cricket ground in mid-summer when the cricket season was at its height, so that the claimant should have realised that there was a risk that cricket balls would from time to time be hit into the garden. Lord Denning explained his reasoning:

> This case is new. It should be approached on principles applicable to modern conditions. There is a contest here between the interest of the public at large; and the interest of a private individual. The public interest lies in protecting the environment by preserving our playing fields in the face of mounting development, and by enabling our youth to enjoy all the benefits of outdoor games, such as cricket and football. The private interest lies in securing the privacy of his home and garden without intrusion or interference by anyone. As between [these] conflicting interests, I am of the opinion that the public interest should prevail over the private interest.

The decision in the case can be described as 'creative law-making' by the court which believed that the old rule led to injustice. The decision has not been followed in later cases, but in *Kennaway v Thompson* (1980) the Court of Appeal acknowledged that the issue of public benefit is relevant to the remedy for nuisance, framing an injunction in such a way as to contrive some kind of balance between the interests of the parties.

The approach to the interpretation of legislation further illustrates how the system itself contributes to maintaining the balance. The rules of statutory interpretation ensure certainty but also allow flexibility.

The use of the Literal Rule can undoubtedly cause injustice but modern courts are more readily using the Mischief Rule and the Purposive Approach, which allow the judge to take a slightly more flexible approach in deciding what the legislation was intended to achieve, and giving effect to that intention.

If the balance is to be maintained there must be equality of access to the courts. The cost of legal proceedings is beyond the reach of many ordinary people unless there is some means of financial assistance. Parliament has passed the Access to Justice Act 1999 which reforms the previous system by the creation of a Community Legal Service intended to widen access to legal advice and help by making it readily available by increasing funding to Advice Centres and by the introduction of the Conditional Fees Scheme. Legal aid is still available but the scope of the Scheme has been changed. It is too early to say whether or not the changes will have the intended effect of ensuring better access to justice for all, regardless of personal wealth.

Court rules of procedure also contribute to easy access. The Woolf Reforms which are coming into effect should ensure that civil cases can be dealt with more quickly, cheaply and efficiently than in the past thus giving an effective remedy for those who believe that they have suffered a legal wrong.

Conclusion

The writer started to study the English law in 1964. Since that time there have been many changes as injustices in all parts of the law have been acknowledged and remedied. Injustice still occurs but the writer has found the approach by the judges and by Parliament sufficiently flexible to hope that justice will in most cases be achieved. The most important development over recent years has been the coming into effect of the Human Rights Act 1998. It was believed that this would in some cases, turn the existing common law and statutory law upside down. Already, a number of important decisions have been given in all areas of the law. These have been referred to throughout this book where they are concerned with the law of tort. There is no reason to suppose that the impact of the Act will decrease over the next few years. The writer can again end the text with the words 'An exciting and interesting time lies ahead!'

13   General questions on tort law

Not all A-level examination boards ask questions in the same way although the standard required from candidates is the same. The following questions are a selection which can be used by any candidate for practice but which will be of particular help to candidates taking the AQA examinations. Answer guidelines are provided at the end of the Answer guide (pp. 302–313).

Question 1

Greentrees Garden Centre Ltd (GGC Ltd) had operated a business for eight years, supplying various agricultural and garden products both to the trade and to the general public. Originally GGC Ltd's premises were sited some considerable distance from the nearest houses but recently a large housing estate has been developed, one edge of which is within 200 metres of the premises. Though there were no problems during the winter, residents in the nearest houses have begun to complain about summer noise and disturbance resulting from the use of equipment such as electric saws and fork-lift trucks, from commercial vehicles arriving and departing and from the large numbers of visitors and frequent queues of cars. These activities are alleged to start at around 7.00 am and to continue until about 9.00 pm.

David bought some timber at the garden centre and was assisting Guranjit, a GGC Ltd employee, to saw it up by guiding it into the electric saw. However, David lost his grip on the timber, a section of which splintered, flew out into David's face and caused him to lose an eye. David's cries of pain attracted the attention of Etesham, another visitor, who had known David for many years. Etesham collapsed as soon as she saw David's injuries and has since suffered from severe anxiety and depression. All GGC Ltd employees had been instructed that only employees were permitted in any area where sawing operations were performed but Guranjit had ignored the instruction because David was a friend and former employee.

(a) Explain whether the residents have any rights against GGC Ltd in respect of the noise and disturbance and consider what remedies they may claim.   (10 marks)

(b) Discuss Guranjit's liability for the injury to David and for the anxiety and depression suffered by Etesham.   (15 marks)

(c) Discuss GGC Ltd's liability for the injury to David and for the anxiety and depression suffered by Etesham.   (10 marks)

(d) What is the significance of the fact that GGC Ltd is a company?
                                                                (5 marks)

(e) Having regard to the rules and remedies which you have explained and applied in answering parts (a)-(c) above, how far do you think an outcome which is just in relation to all the parties will be likely to have been achieved? (10 marks)

(AEB 1997)

Question 2

Lifeline Radio Ltd, a local radio station, broadcast a weekly financial advice programme in which listeners could ring for advice on particular problems. At the beginning and end of the programme, the announcer informed listeners that they should consider getting further advice from a financial adviser if large sums of money were at stake, and that no private advice could be given or private correspondence entered into. Advice was given by Carol, who worked at Lifeline Radio Ltd, and by Walter, who was a well-known financial commentator for newspapers, television and radio.

During one programme, Uma rang in to ask about certain investments which she had made. Though Walter did not reveal that he was not an expert in those particular investments, the advice he gave would normally have been perfectly sound. Unfortunately, changes in the market were taking place about which a specialist in that area would have known, and the advice turned out to be bad. Uma followed it and lost a lot of money. So, too, did Sheila, who had been listening to the programme.

Also during the programme, Carol gave advice to another caller, Fred. Later she telephoned him and gave him further advice about the same matter. This further advice turned out to be very poor and Fred lost a lot of money by following it.

(a) Explain the rules which determine whether a person may be liable for financial loss suffered by another in consequence of the provision of bad advice or incorrect information. (10 marks)

(b) Apply those rules to determine whether Walter is liable for the loss suffered by Uma and Sheila, and whether Carol is responsible for the loss suffered by Fred. (10 marks)

(c) Assuming that both Walter and Carol are liable, explain whether Lifeline Radio Ltd may also be liable for those losses. (10 marks)

(d) If any disputes between the parties involved in these incidents could not be resolved by agreement, explain in which court(s) it seems likely that actions would be tried. (You are not required to discuss appeals.) (5 marks)

(e) Explain what you consider to be the most significant development in the tort of negligence since the House of Lords decided the case of *Donoghue v Stevenson*. (15 marks)

(AQA 1999)

Question 3

Nathan and a very large number of friends are all addicted to watching sport on television. He frequently invites them to his house where they tend to stay until the early hours of the morning. There is always a lot of shouting and cheering and they often drink and talk in the garden and sometimes take a television out there. People in the neighbouring houses are disturbed by this noise and the noise when they leave. Also there are frequent arguments over car parking and access.

To make it more convenient to watch programmes in the garden, Nathan installed a supply of electricity to an outbuilding by running a cable to it from the house. Though he buried the cable in the ground, he did not use the materials or method required by law and he did not have the installation properly checked. Subsequently, he engaged Owen, a gardener, to install some fencing. Whilst drilling holes for fence posts, Owen cut through the cable and was electrocuted and seriously injured. The incident was witnessed by Nathan's neighbour, Richard, who collapsed with shock.

Though he was using the supply to the outbuilding to power his machinery, Owen had not asked Nathan about the electricity cable and Nathan had not attempted to mention it to him.

(a) Discuss what legal action Nathan's neighbours might pursue in respect of the noise and inconvenience and consider how effective any remedies might be. (10 marks)

(b) Consider whether Owen may be able to recover compensation from Nathan for his injuries. (15 marks)

(c) Assuming that Owen were able to do so, explain whether Richard could also recover compensation from Nathan. (10 marks)

(d) Assuming that Owen has little money, how might he be able to pay for legal advice about his case? (5 marks)

(e) To what extent is the influence of policy considerations evident in the rules of law which you have discussed in examining the case of Owen and Richard? (10 marks)
(AEB 1995)

Question 4

Marie's garden was bordered by wooden fences. She was treating these with Wood-u-like, a product made by Smershco International Limited and advertised as 'the safest and easiest way to cherish and care for sheds, fencing and other garden woodwork'.

Lucy, aged four, was an adventurous and inquisitive child who lived next door to Marie. Hearing Marie working in her garden, Lucy squeezed through a tiny space between a gate post and a fence panel to get into Marie's garden. Just as Lucy was squeezing through the gap, Marie's doorbell rang and, leaving a bowl of Wood-u-like standing beside the fence, Marie went to answer the door.

235

Lucy, believing the Wood-u-like to be cola, drank several mouthfuls of it and suffered serious burns to her mouth and throat and damage to internal organs.

The person at the door was Marie's brother, Nigel, who had called round to help her with the work on the fence. He came through into the garden and found Lucy gasping and screaming. He took control of the situation, telling Marie to call an ambulance and fetch Lucy's mother and doing his best to wash the Wood-u-like from Lucy's mouth and hands. As a result of this experience, Nigel suffered severe depression for a considerable period.

(a) Consider what rights Lucy might have against Marie and Smershco.

(25 marks)

(b) Discuss whom Nigel might sue to recover damages in respect of his depression, and consider his chances of success. (25 marks)

(c) Discuss whether the law with regard to liability for causing psychiatric harm is satisfactory. (25 marks)
(AQA 2001/2002 Specimen Paper)

Question 5

Prince and Company were a firm of surveyors. They were asked by Rupert to consider a piece of land he was intending to buy and to advise him on its suitability for his purpose and the price he should pay. Rupert intended to use the land to build an amusement park. Prince and Company prepared their report and were paid by Rupert. Rupert bought the land but was then unable to finance development and sold the land to Simon, who intended to develop an amusement park on the land and relied on Prince and Company's report when deciding that the land was suitable for this purpose.

Building work began and large quantities of gravel were delivered for use for various purposes. The gravel was stored in enormous heaps near the boundary with adjoining land belonging to Thomas, a farmer. A prolonged period of rain made the gravel heaps unstable and they began to slide onto Thomas's land, destroying fences and making grazing land unusable for a complete season.

When the park was completed, residents in two neighbouring villages complained about noise, dust and increased traffic flow. Smells from the burger bar in the amusement park deterred local residents from using the local fish and chip shop; they said that the smell 'put them off' fried food of any kind.

(a) Consider whether Simon has a good cause of action against Prince and Company. (25 marks)

(b) Discuss the possible actions against Simon that might be brought by Thomas and by local people. (25 marks)

(c) To what extent do the torts of nuisance and *Rylands v Fletcher* provide adequate protection for owners of land? (25 marks)
(AQA 2001/2002 Specimen Paper)

14 Sources of tort law

As has been seen throughout this book, tort law is derived from principles of common law and from statute.

Common law

The common law is found in the speeches of judges giving judgment in past cases. These are given in detail in the various series of Law Reports and form a primary source of law. The greater part of tort law is derived from this source through the operation of the doctrine of precedent. An example of the way in which this happens can be seen in the gradual development of the rules relating to nervous shock which can be traced from *Dulieu v White* (1901) to *Page v Smith* (1995) (see Chapter 2).

Statute

The second primary source of law is legislation, in other words the creation of statutes by the operation of Parliament. As yet tort law has not been greatly affected by parliamentary action but as the work of the various law reform bodies continues, more statutes are appearing; examples can be seen in the Occupiers' Liability Acts 1957 and 1984 (see Chapter 4) and in the Animals Act 1971 (see Chapter 7). The Human Rights Act 1998 is already having a substantial effect as it incorporates the European Convention on Human Rights into the law of the United Kingdom. Throughout the book reference has been made to a number of important developments. Statutes do not always clearly state what the rules are and here the judges assist by means of their function to interpret legislation. The reports of judgments in such cases are another primary source which can be very helpful.

The European Union

A third primary source of law is the law which comes from the

European Union. In relation to tort law this is not as yet a major source. It has some effect in the area of consumer protection, the Consumer Protection Act 1987 being passed to give effect to a European Directive (see Chapter 7). The European Union is also active in the field of environmental protection. The Environmental Protection Act 1990 and the Environment Act 1995 give effect to Directives and have added important protection in relation to matters which cannot always be dealt with by using the common law relating to the tort of nuisance (see Chapter 6).

Textbooks

With very few exceptions textbooks are not a primary source of law but provide the writer's interpretation of the primary sources. As you have read this book, you have come across some fairly lengthy sources from both judgments and statutes together with the writer's explanation. The real fun of legal study comes with the ability to use primary sources; for example, reading the full report of *Cambridge Water Co v Eastern Counties Leather plc* (1994) enables the reader to decide the *ratio decidendi* (the binding part of the precedent), in other words that foreseeability of damage is an essential element of the tort of *Rylands v Fletcher*, and to distinguish this from the *obiter dicta* (a persuasive precedent) that storage of chemicals is a classic case of non-natural user. (See Chapter 6 for a full discussion of the case.) It is true that the judgments themselves can cause confusion and this is where a textbook can help even if all it does is to acknowledge where confusion in the law exists!

Some source material and one way to use it

The next part of this chapter consists of the source material on tort law provided by one of the main examination boards, OCR, together with commentary and advice on how to understand and use this kind of material. The selection of sources reproduced provides the basis for synoptic assessment (see Chapter 16 for more on this) for students taking the OCR tort law option, and it will be particularly relevant to them. At the same time, for anyone else studying tort law, the selection of sources, together with the questions and commentary provided, will provide an ideal means of gaining an insight into the nature and use of sources of this kind, enhancing understanding of tort law more generally.

OCR Special Study Material source materials (with commentary)

1 Extract adapted from *Walker and Walker's English Legal System* by Richard Ward (Butterworths, pp 62–3, 75, 76, 34–6, 42, 218–19)

The traditional view of the function of an English judge has been that it is not to make law but to decide cases in accordance with existing legal rules. Few would now deny that judges have a powerful law-making function, but there is no doubt that this traditional declaratory view of the judicial process was the theoretical foundation of binding precedent whereby the judge is not merely referred to earlier decisions for guidance, but also bound to apply rules of law decided by those cases. The operation of the doctrine depends upon the hierarchy of the courts. All courts stand in a definite relationship to one another. A court is bound by decisions of a court above itself in the hierarchy and, usually, by a court of equivalent standing. Given that the doctrine of precedent has binding force within this framework, the question naturally arises of how the law may develop if cases are always to be determined according to ageless principles. In practice there are several ways in which the doctrine retains its flexibility ... two basic principles [should be considered]; first, that superior courts have power to overrule decisions of inferior courts and, in certain cases, to overrule their own earlier decisions, and, secondly, that any rule of law may be changed by statute. Consequently every rule of law is subject to change, either by the judges themselves or by Parliament. Although legislation is the ultimate source of law, in the sense that Parliament has within our constitution the ultimate power to make, or unmake any law, it should not in any way be regarded as a superior source of law. Although judges may well be reluctant to make major changes which involve policy better settled by Parliament, judicial law-making can provide flexibility, and relative speed, because of the demands on parliamentary time.

Every rule of law must have its origin. If it were not created by statute, then it must have been created by a court. Thus where there is no precedent the doctrine breaks down and the judge is bound to reach a decision in accordance with the general principles. Even in modern times cases arise for which there is no precedent. These cases are described as cases of first impression and require the judge to make law rather than to apply it.

Judges do sometimes create new law. For example, Lord
Denning ... virtually did this in *Central London Property Trust v
High Trees House Ltd* ([1947] KB 130). The self-assumed power of
the House of Lords to depart from its own previous decisions
has had the effect of bringing into sharp relief the scope of the
judicial function, for the members of the House are now free, in
effect, to create new law. It is fair to say that certain judges
deem it to be within their function to create new principles of
law while others believe that any far-reaching change should be
left to Parliament, which has greater facilities for testing the
possible repercussions of law reform.

Where the words of a statute are clear and unambiguous,
persons affected by its provisions will regulate their conduct
according to the terms of the statute and the need for judicial
interpretation will not arise. However, if the meaning or extent
of a statute is uncertain or ambiguous litigation is inevitable and
the statute will have to be interpreted. There is a technical
distinction between interpretation and construction.
'Interpretation' is simply the process whereby a meaning is
assigned to the words in a statute. The courts' primary task on
interpretation is to ascertain and give effect to the meaning of
the words used: the first inquiry of a court should be to ask:
'what do the words themselves mean?' 'Construction', on the
other hand, is the process whereby uncertainties or ambiguities
in a statute are resolved. It follows that every statute that comes
before a court is interpreted whereas only uncertain or
ambiguous provisions require construction. The processes are
not usually distinguished by judges since, in the nature of
things, litigation only arises around the wording of a statute
where it is ambiguous or, at least, uncertain.

The main difficulty in such cases is that the intention of
Parliament must be established primarily from the words used
by Parliament, although increasingly extrinsic aids may be
used.

An interesting problem of construction arises when the court is
faced with a factual situation for which the statute has not
provided. It can only be remedied by attributing to Parliament
an intention which Parliament never had. That amounts to a
legislative act on the part of the judiciary and is a function
which the more conservative judges are slow to adapt.

[In *Magor & St Mellons v Newport Corporation* [1952] AC 189
Lord Simonds condemned the approach of Lord Denning of
'filling in the gaps and making sense of the enactment] as 'a
naked usurpation of the legislative function' ... 'If a gap is

disclosed,' Lord Simonds explained, 'the remedy lies in an amending Act.' Nonetheless it is a truism that hard cases make bad law and the courts have, from time to time, been prepared to assume the authority to supply omissions left by the legislature.

Having read the extract, we can see that the passage is about the role of the judges and the development of the law. The extract covers the role played by the judges in the creation and use of precedent, the hierarchy of the courts and the role played by the judges in interpreting legislation. Tort law as a whole provides many examples.

The development of the common law is illustrated particularly by the tort of *Rylands v Fletcher* (see Chapter 6). The tort starts life as a development of nuisance and a tort of strict liability. Over the years the judges have taken policy decisions, which are not always acknowledged to be policy decisions, effectively limiting the usefulness of the tort. This is particularly clear in the way in which the judges have dealt with the issue of natural and non-natural use of land.

Issues relating to statutory interpretation are seen in the law relating to animals governed by the Animals Act 1971. It will be remembered that liability for damage or injury caused by a non-dangerous animal requires the judge to decide whether the animal has an abnormal characteristic which has led to the behaviour causing the damage. Guidance as to the interpretation of this section of the Act (s.2(2)(b)) is found in earlier Court of Appeal decisions (e.g. *Curtis v Betts* [1990] and *Gloster v Chief Constable of Greater Manchester Police* [2000]). Most recently the sub-section has been explained by the House of Lords in *Mirvahedy v Henley and Another* (2003).

As you work through the book, you will find many other examples.

2 Extract adapted from *Street on Torts* by John Murphy, 11th edn (Butterworths p. 282)

Establishing cause and effect in law can be far from easy. Every occurrence is the result of a combination of several different events. Thus an incident resulting in injury to a claimant is the product not simply of the negligent acts and omissions of the defendant, but also of the conditions in which those events took place.

What must be identified is the operative legal cause or causes. And this, it must be recognised, involves considerations of policy as much as it does any strict notion of factual cause and effect. Lord Wright captured the point when he said 'the choice of the real or efficient cause from out of the whole complex of facts must be made by applying common sense standards'.

'Causation', he insisted, 'is to be understood as the man in the street, and not as either the scientist or the metaphysician would understand it.'

It is thus partly as a matter of convenience that the law settles upon a basic 'but for' test of causation whereby the question that the court generally addresses is whether, but for the defendant's negligence, the accident would have occurred. If the question receives a negative answer, and there is no evidential complication in the case, the court will hold the defendant liable (subject to the harm in question being too remote to permit recovery).

This extract from a leading textbook highlights the difficulty faced by the judges in deciding the cause of damage or injury and explains why the 'but for' test in negligence is a simple way of deciding causation. For a full discussion of the rules of causation in negligence, see Chapter 3.

3 Extract adapted from the judgment of Neild J in *Barnett v Chelsea Hospital Management Board* [1969] 1 QB 428

Without doubt the casualty officer should have seen and examined the deceased. His failure to do either cannot be described as an excusable error as has been submitted. It was negligence. It remains to consider whether it is shown that the deceased's death was caused by that negligence or whether, as the defendants have said, the deceased must have died in any event.

Without going in detail into the considerable volume of technical evidence which has been put before me, it seems to me to be the case that when death results from arsenic poisoning it is brought about by two conditions; on the one hand dehydration and on the other disturbance of the enzyme process. If the principal condition is one of enzyme disturbance – as I am of the view it was here – then the only method of treatment which is likely to succeed is the use of the specific antidote which is commonly called B.A.L. Dr Goulding said this in the course of his evidence:

'I see no reasonable prospect of B.A.L. being administered before the time at which he died.'

and at a later point in his evidence:

> 'I feel that even if fluid loss had been discovered death would have been caused by the enzyme disturbances. Death might have occurred later.'

> So if damage would have occurred in any event without the breach of the duty of care on the part of the defendant, then the defendant will not be liable.

In this extract from his judgment Mr Justice Neil explains the factual circumstances of Mr Barnett's death and why the 'but for' test needs to be used. More guidance on this issue can be found in Chapter 3.

4 Extract adapted from the judgment of Lord Reid in *Baker v Willoughby* [1970] 2 WLR 50 HL

> If the latter injury suffered before the date of the trial either reduces the disabilities from the injury for which the defendant is liable, or shortens the period during which they will be suffered by the plaintiff then the defendant will have to pay less damages. But if the later injuries merely become a concurrent cause of the disabilities caused by the injury inflicted by the defendant, then in my view they cannot diminish the damages. Suppose that the plaintiff has to spend a month in bed before the trial because of some illness unconnected with the original injury, the defendant cannot say that he does not have to pay anything in respect of that month; during that month the original injuries and the new illness are concurrent causes of his inability to work and that does not reduce the damages.

Lord Reid explains the effect of a concurrent cause of injury. The extract is not easily understood and demonstrates the practical and legal difficulties which can arise in such a case.

5 Extract adapted from *Modern Tort Law* by Vivienne Harpwood, 5th edn (Cavendish Publishing, pp. 146–50)

> Causation is a question of fact which it is necessary for the claimant to prove. In civil cases, a proposition must be proved 'on a balance of probabilities'. This is sometimes extremely difficult, especially where it is possible for the defendant to argue that there are a number of other causative factors besides the one relied upon by the claimant.

> Some of the cases in this area appear contradictory and there are many difficulties involved in them which make the outcomes seem unfair to the claimants in some instances.

In *Bonnington Castings v Wardlaw* [1956] 1 All ER 615, the claimant suffered pneumoconiosis after years of working in a dusty industry. The claimant claimed that his employers did not provide proper washing facilities or extractor fans for the safety of their employees. There were two main dust sources in the workplace. The claimant could not establish which type of dust he had inhaled most. However, the House of Lords held that because the dust from the swing grinders was at least a contributory cause of the illness, the claimant should succeed for the full amount of his claim. In *McGhee v National Coal Board* [1973] 1 WLR 1, a workman contracted dermatitis as a result of handling brick dust. He could not prove, on a balance of probabilities, that the illness could have been avoided by the use of showers at work but he succeeded in his claim. The reasoning of the court was that because the employee had demonstrated neglect by the defendant of an obvious safety precaution, it followed that when the risk that the precaution could have avoided materialised, the burden shifted to the defendant to disprove a causal link. This was clearly of great advantage to the claimant and placed him in a far more advantageous position than he would have been in under the 'but for' test.

A different approach was taken in *Hotson v East Berkshire HA* [1987] 2 All ER 909. A 13 year old school boy ... injured his knee ... An X-ray had been taken ... and no injury was apparent, so no further exploratory examination was made ... the boy developed a condition known as avascular necrosis [which] results in pain and deformity. Although the boy may have suffered the condition in any case as a result of the injury there was a 25% chance that if it had been properly treated immediately, he would have made a full recovery. It was held at first instance that the claimant should receive 25% of the full award. The House of Lords held that he should receive nothing. He had not been able to establish that the ... defendant's negligence caused his injury, as there was a 75% chance that he would have developed the avascular necrosis even if they had not been negligent in their original treatment.

In *Wilsher v Essex AHA* (1988) the House of Lords decided that, on the medical evidence, there were six possible causes of retrolental fibroplasia, and that excess oxygen was just one of these. The House of Lords would not accept that there could be liability on the basis of the 'material contribution' principle. The *McGhee* principle could not be applied because there were five possible causes of the injury.

In *Fairchild v Glenhaven Funeral Services Ltd* [2002] UKHL 22,
the House of Lords added to the picture, confirming in effect
that causation is not concerned only with factual matters, but
also with policy issues. The case demonstrates that even when
medical science is incapable of establishing certain factual
matters ... the claimant may still succeed in proving causation.
The case involved three appeals by people who had developed
mesothelioma ... after inhaling asbestos fibres at their places of
work. As the disease may not develop until many years after
inhalation ... it can be difficult for a claimant to establish
precisely where and when the fibres were inhaled. The
inhalation of one single particle of asbestos dust has the
potential to cause this particular disease and a claimant wishing
to establish a causal link between exposure to asbestos by a
negligent employer and the damage ... would, on application of
traditional principles of causation, need to demonstrate that a
particular defendant had caused the damage.

In this case the claimants had all worked for several different
employers in jobs where they had been exposed to asbestos
dust.

The House of Lords, influenced by policy considerations ...
held that in the exceptional circumstances of these claimants,
the normal application of the 'but for' test should be relaxed
and each employer could be taken to have made a material
contribution to the risks.

In this extract examples are given of the apparently contradictory
results reached by the courts in four important cases. The cases illustrate
the injustice suffered by the claimant which can be caused by the
rules of causation (*Hotson v East Berkshire HA* [1987] and *Wilsher v
Essex AHA* [1988]) and the injustice which a different approach can
inflict on a defendant (*Bonnington Castings v Wardlaw* [1956] and
Fairchild v Glenhaven Funeral Services Ltd [2002]).

6 Extract adapted from the judgment of Lord Salmon in *McGhee v National Coal Board* [1973] 1 WLR 1 HL

I would suggest that the true view is that, as a rule, when it is
proved, on a balance of probabilities, that an employer has
been negligent and that his negligence has materially increased
the risk of his employee contracting an industrial disease, then
he is liable in damages to that employee if he contracts the
disease notwithstanding that the employer is not responsible for
other factors which have materially contributed to the disease.

In this short extract from his judgment, Lord Salmon suggests that in the case of an industrial injury, an employer may be liable if the employment conditions have materially increased the risk that the employee may suffer injury.

7 Extract adapted from the judgment of Lord Reid in *McKew v Holland & Hannen & Cubitts (Scotland) Ltd* [1969] 3 All ER 1621 HL

> The appellant's case is that the second accident was caused by the weakness of his left leg which in turn had been caused by the first accident. The main argument of the respondents is that the second accident was not the direct or natural and probable or foreseeable result of their fault in causing the first accident.
>
> In my view the law is clear. If a man is injured in such a way that his leg may give way at any moment he must act reasonably and carefully. It is quite possible that in spite of all reasonable care his leg may give way in circumstances such that as a result he sustains further injury. Then that second injury was caused by his disability which in turn was caused by the defender's fault. But if the injured man acts unreasonably he cannot hold the defendant liable for injury caused by his own unreasonable conduct. His unreasonable conduct is *novus actus interveniens*. The chain of causation has been broken and what follows may be regarded as caused by his own conduct and not by the defendant's fault or the disability caused by it.
>
> So in my view the question here is whether the second accident was caused by the appellant doing something unreasonable.
>
> He knew that his left leg was liable to give way suddenly and without warning. He knew that this stair was steep and that there was no handrail. He must have realised, if he had given the matter a moment's thought, that he could only safely descend the stair if he went extremely slowly and carefully so that he could sit down if his leg gave way, or waited for assistance. But he chose to descend in such a way that when his leg gave way he could not stop himself.

Lord Reid, while discussing the situation where consequences of injury make a claimant more likely to suffer from activity which the claimant undertakes after the original injury, differentiates between additional injury caused by doing something reasonable and additional injury caused by doing something unreasonable. The latter may well be viewed as a *novus actus interveniens*.

8 Extract adapted from the judgment of Lord Justice Stephenson in *Knightley v John and Others* [1982] 1 All ER 851

In *The Oropesa* Lord Wright ... said:

> 'To break the chain of causation it must be shown that there is ... something unwarrantable, a new cause which disturbs the sequence of events, something which can be described as either unreasonable or extraneous or extrinsic. I doubt whether the law can be stated more precisely than that.'

Negligent conduct is more likely to break the chain of causation than conduct which is not; positive acts will more easily constitute new causes than inaction. Mistakes and mischances are to be expected when human beings, however well trained, have to cope with a crisis ... if those that occur are natural the wrongdoer cannot, I think, escape responsibility for them simply by calling them improbable or unforeseeable.

In my judgment, too much happened here, too much went wrong, the chapter of mistakes was too long and varied, to impose on John's liability for what happened to the plaintiff in discharging his duty as a police officer, although it would not have happened had not John negligently overturned his car. The ordinary course of things took an extraordinary course. The length and the irregularities of the line leading from the first accident to the second have no parallel in the reported rescue cases, in all of which the plaintiff succeeded in establishing the wrongdoer's liability. It was natural ... probable ... foreseeable ... indeed certain that the police would come to the overturned car ... It was also natural and probable and foreseeable that some steps would be taken in controlling the traffic ... and some things done that might be more courageous than sensible. The reasonable ... observer would anticipate some human errors ... perhaps even from trained police officers. But would he anticipate such a result as this from so many errors as these, so many departures from the common-sense procedure prescribed by the standing orders for just such an emergency as this? I can only say that, in my opinion, the judge's decision carries John's responsibility too far: in trying to be fair to the inspector the judge was unfair to John and gave the wrong answer ...

In this extract Lord Justice Stephenson attempts to explain the circumstances in which an original defendant can be liable for subsequent injury caused by a second negligent act by someone else.

The judge seems to be saying that where the chain of events shows that the nature of the second accident could *reasonably* result from human error, that accident will not be likely to be viewed as a *novus actus*. Blatant disregard of common sense however, may well be an intervening act which limits the defendant's liability for increased injury.

9 Extract from the Law Reform (Contributory Negligence) Act 1945

1   Apportionment of liability in the case of contributory negligence

(1) Where any person suffers damage as the result partly of his own fault and partly the fault of any other person or persons, a claim in respect of that damage shall not be defeated by reason of the fault of the person suffering the damage, but the damages recoverable in respect thereof shall be reduced to such extent as the court thinks just and equitable having regard to the claimant's share in the responsibility for the damage:

Provided that –

(a) this subsection shall not operate to defeat any defence arising under a contract;

(b) where any contract or enactment providing for the limitation of liability is applicable to the claim, the amount of damages recoverable by the claimant by virtue of this subsection shall not exceed the maximum limit so applicable.

(2) Where damages are recoverable by any person by virtue of the foregoing subsection subject to such reduction as is therein mentioned, the court shall find and record the total damages which would have been recoverable if the claimant had not been at fault.

This source simply sets out the statutory provision which allows a judge to apportion damages in proportion to the amount of blame which can be attributed to the claimant and to the defendant. You will recognise that this is the basis of the defence of contributory negligence. Reference can be made to Chapter 5, in which the defence is discussed in some detail.

10 Extract adapted from *Casebook on Torts* by Richard Kidner, 5th edn (Oxford University Press, p. 239)

The principle of contributory negligence is that the damages awarded to a plaintiff who has himself been at fault should be reduced to the extent that his fault has contributed to the accident or the damage. It might seem logical that if a defendant is to be held responsible for his fault, then so should a plaintiff for his, but it should be borne in mind that in practice the effect of a finding of contributory negligence on the part of a plaintiff is entirely different from a finding of fault on the part of the defendant. The reason is that, at least in personal injury cases, a defendant will usually be insured, or may be able to distribute his loss in some other way. Thus a defendant who is made liable will not often bear the burden himself. But where a plaintiff is held to be contributorily negligent and his damages are reduced, he will almost always bear the burden himself. Why should we deliberately undercompensate people in this way? It is doubtful whether the doctrine has any deterrent effect: for example it is highly unlikely that in the past the fact that a person who was not wearing a seat belt would be held contributorily negligent had any effect on the numbers of people who wore seat belts.

The rules for establishing contributory negligence on the part of the plaintiff are not the same as the rules for establishing liability for negligence on the part of the defendant. There is, for example, no room for the concept of duty of care, and the question is rather simply whether the plaintiff has taken proper care for his own safety. One of the most difficult problems relates to causation, i.e. was the act of the plaintiff merely the background against which the negligence of the defendant operated, or did it causally contribute to the accident.

This extract explains the effect of the principle of contributory negligence and discusses whether or not it is fair in the way it affects a claimant. The author considers the different standards by which fault by the claimant and defendant respectively is judged.

11 Extract adapted from the judgment of Lord Denning in *Froom v Butcher* [1976] QB 286 CA

The accident is caused by the bad driving. The damage is caused in part by the bad driving of the defendant, and in part by the failure of the plaintiff to wear a seat belt. If the plaintiff was to blame for not wearing a seat belt, the damage is in part a result of his own fault. He must bear some share in the

responsibility for the damage and his damages have to be
reduced to such extent as the court thinks just and equitable.

Whenever there is an accident, the negligent driver must bear
by far the greater share of responsibility. But in so far as the
damage might have been avoided or lessened by wearing a seat
belt, the injured person must bear some share. But how much
should this be? This question should not be prolonged by an
expensive enquiry into the degree of blameworthiness on either
side, which would be hotly disputed. Suffice it to assess a share
of responsibility which will be just and equitable in the great
majority of cases.

In such case I would suggest that the damages attributable to
the failure to wear a seat belt should be reduced by 15%.

In this extract Lord Denning suggests that the degree of contributory
negligence should be assessed as the extent to which it is fair to hold
the claimant partly to blame for the injuries/damage.

12 Extract adapted from *Law of Tort* by John Cooke, 6th edn (Pearson Publishing, pp. 151–2)

There are two possible ways of assessing the claimant's share in
the responsibility for the damage, causation and
blameworthiness.

If a test of causative potency is used, then logically every case
should end with a 50/50 apportionment, as the conduct of both
the claimant and the defendant is a cause.

Where the comparative blameworthiness or culpability of the
parties is taken into account, then the test is an objective one of
deviating from the standard of behaviour of the reasonable
person.

The requirement that the reduction be just and equitable means
that there is no single test for determining the level of the
reduction of damages.

Can there be a 100% reduction …? If there can be then there is
no practical difference between this defence and *volenti*, as the
claimant receives no damages. In *Pitts v Hunt* [1930] 3 All ER
344, the trial judge felt he was unable to apply *volenti* …
because of the statutory provision. However, he held the
plaintiff to be 100% contributorily negligent. The Court of
Appeal stated that it was impermissible to make a finding of
100% contributory negligence, as the Act states that the plaintiff

must suffer damage partly as a result of their own fault and partly as a result of the defendant's fault. (But see *Jayes v IMI (Kynoch) Ltd.*)

That the argument on 100% reduction is not over is shown in the case of suicide in police custody of *Reeves v Commissioner of Police* [1998] 2 WLR 401. The trial judge had held the deceased to be 100% contributorily negligent, with which Morritt LJ (dissenting) agreed in the Court of Appeal. The majority were hesitant. In the House of Lords it was held that where the deceased was of sound mind he bore at least partial responsibility for killing himself and damages were reduced by 50 per cent.

In this extract, the author discusses the difficulty of assessing the level of contributory negligence and explains why there cannot be a finding that the claimant bears 100% of the blame.

A strategy for using the material

The source material is taken from primary sources (the sources from judgments) and from secondary sources (the sources from textbooks). Having read the material you will have become aware of the complexity of the law relating to the issue of causation in the tort of negligence. The sources also illustrate the theme raised in Source 1, namely the use of precedent for the development of the common law.

At first sight you may find the material daunting, having been used to using textbooks with the user-friendly explanations given by your teacher or lecturer. If you are taking the OCR examination, the sources will be available to you for some months before the examination itself and you will be provided with a clean copy of the material on the day. This means that although you must become very familiar with the material, it does not need to be memorised. The material will form the basis of the examination questions and you will be expected to refer to it in your answers when it is appropriate to do so. The following suggestions might help you to tackle the task of familiarising yourself with the material.

- Read all of the material through without worrying too much about understanding exactly what it all means and what particular issues are raised. This will enable you to get the feel of the material ready for more detailed study.

- Decide on a method of working through the material – the following suggestions may help – and take things steadily. Initially the task may seem immense but by the time you reach the end, you will have a sense of real achievement.

- Read one source at a time, making sure you understand the words used and referring to your textbook to revise that area a little so that you understand the context.

- Make notes on what you have read – both short jottings in the margin of the materials and then more detailed notes on paper. You will find it helpful to have a summary of each of the sources to hand as you attempt practice questions.

- When you have read more than one source, consider why it was included and what the connection may be between two sources.

- Attempt some of the questions below (pp. 255–257) and congratulate yourself that you are in a position to do so with reasonable confidence!

- Finally, think about extra issues which may arise – you can be sure that the examination paper will not have the same questions as those you have used for practice.

The sources and questions

A useful first step would be to make a list of the sources as you scan through the material. You can then tick each one off as you finish work on it. The following items are included:

1 Extract from *Walker and Walker's English Legal System*

2 Extract from *Street on Torts*

3 Extract from the judgment of Neild J in *Barnett v Chelsea Hospital Management Board* (1969)

4 Extract from judgment of Lord Reid in *Baker v Willoughby* (1970)

5 Extract from *Modern Tort Law* by Vivienne Harpwood

6 Extract from judgment of Lord Salmon in *McGhee v National Coal Board* (1973)

7 Extract from judgment of Lord Reid in *McKew v Holland & Hannen & Cubitts (Scotland) Ltd* (1969)

8 Extract from judgment of Stephenson LJ in *Knightley v Johns and Others* (1982)

9 Extract from Law Reform (Contributory Negligence) Act 1945

10 Extract from *Casebook on Torts* by Richard Kidner

11 Extract from judgment of Lord Denning in *Froom v Butcher* (1976)

12 Extract from *Law of Tort* by John Cooke.

Initial thoughts

Source 1 is from a textbook which is one of the leading books on the English legal system. The author discusses the general way in which the law develops. The role of the judges as law-makers is described with reference to both the common law and legislation. The doctrine of precedent and the role of the various courts are briefly explained. The author suggests that these contribute to the flexibility of the common law. In relation to legislation the author explains the role played by the judges in interpretation of a statute. He highlights the distinction between interpretation and construction of statutes and refers to the different views of Lord Denning and Lord Simonds, both of whom were very senior judges.

The source alerts us to the area of law which you have studied for the AS examination and which you will need to revise and develop for the A2. You will have noticed that the source refers to the general development of the law and the role played by the judges.

Source 2 is from a leading textbook on torts in which the author explains the difficulty in establishing causation in law. He identifies that policy considerations are relevant and suggests that the 'but for' test is used 'as a matter of convenience'.

Source 3 is from the judgment in *Barnett v Chelsea HMB*, a case which is used to illustrate how the 'but for' test should be used. Neild J explains the need for a claimant to prove cause and effect.

Source 4 is from one of the judgments given in the House of Lords in *Baker v Willoughby*. Lord Reid explains the important concept of 'concurrent injuries' and the effect it may have on the amount of damages to be paid by the defendant.

Source 5 is another extract from a textbook. The author discusses the difficulties which can arise in establishing causation of fact when there is more than one possible cause. The different approaches taken by the courts in *Bonnington Castings v Wardlaw, Hotson v East Berkshire HA, Wilsher v Essex AHA* and *Fairchild v Glenhaven Funeral Services* are discussed. The author uses the cases to demonstrate the problems which can arise and to suggest that the law may operate unfairly from the claimant's point of view.

Source 6, from a judgment by Lord Salmon, suggests that when an employer has been proved negligent the claimant can successfully claim if all that can be proved is that on the balance of probabilities the employer's negligence materially increased the risk of the injury suffered by the claimant.

Source 7, from Lord Reid's judgment in *McKew v Holland & Hannon & Cubitts*, explains when the claimant's own actions may be seen as a *novus actus interveniens*. The judge suggests that the real question is whether or not the claimant's actions were reasonable or unreasonable. If the action is unreasonable then it will amount to a *novus actus*.

Source 8 is from a judgment by Stephenson LJ, who suggests that a negligent act is more likely to be a *novus actus* than simple error of judgment. The decision must be fair to both the claimant and the defendant. Some human errors can be anticipated but in the particular case, the number of departures from procedure was simply too many and the defendant was not responsible for the injury resulting from the accumulation of errors.

In **Source 9**, the statutory rules governing contributory negligence are set out.

Source 10 is taken from a casebook. A casebook sets out the facts of cases including the important points of the judgments in the cases. The extract is the author's explanation of the way in which the cases show how the law on contributory negligence works.

Source 11, from the judgment of Lord Denning, explains the effect of contributory negligence when a passenger in a car fails to wear a seat-belt. Lord Denning suggests that the passenger is 15% to blame for his injuries.

Source 12 is another extract from a leading textbook which discusses the difficulty of establishing the claimant's share of the blame. The author refers to a long-standing debate as to whether it is possible for someone to be 100% contributorily negligent. He demonstrates, using case law, that contributory negligence cannot amount to 100% as this would mean that there was no practical difference between contributory negligence and *volenti non fit injuria*.

The sources are linked by common themes, the role of judges in development of the common law and interpretation of statutes and the issues of causation and remoteness of damage in the context of negligence. You might find it useful to look at the full judgment of the cases referred to and to read the relevant part of the textbooks from which the sources are taken.

OCR has not published specimen questions on this source material, which will form the basis of questions for the Special Study Paper in June 2005, January 2006 and June 2006. The questions that follow are the writer's suggestion of the type of question which you may face. They are based on those asked by OCR in past AS and A-level papers, and are relevant to the new source material.

Specimen question paper

*Answer **all** questions.*

1. '…if the meaning or extent of a statute is uncertain or ambiguous litigation is inevitable… The main difficulty in such cases is that the intention of Parliament must be established primarily from the words used by Parliament, although increasingly extrinsic aids may be used.' [Source 1]

   Discuss the extent to which the rules of statutory interpretation enable the judges to ascertain the intention of Parliament. [25 marks]

2. Briefly explain the facts of *Wilsher v Essex AHA* [Source 5] and its significance to the development of the rules of causation. [15 marks]

3. Discuss the extent to which the rules of causation in the tort of negligence ensure that liability is appropriately pinpointed where there are several causes of action. [30 marks]

> 4. Bert is a coalminer employed by ABC Ltd. Consider the extent to which ABC Ltd may be liable for Bert's injuries suffered in each of the following separate scenarios. Do not discuss the issue of vicarious liability.
>
> (a) Bert did not hear a warning siren and is injured when a cart full of coal crushes him against the wall of a tunnel. Bert has more than once complained to ABC Ltd that the siren cannot be heard above the noise created by drills used to mine the coal. [10 marks]
>
> (b) Bert suffers a back injury due to the negligence of ABC Ltd. While he is away from work, Bert goes rock-climbing which has been his hobby for some years. On this occasion he slips and falls. As a result his back problem is made much worse and he has to give up work. [10 marks]
>
> (c) Bert has now developed a lung disease (pneumoconiosis), which is caused by exposure to coal dust. He has worked for ABC Ltd for the past year but was employed by other coalmining companies before then. [10 marks]

Tackling the question paper

You must remember that the allocation of marks for the Special Study Paper is different from that in the other two papers. The total marks available for the paper are 100 but this is divided into 40 marks for Assessment Objective 1, the demonstration of your knowledge and understanding; and 60 marks for Assessment Objectives 2 and 3, demonstrating your ability to analyse, evaluate and apply the law using appropriate language, grammar and punctuation. As always, the first thing to do is to read the question paper very carefully. Remember that the actual allocation of marks to each question may change from examination to examination. Each question must be answered fully. You have one hour and thirty minutes to answer all the questions. Questions carrying the most marks are more complex and will take more time to answer.

You need to write concisely and to the point in order to achieve the best possible marks within the time allowed. You should refer to the source material where it is relevant to do so but you do not need to copy out long sources – do the same as the examiner does and use a small quotation or identify the relevant bit by reference to the number of the source and the lines where it appears. You may also find that the same factual material, for example the statutory provisions which govern contributory negligence or a statement of the basic 'but for' test, is relevant to more than one question. You do not need to write it out more than once; simply refer back to the answer in which you have already given the information.

Question 1

This question is based on Source 1 and requires you to draw on the knowledge that you acquired for the AS examination about the judges' use of the rules of statutory interpretation. Answer the question fully using what you know about the operation of the rules of statutory interpretation and referring to the source material which you have studied. A good answer might include:

- an explanation of when the need for interpretation may arise – you could refer here to the fourth paragraph of Source 1;

- an explanation of the rules of statutory interpretation (literal, golden, mischief and purposive) with use of cases to show how the rules work;

- a discussion of the potential for injustice which particularly arises where the literal rule is used;

- consideration of whether the use of the purposive approach and extrinsic aids such as *Hansard* enable the judges to give effect to the intention of Parliament more easily;

- you could refer to the Law Reform (Contributory Negligence) Act 1945 s.1 (Source 9) and the issue raised by Source 12 – can the statute be interpreted to allow a finding that a claimant was 100% contributorily negligent? – and you could also refer to the inconsistent decisions made by the judges referred to in Source 12;

- you need to reach a conclusion that answers the question – you could comment that the injustice which can be caused by use of the literal rule is unlikely to be what Parliament really intended, that the use of the purposive approach may mean that the judges get closer to what Parliament intended and finally that whether or not the intention of

Parliament can be ascertained to a large extent depends on which approach the judges choose to use.

Question 2

This question looks very straightforward and you could spend a lot of time on the answer. Note that only 15 marks are allocated, which means you cannot take too long. The examiner has tried to help by telling you that the facts of the case only need to be stated briefly, so do not waste time by writing out the facts in detail. A brief summary is all that is required. The more important aspect of the question is the second part, where you need to discuss the importance of the case in connection with the issue of causation. A good answer could:

- summarise the facts of the case;

- identify that the decision was reached by the application of the 'but for' test – it would be appropriate to refer to Source 3, where the test is explained (*Barnett v Chelsea & Kensington HMC*);

- suggest that the case marked a move by the courts from the more liberal approach taken in *Bonnington Castings v Wardlaw* and *McGhee v NCB*, making it more difficult for a claimant to establish causation – here you could refer to the discussion set out in Source 5;

- discuss the approach taken in *Fairchild v Glenhaven Funeral Services* and contrast this with the approach in *Wilsher v Essex AHA*;

- suggest that *Wilsher* illustrates the approach to be taken where there is more than one possible cause of the injury while *Fairchild* is likely to apply only where the specific cause can be identified.

Question 3

This is a wide-ranging question requiring you to discuss the effect of the rules relating to causation. You need to remember that most of the marks will be awarded for Assessment Objective 2: discussion and evaluation of the rules to demonstrate how far the rules allow a fair allocation of responsibility for damage. You will be able to make use of the source material but you may wish to refer to other information that has been covered for the other papers. A good answer could:

- explain the 'but for' test that may show separate causes of the damage – it may be appropriate to refer back to your answers to Questions 1 and 2 in which you are likely to have explained the test;

- discuss the situation where there are multiple causes, referring to the distinctions between *Wilsher* and *Fairchild* that you will already have discussed in answer to Question 2;

- explain the effect of the claimant's own contribution to the damage – here you could refer to Source 9 and to the discussion in Source 10 in which the author argues that the rules may be unfair to the claimant;

- reach a conclusion about whether or not liability is fairly allocated where more than one defendant may be liable and where the claimant has contributed to the damage.

Question 4

The question is divided into three parts. The format of this question can vary so that only one problem needs to be discussed or it can be divided into a number of separate scenarios each of which carries a proportion of the total marks for the question.

Part (a) raises the issue of the extent to which an employee can be said to be contributorily negligent or *volenti* to dangers rising from the employment. A good answer could:

- refer to the fact that the judges are reluctant to reach a conclusion that an employee is partly or wholly to blame for injuries caused by an unsafe system of work – you could refer here to cases such as *Smith v Baker* (1891) and *Jones v Livox Quarries* (1952), which are referred to in Chapter 5;

- remember to reach a conclusion based on the law which you have discussed.

Part (b) is clearly about the issue of whether the claimant's action is a *novus actus interveniens*. A good answer could:

- explain the effect of a *novus actus* – it can break the chain of causation releasing the defendant from liability – it would be appropriate to refer to Source 7;

- discuss the requirement that a claimant's act needs to be unreasonable if it is to amount to a *novus actus* – here you could again refer to Source 7 in which Lord Reid explains the requirement – you could also identify that the facts of the case referred to in Source 7 are broadly similar to those given in the scenario;

- the discussion could appropriately refer to Source 8 in which the concept of a *novus actus* is discussed in more general terms;

- reach a conclusion as to whether the claimant is likely to be awarded damages.

Part (c) should immediately bring *Fairchild v Glenhaven* to mind as the claimant has worked for several employers and the disease could have been caused at any time during his employment. A good answer could:

- identify that the facts given appear to be similar to those of *Fairchild*;

- it would be appropriate to refer back to your answer to Question 2 where you have discussed the 'but for' test and the explanation given in Source 5;

- reach a conclusion based on your arguments.

Conclusion

Careful study of the source materials and revision of the relevant parts of the textbooks, for AS as well as the law of torts, should enable you to meet any questions set on the source material with confidence. You will be given credit for up-to-date knowledge – an incentive to read newspapers and use other resources mentioned at the end of the book.

15   Key skills

Be reassured – key skills are nothing new. They are really ongoing skills that you will have largely acquired in your journey through education. Just as it is expected that you can write an essay in order to pass A-level law, so it is also expected that you can read, summarise, form an argument, present your work in a reasonable way and so on.

What is new is the increasing requirement to show that you have achieved a reasonable level of proficiency in these skills. To a prospective employer, or a university admissions tutor, these skills are an integral and essential part of your attainment. This is an encouragement to think positively and enthusiastically about key skills, because if you are studying A-level subjects, you should find it a reasonably straightforward task to assemble the evidence needed.

The government and examination boards have set out guidelines on what is expected and how this can be achieved. There follow some suggested activities which can be included in your portfolio of key skills and which can, as a routine part of your study, help you to provide evidence that you are working at an appropriate level in the particular areas of skill.

A-level students will generally be assessed in relation to key skills at level 3. It may not be obvious that skills other than communication can be assessed through the study of law. This chapter aims to provide both teachers and students with some ideas of the ways in which the study of law can in fact be used to build the necessary portfolio in relation to other skills.

Key skills to be assessed

The main key skills at level 3 are:

- C3 Communication
- N3 Application of number
- IT3 Information technology

The wider key skills at level 3 are:

- WO3 Working with others
- LP3 Improving own learning and performance
- PS3 Problem solving

To achieve a qualification in key skills, both internal and external assessment is involved. You will have to compile a portfolio of tasks undertaken across your studies, showing evidence that you are competent in each area of skill. This need not be a particularly difficult task, or much more than you would do in the normal course of studying at A-level. The ideas here will provide opportunities for you to demonstrate that you have the skills within the various categories, which you can use to compile your portfolio. It is difficult in an essay based subject to show evidence of the skill of application of number, but there are many opportunities for using the other skills in achieving your goal of success in A-level law. The following are suggestions, pointing you to an area of study covered in most cases by this book where you can find material to help you. A few suggestions go beyond this book a little, linking into areas useful as revision for the synoptic assessment at the end of your course.

Communication

C3.1a – Contribute to a group discussion about a complex subject.

The law of torts presents a number of complex subjects, for example

- To what extent do the rules relating to self-defence in the context of trespass to the person ensure that justice is achieved both from the point of view of the claimant and the defendant? (Chapter 1)

- Is the law relating to compensation for nervous shock satisfactory? To what extent does it achieve justice for the victims? (Chapter 2)

- In relation to compensation for personal injury, would a non-fault based system provide a solution to the problems presently encountered by claimants? (Chapters 2 and 3)

- Using the rules for claims for nervous shock or negligent misstatement, consider whether the courts are justified in taking account of 'policy issues'. (Chapters 1–3 and 5)

- Is the problem of environmental pollution adequately dealt with by means of the law relating to nuisance? (Chapter 6)

- 'Every dog is allowed one bite!' To what extent is this true having regard to the Animals Act 1971? (Chapter 7)

- The doctrine of vicarious liability serves a useful purpose but is it fair to an employer whose employee disobeys specific instructions or who is careless in the way in which their duties are carried out? (Chapter 8)

- In what circumstances might a court be persuaded to allow a claim after the limitation period has expired? Does this enable both the claimant and the defendant to feel that justice has been done? (Chapter 11)

C3.1b – Make a presentation about a complex subject, using at least one image to illustrate complex points.

Matters which could be used for this purpose include

- explaining the elements of the tort of *Rylands v Fletcher* using a diagram;

- explaining the difference between strict liability and fault-based liability using a diagram.

Remember that an image might be a diagram or a flow-chart or a transparency for use on an overhead projector.

C3.2 – Read and synthesise information from two extended documents that deal with a complex subject. One of these documents should include at least one image.

There are many documents which could be used for this purpose, for example

- The Report by the Royal Commission on Civil Liability and Compensation for Personal Injury (Cmnd 7054, 1978) (the Pearson Report);

  The law report of a leading case such as *Cambridge Water Co v Eastern Counties Leather* (1993).

  Both documents referred to raise complex questions for analysis and discussion.

C3.3 – Write two different types of documents about complex subjects. One piece of writing should be an extended document and include at least one image.

The examination requires you to deal with essay questions and problems. This allows the opportunity to fulfil this objective, for example

- writing a full essay on the principles of the Occupiers' Liability Acts 1957 and 1984;

- drafting advice to a potential claimant based on a scenario concerned with a particular problem arising from one part of the syllabus, e.g. a claim for damages for nervous shock.

Information technology

IT3.1 – Compare and use different sources to search for, and select, information required for two different purposes.

Information technology provides a wealth of opportunities to search for and obtain information, for example

- Search the web sites provided by daily newspapers such as *The Times* for law reports.

- Look at government or European Union web sites for current policy and proposed changes to the law on matters such as the environment.

- Use a CDROM (for example, *The Times* reports – Lawtex) to research a topic of tort law.

IT3.2 – Explore, develop and exchange information and derive new information to meet two different purposes.

- Design a mini project, involving the creation of a database of cases in tort law, using one field to contain a key word to identify the main topic of the case. You could work as a team on this, so that a larger number of cases can be entered. This could be used for:

  - fellow students to access a set of cases on a topic by performing a query;

  - the production of a law magazine (again, working as a team);

  - e-mailing a list of cases on a particular topic in response to requests by other law students.

IT3.3 – Present information from different sources for two different purposes and audiences. Your work must include at least one example of text, one example of images and one example of numbers.

This could be done by defining the target audience and explaining, for example, the concept of consent to (a) a group of sports-persons and (b) a group of health care professionals.

Working with others

This requires you to follow through at least two substantial activities that each include tasks for WO3.1, WO3.2 and WO3.3.

WO 3.1 – Plan [an] activity with others, agreeing objectives, responsibilities and working arrangements.

WO 3.2 – Work towards achieving the agreed objectives seeking to establish and maintain cooperative working relationships in meeting individual responsibilities.

WO 3.3 – Review the activity with others against the agreed objectives and agree ways of enhancing collaborative work.

Suggested activities

The organisation of a moot based on a given scenario (many of the problem questions at the ends of chapters are suitable for this). The stages could be:

- Meet as a group and organise the breakdown of tasks, e.g. there will need to be agreement on pairs or small groups researching different legal aspects of the problem, including obtaining case details and references to be cited, and preparing speeches for presentation. Appoint a leader to coordinate the exchange of information and to coordinate communication. Establish a communication route – use e-mail if practical. Agree on deadlines, and on the method of recording the information.

- Carry out the research in agreed groups. Cooperate with members of the group in sharing information and the burden of recording, so that deadlines are met. Monitor problems with working relationships, to ensure that goals are achieved. Review progress and goals, changing plans by agreement if necessary.

- Hold the moot, inviting others to attend. You could ask a teacher or a fellow student to preside.

- Arrange a post-moot discussion group to give feedback. Encourage this to include positive criticism, with suggestions for improvement.

Make a presentation on a given topic of general interest from the syllabus, e.g. how the law protects the environment. This could be for presentation to the year group.

- Meet as a group and organise the distribution of tasks, e.g. there will need to be agreement on pairs or small groups researching different legal aspects of the problem, including obtaining case details and references to be cited, and preparing material for presentation, e.g. text of oral presentation, OHP (overhead projector) text, OHP illustrations (alternatively prepare text and illustration for a Powerpoint presentation, if facilities for this are available on the computer network). Appoint a leader to coordinate the exchange of information and to coordinate communication. Establish a communication route – use e-mail if practical. Agree on deadlines, and on the method of recording the information.

- Carry out the research in agreed groups. Cooperate with members of the group in sharing information and the burden of recording, so that deadlines are met. Monitor problems with working relationships, to ensure that goals are achieved. Review progress and goals, changing plans by agreement if necessary. Ensure that the style of presentation is consistent.

- Give the presentation, inviting others to attend.

- Arrange a post-presentation discussion group to give feedback. Encourage this to include positive criticism, with suggestions for improvement. Alternatively this could be done by a questionnaire completed by those attending.

Problem solving

PS3.1 – Recognise, explore and describe the problem, and agree the standards for its solution.

PS3.2 – Generate and compare at least two options which could be used to solve the problem, and justify the option taken forward.

For this skill you need to follow through a complex activity which involves identifying a problem and providing a solution. The key skills syllabus requires you to implement a solution. While it is easy to find a problem scenario from tort law, it is not possible to implement any solution, as only a theoretical solution based in the law relevant to the problem can be reached.

At least fifty per cent of the A-level examination requires candidates to solve problems by analysing and applying relevant law to specific scenarios. You could, in addition to answering the question, review the steps by which you have progressed to the potential solution, considering whether the task could have been approached in a different way.

Improving own learning performance

These objectives must be achieved over a period of time and must include study-based learning, activity-based learning and an example of learning from two different contexts to meet the demands of a new situation.

LP3.1 – Agree targets and plan how these will be met, using support from appropriate others.

LP3.2 – Use the plan, seeking and using feedback and support from relevant sources to help meet targets, and use different ways of learning to meet new demands.

LP3.3 – Review progress in meeting targets, establishing evidence of achievements, and agree action for improving performance using support from appropriate others.

The study of law generates opportunity for this tutor-support based skill by, for example, requiring you to undertake a research assignment on a substantive area of law. This can perhaps be linked to the achievement of other key skills like communication and information technology which would require support to ensure underpinning knowledge, as well as guidance on the use of source material.

Suggested activity

You can monitor progress in many ways, but each should include appropriate feedback, recording of achievement and setting of targets:

- through essay writing and solving scenario-type problems as homework assignments
- through timed essays
- through case tests
- through oral and practical contribution to group activities
- by extended work on an area of interest or one in which problems arise
- by attending court or student conferences, and writing appropriate notes and reports
- by aiming to improve hand written presentation or ICT skills.

Remember that the total portfolio of evidence that you compile for assessing key skills can come from any area of your studies – it does not all have to come from the study of law. However, your choice to study law as a subject will provide you with fine opportunities in the above categories.

16   Examinations and assessment

All examination boards aim to test candidates' knowledge of the particular subject, and also candidates' ability to look at the area critically or to use the knowledge they have gained to solve problems.

The content of the specifications

The two major boards examining the law of torts at A-level take a very different approach. AQA include substantive law (relating to liability in negligence for physical damage to people and damage to property, duty, breach and loss and the issue of capacity) in Module 3 of the AS examination. The topic appears again as part of Module 5, which includes other aspects of negligence, occupiers' liability, nuisance, strict liability and defences.

OCR requires candidates to study the substantive law in only one major area, one of these options being the law of tort. Module 10 covers negligence, occupiers' liability, defences and vicarious liability, Module 11 the torts relating to land, liability for animals, trespass to the person, remedies and the nature of tort.

Ethical, cultural and political issues

The new A-level specifications require candidates not only to demonstrate ability to explain and handle the substantive law, but also to recognise the influences of morality, ethics and culture, as well as politics, which affect the development of the law and its application by the courts. The boards take a different approach to this requirement.

AQA set questions which specifically direct the candidate to consider a particular aspect of such issues, for example

> With reference to any area(s) of law, distinguish between law and morals. Consider how far it may be said that the law upholds the moral values of society.
>
> (Unit 6, AQA specimen paper, question 2)

Candidates are expected to explain the concepts of 'law' and 'morals' and to discuss the problem of identifying 'moral values of society' illustrating the points made by reference to examples of laws with and without moral content and laws on debatable moral issues.

OCR expect candidates to discuss such issues within the context of a specific tort; for example

> To what extent is it true to describe the doctrine of vicarious liability
> as being based on 'social convenience and rough justice'?
>
> (Unit 10, OCR specimen paper question 2)

In addition to the factual information defining and explaining the doctrine, candidates are also expected to discuss the reasons for the doctrine and to consider the fairness, or justice, of imposing such liability.

Throughout this book, the author has made appropriate links between tort law and these broader issues, providing essential information and relevant comments, encouraging students to think for themselves about the ways in which the law is influenced by society and its beliefs.

Synoptic assessment

The A-level examination is taken after, or at the same time as, the AS examination which covers the structure and development of the English legal system. The boards expect candidates to draw on the knowledge acquired as part of their AS study to demonstrate how the substantive law 'slots into' the whole legal system. The boards, in the specifications, make it clear that their approach is very different but the objective is the same. The synoptic element must account for at least twenty per cent of the total marks available for the A-level.

AQA achieve this by means of a module (Module 6) which requires candidates to write two longer essays. The subjects of the essays require candidates to draw on material studied not only in the A-level modules (Modules 4 and 5) but also on material studied for the AS (Modules 1, 2 and 3). The questions are framed to allow candidates to concentrate on an area of choice within the context of the question, for example

> Explain, by reference to any area of law you have studied, what a
> 'policy issue' is. In deciding cases through the mechanism of
> precedent, how much consideration can and should judges give
> to policy issues?
>
> (Unit 6, AQA specimen paper question 1)

This enables candidates to look to the law relating to nervous shock, and also requires them to look back to the AS to discuss the issue of precedent.

OCR take a different approach requiring candidates to demonstrate ability to read extended passages of law, which identify the areas of substantive law which will be assessed and also the relevant area from the AS syllabus. The material is provided well in advance of the examination, and clearly signposts the areas of substantive law and the aspects of AS law on which questions are likely to be set. Candidates are required to answer the questions set and are not given any choice.

For a more detailed coverage of the OCR synoptic paper, see Chapter 14 on the sources of tort law.

Examination technique generally

Candidates for all boards must remember that the marks for each question are divided to ensure that the assessment objectives are met:

- Assessment Objective 1 requires candidates to demonstrate knowledge and understanding of the relevant law.

- Assessment Objective 2 requires candidates to demonstrate ability for analysis, evaluation and application of the relevant law.

- Assessment Objective 3 is concerned with the skills of communication and presentation.

Essay questions

With essay questions the examiner seeks to guide the candidate on the approach to be taken, indicating the 'slant' of the question. While writing the essay, it is a very good idea to bear in mind, all the time, what the slant is so that each part of your answer addresses the actual question. Examiners' reports frequently draw attention to the fact that simply writing all you know about a particular area rarely enables a candidate to obtain very good marks as the marks awarded for Assessment Objective 2 are usually limited in such cases. As a general rule a candidate needs to

- state the law clearly and concisely

- explain how it works

- address the specific question which may require critical evaluation or analysis

- reach a conclusion which is supported by the arguments given.

When referring to cases, it is rarely necessary to give the facts in detail. The name of the case, its date and a brief summary are usually all that is needed as the important thing, for which most marks will be awarded, is the point of law for which the case is authority or an example.

Statutes should be referred to by title and date and used as authority for the rules of law created by a particular Act.

Problem questions

Remember that the examiner has framed these questions to try to enable candidates to demonstrate how the law might work in a given situation. Candidates who write out the facts given, albeit in slightly different words, or whose arguments are concerned mainly with facts or common sense rarely do very well. As a general rule candidates need to:

- state the relevant law clearly and concisely

- explain how it works

- apply it to the facts given by the examiner

- reach a conclusion which is supported by the arguments.

Specimen questions, both essays and problems, have been given throughout this book and at the end you will find suggestions on points to be considered in your answer.

Finally

Watch your time. You must answer the number of questions which the examination paper specifies. If you are running out of time, brief notes will get you some marks provided relevance to the question is shown – merely listing, for example, the defences to private nuisance rarely gets many marks but a brief comment as to which defences are relevant to the particular question might enable some marks to be given for each of the Assessment Objectives.

Last of all
Good luck!

APPENDIX
Convention for the Protection of Human Rights and Fundamental Freedoms (as amended by Protocol No. II)

The following extracts from the Convention are those which are most likely to influence the development of the law of torts.

Article 3

Prohibition of torture

No one shall be subjected to torture or to inhuman or degrading treatment or punishment.

Article 5

Right to liberty and security

1. Everyone has the right to liberty and security of person. No one shall be deprived of his liberty save in the following cases and in accordance with a procedure prescribed by law:

   (a) the lawful detention of a person after conviction by a competent court;

   (b) the lawful arrest or detention of a person for non-compliance with the lawful order of a court or in order to secure the fulfilment of any obligation prescribed by law;

   (c) the lawful arrest or detention of a person effected for the purpose of bringing him before the competent legal authority on reasonable suspicion of having committed an offence or when it is reasonably considered necessary to prevent his committing an offence or fleeing after having done so;

      (d) the detention of a minor by lawful order for the purpose of educational supervision or his lawful detention for the purpose of bringing him before the competent legal authority;

      (e) the lawful detention of persons for the prevention of spreading of infectious diseases, of persons of unsound mind, alcoholics or drug addicts or vagrants;

      (f) the lawful arrest or detention of a person to prevent his effecting an unauthorised entry into the country or of a person against whom action is being taken with a view to deportation or extradition.

2. Everyone who is arrested shall be informed promptly, in a language which he understands, of the reasons for his arrest and of any charge against him.

3. Everyone arrested or detained in accordance with paragraph 1(c) of this article shall be brought promptly before a judge or other officer authorised by law to exercise judicial power and shall be entitled to trial within a reasonable time or to release pending trial. Release may be conditioned by guarantees to appear for trial.

4. Everyone who is deprived of his liberty by arrest or detention shall be entitled to take proceedings by which the lawfulness of his detention shall be decided speedily by a court and his release ordered if the detention is not lawful.

5. Everyone who has been the victim of arrest or detention in contravention of the provisions of this article shall have an enforceable right to compensation.

Article 8

Right to respect for private and family life

1. Everyone has the right to respect for his private and family life, his home and his correspondence.

2. There shall be no interference by a public authority with the exercise of this right except such as is in accordance with the law and is necessary in a democratic society in the interests of national security, public safety or the economic well-being of the country, for the prevention of disorder or crime, for the protection of health or morals, or for the protection of the rights and freedoms of others.

Article 10

Freedom of expression

1. Everyone has the right to freedom of expression. This right shall include freedom to hold opinions and to receive and impart information and ideas without interference by public authority and regardless of frontiers. This article shall not prevent states from requiring the licensing of broadcasting, television or cinema enterprises.

2. The exercise of these freedoms, since it carries with it duties and responsibilities, may be subject to such formalities, conditions, restrictions or penalties as are prescribed by law and are necessary in a democratic society, in the interests of national security, territorial integrity or public safety, for the prevention of disorder or crime, for the protection of health or morals, for the protection of the reputation or rights of others, for preventing the disclosure of information received in confidence, or for maintaining the authority and impartiality of the judiciary.

Article 13

Right to an effective remedy

Everyone whose rights and freedoms set forth in this Convention are violated shall have an effective remedy before a national authority notwithstanding that the violation has been committed by persons acting in an official capacity.

Answers guide

End of chapter questions

Chapter 1 Trespass to the person

Question 1

You need to identify which tort or torts may be involved, explain and apply the relevant law to each scenario and reach a reasonable conclusion based on the detail you have given. A good answer could include:

- Definition of assault, battery and false imprisonment.

- In relation to assault:
  Cedric's gesture is accompanied by words – a discussion of the effect of words is appropriate (*Tuberville v Savage*).
  Discuss the requirement that the victim believe the threat and that it is capable of being carried out (*Thomas v NUM*).

- In relation to battery:
  There are two elements here, the beer thrown over Cedric who then punched Albert.
  The requirement of personal contact needs to be stated (*Pursell v Horn, Cole v Turner*).
  The issue of hostility is relevant (*Wilson v Pringle, F v West Berks HA*) – on the facts this is clearly demonstrated.
  Discuss possible defences – Cedric could claim self-defence for the punch – the issue of proportionate force needs to be explained (*Revill v Newbury*).

- In relation to false imprisonment:
  State the need for total restraint (*Bird v Jones*).
  Consider whether or not there is a reasonable and safe means of escape (*Robinson v Balmain Ferry*).

Question 2

The question needs to be read carefully as it is about only one element of trespass to the person, namely battery. You need to explain the relevant law, apply it to the facts given and reach a conclusion based on the law which you have explained. A good answer could include:

- Definition of battery.

- An explanation of the need for consent to medical treatment where patient has mental capacity (*Ms B v An NHS Trust, Re C (Adult: Refusal of Treatment)*).

- An explanation of the rules relating to adults who lack capacity – treatment can only be given if urgently necessary to save life – Helen clearly regains capacity once the anaesthetic wears off.

- Helen has consented to caesarean section – the issue is, has she consented to the sterilisation?

- Sterilisation is not apparently urgent to save life.

- Keith is probably liable for battery.

Question 3

This question requires you to consider the tort from a particular viewpoint which makes the defences very relevant. A good answer could include:

- A definition of the tort and its constituent parts – assault, battery and false imprisonment and an explanation of the problems arising from the application of the law which can be said to make it less effective:
  Assault – the requirement that the threat be capable of being carried out (*Thomas v NUM*), the question of whether words alone can be an assault (*Tuberville v Savage, Mead's Case, R v Wilson, R v Ireland*).
  Battery – the issue of hostility (*Wilson v Pringle, F v West Berks. HA*).
  Imprisonment – the requirement of total restraint (*Bird v Jones*).

- Discuss the constraints put on the law by the defences:
  Self-defence which allows proportionate force to be used against another (*Revill v Newbury, R v Martin*).
  Lawful authority giving outline details of PACE and the Mental Health Act.
  Contractual obligation in relation to false imprisonment (*Robinson v Balmain Ferry, Herd v Weardale etc Co*).
- Use the material to support a conclusion as to the effectiveness of the tort.

Question 4

This question requires you to discuss the way in which the rules relating to trespass to the person are applied by the courts and whether they do in fact protect personal liberty etc. A good answer could include:

- A definition of the tort and its constituent parts – assault, battery and false imprisonment – and an explanation of the problems arising from the application of the law which can be said to make it less effective.
  Assault – the requirement that the threat must be capable of being carried out (*Thomas v NUM*), the question of whether words alone can be an assault (*Tuberville v Savage, R v Wilson, R v Ireland*).
  Battery – the issue of hostility (*Wilson v Pringle, F v West Berks AHA*).
  False imprisonment – the requirement of total restraint (*Bird v Jones*).

- The tort is actionable *per se* – does this mean that it is more effective as damage does not need to be proved.

- Consider whether, in relation to false imprisonment, the fact that knowledge of the restraint is not necessary may make it more effective (*Meering v Grahame-White Aviation*).

- Discussion of the defence of consent particularly in the context of sport (*Condon v Basi*) and in the context of medical treatment (*Re T, Sidaway v Bethlem Royal Hospital*).

- Consider the problems of defining what amounts to reasonable force in the context of the defence of self-defence (*Revill v Newbery*).

Chapter 2: Negligence – the duty of care

Question 1

The question sets a scene involving potential claims for negligence and in particular nervous shock. You are told that the defendant acted negligently, an indication that the detailed rules of duty, breach and damage do not need to be discussed. The problems suffered by the potential claimants are all psychological in origin which indicates that the claims will be for nervous shock. A good answer could:

- Give a brief definition of negligence and identify that the question is concerned with claims for nervous shock.

- Identify all the claimants as secondary victims.

- In relation to Steven:
  He fulfils the *Alcock* requirement of close ties of love and affection – he is Jessica's father so that such ties are presumed.
  He was being treated for depression prior to the accident – does this mean that he is not a person of normal fortitude (*Page v Smith*)?
  Proximity is not a problem – he was present at the scene.

- In relation to Natasha:
  She was merely a friend and will have to prove close ties to Jessica akin to a family relationship (*Alcock*).

- In relation to Mary:
  As Jessica's mother she is presumed to have the necessary close ties.
  She needs to have been present at the scene or at the immediate aftermath.
  Identifying a body at a mortuary was not held to suffice in *Alcock*.
  Immediate aftermath extends for the period during which the victim remains in the same state as immediately after the accident (*McLoughlin v O'Brian, Taylor v Somerset HA*).
  Mary is unlikely to succeed in her claim.

- In relation to Rosemary:
  She will have to prove close ties of love and affection as she is Jessica's grandmother.
  Nervous shock means identifiable psychiatric illness – tearfulness and withdrawal may not suffice.

The means by which she learned about the accident are relevant.

Pictures on TV will not normally suffice if the rules as to ensuring that victims cannot be identified are followed (*Alcock*).

Judges in *Alcock* indicated that clearly identifiable live pictures on TV might suffice to meet the requirement for proximity.

Question 2

You will identify this as a question based in negligent mis-statement. A good answer could:

- Set out the necessary criteria for liability:

  The existence of a special relationship between claimant and defendant (*Hedley Byrne v Heller*).

  Knowledge by the defendant of the purpose for which the information is required (*Caparo v Dickman*).

  The need for reliance on the information by the claimant – was such reliance reasonable (*Caparo*).

  Did the defendant assume responsibility (*Henderson v Merrett*)?

- In relation to Molly:

  Are surveyors in a different position to some others?

  Smith v Eric Bush held that a surveyor preparing a report for a building society on which he knew the purchaser would be likely to rely had liability to the purchaser.

  Molly probably liable.

- In relation to Thomas:

  The facts given are almost identical to those in *Caparo.*

  Apply the *Caparo* criteria to conclude Thomas probably not liable.

Question 3

You are asked to discuss Lord Atkin's neighbour principle and to decide whether or not it has been successful. A good answer could:

- Identify the three elements of negligence – duty, breach and damage.

- Explain that the question is about the first element and in particular when a duty of care is owed.

- Explain the neighbour principle – need for reasonable foresight of harm to those reasonably foreseeable as being at risk.

- Consider later development – the two stage test from *Anns v Merton BC.*

- Discuss the modern three stage test from *Caparo v Dickman* – foreseeability of damage, proximity between parties, just and equitable to impose duty.

- Consider the influence of policy to limit class owed duty of care – negligent mis-statement (*Hedley Byrne v Heller, Caparo v Dickman, Henderson v Merrett Syndicate*) – nervous shock (*McLoughlin v O'Brian* leading to tightening of rules in *Alcock v Chief Constable of S. Yorks, Page v*

Smith, White v Chief Constable of S. Yorks, N. Glamorgan NHS Trust v Walters).

- Use the material to reach a conclusion as to whether or not Lord Atkins' neighbour principle has been successful.

Question 4

The question requires you to consider the basic principles of liability for negligent mis-statement and to consider whether the rules protect a person from unlimited liability. A good answer could:

- Explain development of the criteria for liability:

    Reliance by claimant on defendant's skill and judgment (*Hedley Byrne v Heller*).

    Requirement of a special relationship (*Hedley Byrne v Heller, Smith v Eric Bush*).

    Knowledge by defendant of the purpose for which the statement is to be used (*Caparo v Dickman*).

    Did the defendant assume responsibility to the claimant (*Henderson v Merrett*)?

- Discuss the general intention of the courts to limit the possibility of indeterminate liability for tortious acts.

- Note that the earlier reliance on the test of foresight alone allowed an increasing number of claimants to make a claim.

- Consider whether the limits introduced by *Caparo* have limited expansion by substituting a narrower test for liability.

- Discuss the doctrine of assumption of responsibility – does this expand or limit potential liability.

Question 5

The question requires you to consider the position of various categories of potential claimants for nervous shock arising from the defendant's negligence. A good answer could:

- Give a very brief definition of negligence stating that the question is concerned with the issue of duty.

- Explain the meaning of nervous shock as identifiable psychiatric illness (*Hinz v Berry*).

- Describe the division of claimants into categories of primary and secondary victims (*Page v Smith*).

- State that primary victim need only prove that injury, physical or psychiatric, was reasonably foreseeable.

- Consider the criteria to be met by secondary victims (*Alcock v Chief Constable of S. Yorks*):
  Relationship with the primary victim of close ties of love and affection, presumed only in case of spouses and parent/child (*McFarlane v EE Caledonia*).
  Proximity to the accident or the immediate aftermath in time and space (*McLoughlin v O'Brian, McFarlane, Alcock, Taylor v Somerset HA*).
  Shock must be caused by single traumatic incident.
  Claimant must be a person of reasonable fortitude and psychiatric injury must be reasonably foreseeable (*Page v Smith, Bourhill v Young*).

- In connection with rescuers:
  State the need for participation in the aftermath (*McFarlane, Chadwick v British Rail*).
  In the case of 'professional rescuers' state the need for the rescuer to have been objectively exposed to danger (*White v Chief Constable S. Yorks*).

- Points for discussion arising from the material could include:
  That the law is satisfactory in the case of primary victims.
  Is it reasonable to require a secondary victim to be a person of reasonable fortitude?
  Do policy reasons (encouraging people to be helpful) justify the different treatment of rescuers?
  Is the requirement of close ties of love and affection reasonable – a bystander could suffer just as badly but would be unable to claim?
  Does the policy decision to restrict potential claims (the floodgates argument) justify the rules?

Question 6

This question is similar to Question 4 and much of the same information needs to be given. You are required to approach the topic from a different angle, that of the fairness or otherwise of the distinction between primary and secondary victims. A good answer could:

- Give a very brief definition of negligence stating that the question is concerned with the issue of duty.

- Explain the meaning of nervous shock as identifiable psychiatric illness (*Hinz v Berry*).

- Describe the division of claimants into categories of primary and secondary victims (*Page v Smith*).

- State that primary victim need only prove that injury, physical or psychiatric, was reasonably foreseeable.

- Consider the criteria to be met by secondary victims (*Alcock v Chief Constable of S. Yorks*):
  Relationship with the primary victim of close ties of love and affection, presumed only in case of spouses and parent/child (*McFarlane v EE Caledonia*).

Proximity to the accident or the immediate aftermath in time and
space (*McLoughlin v O'Brian, McFarlane, Alcock, Taylor v Somerset HA*).
Shock must be caused by single traumatic incident.
Claimant must be a person of reasonable fortitude and psychiatric
injury must be reasonably foreseeable (*Page v Smith, Bourhill v Young*).

- Points for discussion arising from the material could include:
That the law is satisfactory in the case of primary victims.
That the result of the rules mean than secondary victims suffer
injustice.
Is it reasonable to require a secondary victim to be a person of
reasonable fortitude – the illness may well be the same as that
suffered by a primary victim?
Is the requirement of close ties of love and affection reasonable – a
bystander could suffer just as badly but would be unable to claim?

- Does the policy decision to restrict potential claims (the floodgates
argument) justify the restrictions?
Case law indicates that there would be many claims if reasonable
foreseeability were used as the only criteria for secondary victims
(*Wigg v BRB, Attia v British Gas, Dooley v Cammell Laird*).

Chapter 3: Negligence – breach of duty, causation and damage

Question 1

This problem requires a discussion of the rules relating to negligence, including
the consequences of an intervening action (*novus actus interveniens*). A good
answer could include:

- A definition of negligence.

- A statement that case law supports the conclusion that road users owe
a duty to each other and a hospital to its patients.

- Consider how the issue of breach of duty is decided:
The reasonable man test (*Blyth v Birmingham Waterworks*).
The test for 'professionals' set out in *Bolam* and further explained in
Bolitho.

- Explain the need for consequential damage.
The 'but for' test (*Barnett v Chelsea & Kensington HMC*).
Is the damage too remote (*The Wagon Mound*)?

- Identify that there are two potential causes of action and explain the
rules relating to an intervening action:
If the second action was reasonable and foreseeable defendant remains
liable.
If second action was unreasonable and unforeseeable, the chain of
causation is broken.

- Consider that both the driver and the hospital owe Yasmin a duty of care.

- Discuss the consequences of the delay in treatment:
  If the chance of recovery was in any event improbable, driver remains liable (*Hotson v East Berks AHA*).
  Was there a more than fifty per cent chance of recovery if she was treated without delay? If so, an intervening act has occurred and the hospital, not the driver, is liable for the additional loss.

- Explain the defence of contributory negligence
  Did Yasmin in part cause her own injury (she was riding at night without lights)?
  If so, explain that she will lose a percentage of her damages which reflects the percentage by which she is to blame.

Question 2

The question is about negligence. You are required to explain the rules of negligence and to apply them to the facts given to reach a conclusion which answers the question. A good answer could:

- Explain the elements of the tort – duty, breach and damage.

- Identify that by applying the neighbour test Eddie probably owes a duty of care to a passer-by.

- Discuss the standard by which Eddie's work will be judged – the standard of the reasonable man (*Blyth v Birmingham Waterworks*).

- Consider that Eddie's inexperience is no excuse (*Nettleship v Weston*) and that he will be assessed by reference to the Bolam principle.

- Explain that damage must result from the breach applying the 'but for' test (*Barnett v Chelsea & Kensington HMC*).

- Conclude that Eddie will probably be liable to the passer-by.

Question 3

The question requires you to discuss the extent to which the rules relating to remoteness of damage limit entitlement of compensation. A good answer could:

- Define negligence briefly and identify the question as being concerned with the third element of damage.

- State the 'but for' test (*Barnett v Chelsea & Kensington HMC*).

- Consider the effect of two independent factors, each of which contributes to the total injury (*Baker v Willoughby, Jobling v Assoc. Dairies*).

- Discuss the relevance of causation (*McGhee v NCB, Wilsher v Essex AHA*).

- Explain that the risk of the type of damage must be foreseeable (*The Wagon Mound, Hughes v Lord Advocate*).

- Describe the 'egg shell skull' principle (*Smith v Leech Brain, Doughty v Turner*).

- Use the material to reach an appropriate conclusion.

Question 4

This question is concerned with negligence and in particular the rules relating to a contributory act or to an intervening act (*novus actus interveniens*). A good answer could:

- Give a brief definition of negligence and state that the question is concerned with the third element of damage.

- Describe and explain the 'but for' test (*Barnett v Chelsea v Kensington HMC*) which may disclose more than one cause of the damage.

- Explain the concept of an intervening cause – it may contribute to the damage or be an independent cause in which case it breaks the chain of causation.

- Consider the rules where there are two successive and sufficient causes:
  Liability for an additional injury lost in the consequences of the first injury may negate the liability for the second injury (*Performance Cars v Abrahams, Carslogie v Norwegian Govt.*).

- Discuss the requirement that the claimant should not be in a better position than they would have been had the torts not occurred (*Baker v Willoughby, Jobling v Ass. Dairies*).

- Explain that reasonable actions by the claimant are unlikely to break the chain of causation (*Sayers v Harlow UDC, Wieland v Cyril Lord Carpets*).

- Conclude perhaps that the law in this area is confused!

Question 5

The question requires you to consider one aspect of the elements required to establish a claim for negligence – breach of duty. You are asked to discuss whether the rules encourage people to be more careful and to avoid activities which might endanger others. A good answer could include:

- A brief statement of the elements of negligence – duty, breach and consequential damage – and identification that the question is concerned with the element of breach.

- State the basic test, i.e. that of the reasonable man (*Blyth v Birmingham Waterworks*).

- Discuss whether the fact that no allowance is made for individual idiosyncrasies is reasonable (*Nettleship v Weston*).

- Consider the factors taken into account:
  How likely is the risk to materialise (*Bolton v Stone*)?
  How serious are any likely consequences (*Paris v Stepney BC*)?
  Were precautions practicable (*Latimer v AEC*)?
  Discuss the problems posed by children (*McHale v Watson, Mullin v Richards*).
  Are there and should there be different standards for professionals?
  Explain the *Bolam* test.
  Consider if *Bolitho* is sufficient to prevent professionals being judge in their own cause.
  Consider whether the availability of insurance, compulsory in some cases, means that any deterrent effect is diminished.

Question 6

This question asks you to consider the second element which the claimant must prove to establish a claim for negligence. A good answer could include much of the material suggested for Question 5 but the approach needs to be different. This time you are asked to consider whether the concept of the reasonable man is realistic and fair. You could include:

- A brief statement of the elements of negligence – duty, breach and consequential damage – and identification that the question is concerned with the element of breach.

- State the basic test, i.e. that of the reasonable man (*Blyth v Birmingham Waterworks*).

- Discuss whether the fact that no allowance is made for individual idiosyncrasies is reasonable (*Nettleship v Weston*).

- Consider the factors taken into account:
  How likely is the risk to materialise (*Bolton v Stone*)?
  How serious are any likely consequences (*Paris v Stepney BC*)?
  Were precautions practicable (*Latimer v AEC*)?
  Discuss the problems posed by children (*McHale v Watson, Mullin v Richards*).
  Are there and should there be different standards for professionals?
  Explain the *Bolam* test.
  Consider if *Bolitho* is sufficient to prevent professionals being judge in their own cause.

- Discuss whether or not the test is realistic as it ignores individual idiosyncrasies.

- Consider the purpose of the tort – to compensate those who have been injured by a standard of behaviour less than they are entitled to expect.

- Is the principle of justice served or does the principle of utilitarianism weigh more?

Chapter 4: Negligence and dangerous premises

Question 1

The first step is to identify that the question is about the Occupiers' Liability Act 1957. You are required to state the relevant statutory provisions and apply these to the facts given in order to reach a conclusion. A good answer could:

- Explain the meaning of occupier (*Wheat v Lacon*) and conclude that Jay is an occupier.
  Set out the duty to ensure the safety of visitors (s.2).
  Explain that the occupier will be judged by the usual negligence standard of the reasonable man.
  Explain the rules relating to children:
  They are expected to be less careful than adults.
  Consider the need for supervision of young children (*Phipps v Rochester Corp., Simkiss v Rhondda BC*).
  Sally is seven – would it be reasonable for her to be supervised in a private home?

- Identify Helen as an expert visitor:
  Explain that she is expected to guard herself against the risks inherent in firefighting (s.2(3)(b), *Roles v Nathan*).
  Explain that Jay is liable to her if her injury was caused by his negligence (on the facts given this is the case) (*Salmon v Seafarers Restaurants, Ogwo v Taylor*).

- State the position of independent contractors:
  Occupier not liable for their negligent actions provided reasonable care taken to choose competent contractors, reasonable care taken to ensure work is satisfactory.
  Provided Jay took reasonable care, he will not be liable to Pat but the fact that the trench in his garden was left uncovered may suggest that Jay did not ensure that the work was satisfactory.

Question 2

The question is concerned with occupiers' liability in relation to two categories of visitors, a lawful child visitor and an unlawful adult trespasser. You are required to state the relevant law and apply it to the facts given in the scenario to reach a conclusion.

- In relation to Indira identify that the 1957 Act applies.

- Give details of the general duty to ensure safety of visitors (s.2).

- Explain that children are expected to be less careful than adults (s.2(3)(a)).

- Consider the concept of an allurements (*Glasgow Corp. v Taylor*) – a chimpanzee would probably be an allurement to a young child.

- Discuss the issue of adult supervision (*Phipps v Rochester Corp*).
  The age of the child is relevant.
  Consider the nature of the premises – are children generally likely to be allowed to run around?
  Indira is too young to be able to read the warning notices but were these sufficient to alert the parents to the need for close supervision?

- Identify Gareth as an unlawful visitor (a trespasser) and state that the 1984 Act applies.

- Explain occupier's duty to take reasonable precautions to protect trespasser from known dangers when it is likely that a trespasser may come into the vicinity of the danger:
  Applying this to the facts, Gareth scaled two fences after the zoo was closed.
  The lions are a known danger.
  Should the zoo reasonably have anticipated that a trespasser would enter the zoo and might come into contact with the lions?
  Were the fences a sufficient safeguard?

Question 3

This question is actually very straightforward requiring you to state the principles contained in both Acts and to discuss how successful they are in protecting both lawful and non-lawful visitors. A good answer could:

- Explain matters which the Acts have in common – the meaning of occupier (*Wheat v Lacon*).

- Distinguish between lawful and non-lawful visitors.

- State that OLA 1957 only applies to lawful visitors.

  Set out the duty owed under s.2 to ensure the safety of visitors.

  Explain the rules relating to special categories of visitors – experts expected to take reasonable care for own safety in respect of risks inherent to their job (*Roles v Nathan, Ogwo v Taylor*).

  Discuss the problem of children – less careful than adults, the concept of allurements (*Glasgow Corp. v Taylor*), the role of parents (*Phipps v Rochester Corp., Simkiss v Rhondda BC*).

- State that OLA 1984 applies to non-lawful visitors, usually trespassers.

  Set out the rules for the existence of a duty to such visitors.

  Explain the need for knowledge of the danger and the risk that a trespasser may come into the region of the danger.

  Discuss the duty of common humanity (*BRB v Herrington*).

- In relation to both Acts consider whether the rules relating to warning notices diminish the protection.

- Discuss whether the defences of voluntary assumption of risk and contributory negligence, especially in relation to children, diminish the statutory protection.

Question 4

This question requires you to gave a clear statement of the duty owed under each Act. In considering whether the duties can be justified, the issue of defences becomes relevant. A good answer could:

- Explain matters which the Acts have in common.
  The meaning of occupier (*Wheat v Lacon*).
  Distinguish between lawful and unlawful visitors.

- In relation to Occupiers' Liability Act 1957:
  State that it applies only to lawful visitors.
  Set out the duty to ensure the safety of visitors (s.2).
  Explain that the occupier will be judged by the usual negligence
    standard of the reasonable man.
  Explain the rules relating to special categories of visitors:
  Experts expected to take reasonable care in relation to the area of their
    expertise (*Roles v Nathan, Ogwo v Taylor*).
  Children less careful than adults.
  Explain the concept of an allurement (*Glasgow Corp. v Taylor*).
  Consider the need for supervision of young children (*Phipps v Rochester
    Corp., Simkiss v Rhondda BC*).
  Independent contractors generally liable for dangers which they create.
  Discuss the effect of warning notices including reference to Unfair
    Contract Terms Act.

- In relation to Occupiers' Liability Act 1984:
  State that it applies to unlawful visitors.
  Explain the duty owed by the occupier to take reasonable precautions
    to prevent unlawful visitors from being injured by known dangers
    (ss.1(3) & (4)).
  Discuss the concept of a duty of common humanity (*BRB v Herrington*).
  Discuss the effect of warning notices including reference to Unfair
    Contract Terms Act.

- Discuss possible defences.
  Voluntary assumption of risk which is a complete defence but difficult
    to establish where the visitor is a child.
  Contributory negligence which will divide blame but in the case of a
    child visitor will depend on the age of the child.

- Discuss the principle of justice/fairness:
  Duty to lawful visitors can be argued to be fair.
  Duty to unlawful visitors more difficult as the visitors are themselves in
  the wrong.

Chapter 5: Negligence – defences, remedies and policy issues

Question 1

The question requires discussion of the elements of negligence and of the defence of contributory negligence. A good answer could:

- Define negligence, stating the elements of duty, breach and damage.

- State that both Susan and James owe a duty of care to other road users.

- In relation to Susan on the facts given it would appear that she is in breach of her duty of care.

- James' claim may be affected by the fact that he was driving without lights – does this amount to contributory negligence?

  State that contributory negligence is governed by Law Reform (Contributory Negligence) Act 1945.

  Explain that defence allows court to take into account the extent to which the claimant was himself to blame and to reduce damages by appropriate percentage (s.1).

  Discuss what amounts to contributory negligence:

  Did James fail to take reasonable care for his own safety by driving without lights (*Jones v Livox Quarries*)?

- In relation to Peter, state that defence of *volenti* not available as Road Traffic Act 1988 s.149 applies.

- Apply the rules relating to contributory negligence:

  Did Peter know, or ought he to have known, that Susan was unfit to drive because of alcohol?

Question 2

The question is about the defences of contributory negligence and voluntary assumption of risk. It clearly states that Ann admits negligence on the part of the Centre so this does not need to be discussed. A good answer could:

- Define contributory negligence – failure to take reasonable care for one's own safety (*Jones v Livox Quarries*).

- State the provisions of Law Reform Contributory Negligence) Act 1945 – explain how rules work – blame apportioned between tort feasor and victim.

- Define voluntary assumption of risk – freely doing something in knowledge of likelihood of injury – explain how rules work – complete defence.

- In relation to contributory negligence, matters for discussion include:

  Should Billy reasonably have foreseen that he was putting himself at risk – on the facts given, yes.

  Did he act as a reasonable and prudent man would do – on the facts, probably not.

Conclude that he may well have been contributorily negligent.

State that damages will be reduced by the appropriate proportion for which he is to blame.

- In relation to voluntary assumption of risk matters for discussion include:

  Was Billy under any pressure to take the risk – on the facts given, probably not.

  Did he know the risk – on the facts given, he had only been warned not to use the equipment without supervision – was this enough for him to understand the risk?

  Conclude that the defence will probably not succeed.

Question 3

The question requires you to compare and contrast the two defences. A good answer could:

- State that *volenti* is now referred to as voluntary assumption of risk.

- Consider the issues for the court:
  Did claimant understand the nature and extent of the risk?
  Was the assumption truly voluntary (*Smith v Baker, ICI v Shatwell*)?

- Discuss the position of special categories of claimants:
  A young child is unlikely to have assumed the risk.
  A sports person agrees to the risks inherent when the game is played according to the rules (*Condon v Basi*).
  Rescuers are not considered to have voluntarily assumed risk if the rescue is necessary to save life, limb or property (*Chadwick v BRB*).

- Explain the effect of the defence – a complete defence and the claimant will get no compensation.

- Comment that the defence cannot be used where Road Traffic Act 1988 s.149 applies.

- State that contributory negligence is governed by Law Reform (Contributory Negligence) Act 1945.

- Explain that defence allows court to take into account the extent to which the claimant was himself to blame and to reduce damages by appropriate percentage (s.1).

- Discuss what amounts to contributory negligence.
  Did claimant fail to take reasonable care for their own safety (*Jones v Livox Quarries*)?
  In an emergency, was the action reasonable having regard to the perceived risk (*Jones v Boyce, Sayers v Harlow UDC*)?

- Consider the position of children (*Gough v Thorne*).

- Matters for discussion could include:
  The different effects of the defences.
  The common approach to the issue of children.
  The justice of the effect of contributory negligence in apportioning
   blame (*Morris v Murray*).
  The fact that *volenti* has been used less frequently since 1945 when
   contributory negligence became available.
  Confusion caused by a tendency to refer to both defences as 'consent'.

Chapter 6: Torts protecting land

Question 1

The question requires you to explain the tort and apply the rules to reach a
conclusion based on the law and on the facts given in the scenario. A good
answer could:

- Define the tort of private nuisance.

- Distinguish between physical damage (the soot) and personal
  discomfort (the lack of sleep) (*St Helens Smelting v Tipping*).

- Explain the matters taken into account by the court to decide if an
  activity is reasonable.
  Location (*St Helens Smelting v Tipping*).
  Abnormal sensitivity (*Robinson v Kilvert*) – not relevant on the facts
   given.
  Duration (*Andreae v Selfridge*) – the time at which the work is done is
   very relevant.
  Malice (*Christie v Davey*) – would be relevant if Ron and Ethel tried to
   get their own back.

- Explain that only a person with an interest in land can sue (*Malone v
  Laskey*).

- Apply the rules to reach an appropriate conclusion – Jay is probably
  liable.

- Consider the remedies which may be available and their effectiveness.

- Discuss whether other courses of action, e.g. the use of ADR or
  conciliation services, might be more effective in solving the problem.

Question 2

The question requires you to consider the tort of private nuisance and to
apply the rules to the facts given. A good answer could:

- Define the tort and explain the matters taken into account by the court
  giving much the same factual material as for Question 1.

- On the facts given the issue of malice is irrelevant although it can
  briefly be mentioned.

- Consider whether on the facts given and applying the rules the interference can be described as substantial and unreasonable.

- Explain the remedies to conclude that an injunction may be granted to limit the hours of work and to restrict the number of parties.

Question 3

This question requires you to discuss the tort of *Rylands v Fletcher* and to apply the rules to the facts given. A good answer could:

- Define the tort stating the need for accumulation of a dangerous substance and its escape.

- Explain that it must be foreseeable at the time of the accumulation that it could cause damage if it escaped (*Cambridge Water v Eastern Counties Leather*).

- Discuss the need for non-natural use of land (*Rylands v Fletcher, Rickards v Lothian, Read v Lyons, British Celanese v Hunt, Cambridge Water v Eastern Counties Leather, Transco v Stockport*).

- Explain the meaning of 'escape' (*Read v Lyons*).

- Explain the defence of act of a stranger which could apply to the facts given – was the interference by the children foreseeable – on the facts given probably not but should Giles have dealt with the problem of the damage done by the children once he was aware of it (*Box v Jubb*).

- Decide whether Pam is likely to be awarded damages.

Question 4

The question requires you to give essentially the same factual information as for Question 3. In addition a good answer could:

- Explain the relevant defences – Act of God (*Nichols v Marsland, Greenock Corp. v Caledonian Rlwy*) – Act of a stranger (*Perry v Kendricks Transport*).

- Generally matters for discussion include whether or not there has been an accumulation; are the accumulated materials dangerous; is it foreseeable that they could cause damage (*Cambridge Water v Eastern Counties Leather*).

- Does the pile of waste constitute non-natural use – probably not on the basis of *Transco v Stockport*; is the storage of explosives a non-natural use – probably yes on basis of *Transco v Stockport*.

- Has there been an escape – on facts given, yes in respect of both materials.

- In relation to the slip, if liability imposed in spite of *Transco*, relevant defence for discussion is Act of God – exceptionally heavy rain not an unforeseeable natural phenomenon (*Greenock Corp. v Caledonian Rlwy*).

- In relation to explosion, the relevant defence is act of a stranger (*Rickards v Lothian*) – Ross had knowledge of children crossing site; is this enough to give him warning of possible vandalism?

- Apply law to reach appropriate conclusions.

Question 5

The question requires you to give a clear statement of the tort and to evaluate it from the particular aspect of protection of privacy. A good answer could:

- Define the tort as wrongful entry onto the land of another and state that it is actionable *per se*.

- Explain the meaning of 'land' to include subsoil below (*Hickman v Maisey*) and air space above (*Bernstein v Sky Views*).

- State the requirement of direct interference.

- Discuss the defences.
  Lawful authority, e.g. PACE, Access to Neighbouring Land Act.
  Permission given by occupier.
  Necessity (*Cope v Sharpe*).

- Explain possible remedies:
  Injunction.
  Damages.
  Re-entry.

- Relevant matters for discussion include
  Is the fact that it is actionable *per se* an advantage?
  How effective are the remedies?
  The cost and delay in taking legal action.
  The potential impact of the Human Rights Act.

Question 6

This question is virtually identical to Question 3. You would be expected to cover the same points in a good answer.

Question 7

The question is about the tort of trespass to land and requires you to state much the same factual information as Questions 5 and 6. The question requires you to look at the tort from a different point of view and in addition to the factual material a good answer could discuss:

- Whether the fact that the tort is actionable *per se* is an advantage.

- Whether the risk of liability for trespass to the person or breach of the special rules relating to residential occupation mean the remedy of self-help is ineffective.

- Other matters which could be mentioned include the cost and delay in taking court action and the potential helpful impact of the Human Rights Act 1998.

Question 8

This question requires you to explain the tort of private nuisance and to evaluate it as a tool to protect the environment. A good answer could:

- Define the tort.
  Distinguish between physical damage and interference with use and enjoyment (*St Helens v Tipping*).
  Explain the factors taken into account to decide if defendant's actions are reasonable:
  Locality (*Sturges v Bridgman, Halsey v Esso Petrol*).
  Claimant's sensitivity (*Robinson v Kilvert*).
  Duration (*Andreae v Selfridge, De Keyser's Royal Hotel v Spicer*).
  Malice on the part of the defendant (*Christie v Davey, Hollywood Silver Fox Farm v Emmett*).

- Discuss the difficulties faced by claimant:
  Need for an interest in the land (*Malone v Laskey*).
  Cost and delay of legal action.

- Explain the defences:
  Prescription (*Sturges v Bridgman*).
  Statutory authority (*Allen v Gulf Oil*).
  Planning consent if it changes the character of the area (*Gillingham BC v Medway Docks, Wheeler v Saunders*).

- State the remedies of injunction and damages.

- Consider the rules governing the grant of injunction (*Shelfer v City of London Electric Lighting*).

- Discuss the extent to which public benefit may be relevant in deciding a remedy (*Kennaway v Thompson, Miller v Jackson*).

- Relevant matters for discussion as to effectiveness include:
  The difficulties faced by claimant.
  The need to prove interference with use and enjoyment of land.
  The apparent injustice that the fact that the claimant moved to the nuisance is irrelevant.
  Public benefit is only relevant to the nature of the remedy.
  Consider whether alternative solutions e.g. statutory nuisance, ADR or conciliation schemes might be more effective.

Question 9

To answer this question you need to explain the tort and consider the kinds of activities which might be covered as well as the extent to which the defences assist in balancing interests between neighbours. Much of the factual material is the same as that required for Question 8. Additionally, a good answer could:

- Explain that any activity can amount to a nuisance if the criteria are satisfied.

- Consider whether public benefit should play a greater part.

- Discuss whether the existence of planning consent should be decisive.

- Explain that there is no remedy for a lawful action.

- Discuss the effect of moving to the nuisance and the defence of prescription.

- Consider the effectiveness of the remedies.

Question 10
This question requires you to analyse and evaluate the tort from the specific viewpoint of protection of the environment. A good answer could:

- Define the tort and explain the various elements:
  Accumulation (*Rylands v Fletcher*).
  Foreseeability that the thing may cause damage if it escapes (*Cambridge Water v Eastern Counties Leather*).
  Escape (*Read v Lyons*).
  Non-natural use of land (*Read v Lyons, British Celanese v Hunt, Cambridge Water v Eastern Counties Leather*).

- State the defences:
  Consent (*Peters v Prince of Wales Theatre*).
  Fault of claimant.
  Act of God (*Nichols v Marsland, Greenock Corp. v Caledonia Rlwy*).
  Act of a stranger (*Perry v Kendricks Transport*).
  Statutory authority.
  Necessity.

- Discuss the problems created by the concept of non-natural user.
  Read v Lyons and *British Celanese v Hunt* suggest that the local environment and public benefit are relevant.
  Cambridge Water suggests *obiter* storage of chemicals a classic case of non-natural user.

- Consider the need for foreseeability:
  Has the introduction of the requirement in *Cambridge Water* lessened the effectiveness of the tort?
  Is there an element of fault required in the light of knowledge at the time of the accumulation?

- Discuss whether legislation, e.g. Environmental Protection Act, and enforcement by Environmental Protection Agency and local authorities is more effective given the uncertainty, costs and delay of private civil action.

Question 11

This question requires you to give much the same information as for the answer to Question 10. The question was in the examination for 1993 and it is now more usual for the examiner to give you a clearer idea of what it is that needs to be discussed.

Chapter 7: Strict liability

Question 1

This question requires you to state and apply various rules set out in the Consumer Protection Act. A good answer could:

- Identify that Celia and her parents have no contractual relationship with the toy shop.

- State that Celia may have a claim under s.2(1) if a defect in a product has caused her injury.

- Define the term *product* under s.1(2) and identify the toy as a product.

- Consider the requirement that the product be defective under s.3 explaining the meaning of *defective*.

- Explain the categories of damage covered by the Act.

- Discuss the appropriate defendant applying ss.2(2) and (3).

Question 2

The question requires you to state and apply the relevant provisions of the Animals Act. A good answer could:

- State that the first point to be decided is whether a dog is a dangerous or non-dangerous animal – s.6(2).

- Identifying dog as non-dangerous, state the criteria for liability under s.2(2).

- Consider that dog is described as large and strong so s.2(2)(a) satisfied (*Curtis v Betts*) and liability could arise for injury to Belinda (*Smith v Ainger*).

- S.2(2)(b) appears to be satisfied as dog attacks smaller dogs and people.

- Characteristic is known to Ahmed and his parents.

- Discuss who is keeper – on facts given, Ahmed's parents – s.6(3).

- Apply law to decide if Belinda and Darren are likely to be successful – probably yes.

Question 3

The question requires you to explain the provisions of the Act and to evaluate the rules to decide a particular issue – does the Act impose strict liability for non-dangerous species? A good answer could:

- Explain the principle of strict liability.

- Define the meaning of non-dangerous species.

- State the criteria for liability.
  Damage of a type which animal was likely to do if not restrained or was likely to be severe.
  Damage due to peculiar characteristics of the animal.
  Knowledge by keeper defining the term 'keeper'.

- Consider problems raised by phrase 'was likely' – does it mean 'more probable than not' or 'there is a risk that it will happen'?

- Discuss the meaning of 'characteristics' and the need for causal link between characteristic and the damage.

- State the defences:
  Default of claimant.
  Trespass by claimant.
  Contributory negligence/voluntary assumption of risk.

- Consider whether in light of difficulties of interpretation and defences Act imposes strict liability.

Question 4
This is a wide-ranging question which allows you to concentrate on one area of strict liability, either the Animals Act or the Consumer Protection Act or both. You are required to describe the concept of strict liability and, having given detail of the chosen area of law, decide whether or not the concept is important today. At the time the question was set, 1992, the tort of *Rylands v Fletcher* would also have been relevant but *Cambridge Water v Eastern Counties Leather* has imposed a requirement of foreseeability and therefore the tort no longer qualifies as one of strict liability. A good answer could:

- Explain the concept of strict liability.

- State and explain the provisions of the relevant area(s) of legislation.

- State the defences available to each Act.

- Decide whether in the light of the limitations set out in the statute(s) and the defences the legislation is important in the twenty-first century.

Chapter 8: Vicarious liability for the acts of others

Question 1
The question requires you to explain and apply the doctrine of vicarious liability in order to suggest solutions to the problems described. You are told that Mike is employed by the garage and that he has been negligent. This means that you do not need to set out the tests for employment in detail nor do you need to give detail of the tort. A good answer could:

- State the doctrine of vicarious liability.

- Explain the concept of the scope of employment (*Whatman v Pearson*).

- Discuss the effect of an express prohibition by the employer (*Twine v Bean's Express, Rose v Plenty*).

- Explain the effect of an unauthorised act (*Century Ins. v N. Ireland RTB*).

- Apply the rules to the facts given to conclude whether or not the garage has vicarious liability for Mike's acts.

Question 2

This question requires you to explain and apply the doctrine of vicarious liability in order to suggest a solution to the problem described. A good answer could:

- Define the doctrine recognising that it applies to the tort of trespass to the person committed by Bob.

- Recognise that the question is unclear as to whether or not Bob is an employee – the tests for employment (control, integration, intention) are relevant and must be explained.

- Distinguish between liability for an employee and an independent contractor – if Bob is not an employee, Andy is not liable.

- Consider the meaning of 'course of employment' (*Whatman v Pearson, Storey v Aston, Smith v Stages, Beard v London General Omnibus*).

- Discuss the effect of an express prohibition (*Twine v Beans Express, Rose v Plenty*) and of disobedience by employee (*Limpus v London General Omnibus, Iqbal v LTE*).

- Apply the rules to conclude that if Bob is an employee, Andy will be liable.

Question 3

This question is straightforward – can liability for someone else's wrongdoing be justified? A good answer could:

- Explain the doctrine of vicarious liability.

- State that it is of most importance in the context of employment.

- Set out the tests for employment:
  Control test.
  Integration test.
  Multiple factor test.

- Explain that doctrine only applies to acts done within the course of employment. Relevant points for discussion could include the question of liability for disobedient or careless acts, the concept of a frolic.

- State the limitation on the employer's right to obtain reimbursement.

- Consider why the doctrine exists:
  Employer gets profit and should bear loss.
  Employer probably insured.
  Costs can be shared among customers/clients.
  Employer should have been more careful in selecting, training and
    supervising employees.

- Discuss the reality that employer cannot have total control over what
  employee does and the problems created by the employment rights
  legislation.
  Use the material to reach a conclusion.

Question 4

The question draws your attention to the fact that there have been recent
developments in relation to vicarious liability and asks whether the doctrine
has become fairer from the view of the employer. A good answer could:

- Define the doctrine.

- You are told to consider the employment situation so it is not necessary
  to do more than mention the tests for employment. The focus of the
  answer should be on the scope of employment.

- Explain that the employer is liable for activity within the course of
  employment or closely connected to it – *Whatman v Pearson, Ruddiman
  v Smith, Lister v Helsey Hall, Storey v Ashton, General Engineering Services v
  Kingston & St Andrew Corp.*

- Explain potential liability for employee's carelessness – *Century Ins. v
  N. Ireland Road Transport Board*; for employee's disobedience – *LCC v
  Catermoles Garages, Limpus v London General Omnibus, Iqbal v London
  Transport*; for employee's criminal activity – *Lloyd v Grace Smith, Morris
  v Martin, Lister v Helsey Hall, Fennelly v Connex South Eastern* contrasting
  with *Warren v Henly's Ltd.*

- Discuss the extent to which the recent cases of *Lister v Helsey Hall* and
  Fennelly v Connex South Eastern have made it almost impossible for the
  employer to escape liability for an employee's criminal activity.

- Decide whether the result is to make the doctrine of vicarious liability
  less fair.

Chapter 9: Protecting reputation

Question 1

This question requires you to explain and apply the rules relating to defamation
in order to reach solutions to the problems. A good answer could:

- Define the tort.

- Explain libel:
  A statement in permanent form.

Actionable *per se.*
Would appear to apply to the article in the newspaper.

- Explain slander:
  A statement in transient form.
  Generally not actionable *per se.*
  In this case imputation of unfitness in profession and accusation of imprisonable offence therefore actionable *per se.*

- Discuss the meaning of defamatory, the need for reference to claimant and publication.

- Consider relevant defences:
  In relation to Sally on the facts the only possible defence is justification.
  In relation to the newspaper:
  The report is apparently an account of what happened at the criminal trial – the defence of privilege applies provided the report is accurate – newspaper not liable.
  If report inaccurate, small print makes the truth clear and on basis of *Charleston v News Group Newspapers* – newspaper not liable.

Question 2

The question requires you to consider the tort of defamation from the point of view of the protection of privacy. A good answer could:

- Explain that there are two parts – libel and slander and give a definition of each.

- State the elements required for liability:
  The requirement that the statement be defamatory and explain the meaning of the term (*Byrne v Deane*).
  The need for reference to the claimant.
  Claimant may be named.
  Consider the concept of innuendo (*Cassidy v Daily Mirror, Newstead v London Express, Hulton v Jones*).
  The statement must be published.

- Discuss the defences, in particular:
  Truth/justification.
  Fair comment.
  Absolute privilege.
  Qualified privilege.

- Consider the remedies of injunction and damages.

- Matters for discussion could include:
  Privacy implies ability to prevent publication – unlikely to be able to act quickly enough to obtain the necessary injunction.
  Truth is always a defence – you might not want true facts to be made public but the tort cannot prevent it.
  The defence of fair comment appears to include any matter in which

the public is interested – should this include a person's private life as opposed to public life?

Possible changes which may arise under the Human Rights Act 1998.

Question 3

The question is very similar to Question 2 and requires much of the same factual information. The difference lies in the 'angle' you are asked to consider, i.e. the tort's effectiveness in protecting reputation. In addition to the factual material a good answer could discuss:

- The fact that a reputation can be destroyed by publication of the truth – the tort will not prevent this.

- Reputation can also be adversely affected by comment which might be protected by the defence of honest comment.

- Privilege allows the publication of reports of court proceedings – some people may not read the facts which appear later in the trial to exonerate the victim/accused.

Chapter 10: Breach of statutory duty

Question 1

The question requires you to explain the law and to evaluate it from the point of view of a claimant. A good answer could:

- Explain that the tort relates to duties imposed by statute.

- Consider that problems only arise when the Act makes no mention of the possibility of compensation claims by individuals affected.

- State that the issue is one of interpretation of the statute.
  Briefly explain the literal rule.
  Briefly explain the mischief and purposive rules.

- Set out the questions the court will ask:
  Was the Act designed to benefit a particular class – if it was intended to benefit the public generally an individual may well have no claim (*Atkinson v Newcastle Waterworks*)?
  Is the damage suffered by the claimant covered by the Act i.e. is it of the type or kind that it was intended to prevent (*Gorrie v Scott*)?
  What remedy is provided by the Act and is it adequate (*Groves v Lord Wimborne, Ex parte Island Records Ltd, X & Others v Bedfordshire CC & other appeals, Z v UK*)?

- Relevant matters for discussion could include:
  Lord Denning's view in *Ex parte Island Records* that any breach should enable an individual who suffers loss to obtain damages.
  The more restrictive view taken by the House of Lords in *X & Others v Beds. CC*.
  The possibility that *Z v UK* means that an effective remedy under the Human Rights legislation may be available.

Whether the availability of remedies under EU law may be of assistance.

The proposals for reform suggested by the Law Commission.

General questions on tort law

Question 1

(a) The question requires you to consider the tort of private nuisance, public nuisance and possible remedies available to the residents. A good answer could:

• Define the tort of private nuisance.

• Distinguish between physical damage and personal discomfort (*St Helens Smelting v Tipping*).

• Explain the matters taken into account by the court to decide if an activity is reasonable:
Location (*St Helens Smelting v Tipping*).
Abnormal sensitivity (*Robinson v Kilvert*) – not relevant on the facts given.
Duration (*Andreae v Selfridge*) – the time at which the work is done is very relevant.
Malice (*Christie v Davey*).

• Explain that only a person with an interest in land can sue (*Malone v Laskey*) – is the area in which cars are queuing owned by the claimants?

• Consider the possibility that the problems could amount to a public nuisance.
Define public nuisance.
Explain that a class of persons in the locality need to be affected.
State that victims who have suffered more damage than others may be able to claim even if they do not have an interest in land (*Halsey v Esso Petrol*).

• Consider the remedies which may be available and their effectiveness.

(b) The question requires you to discuss the issue of liability for negligence and nervous shock. A good answer could:

• In respect of David's claim, define negligence and explain the elements:
The requirement that the defendant owes the claimant a duty of care (*Donoghue v Stevenson*).
The need for breach of duty setting out the test of the reasonable man (*Blyth v Birmingham Waterworks*).
Matters taken into account in assessing standard of care relevant to the question i.e. degree of seriousness of risk (*Paris v Stepney BC*), likelihood of it happening (*Bolton v Stone*).

The need for consequential damage including the 'but for' test (*Barnett v Chelsea & Kensington HMC*) and the requirement that the damage is not too remote (*The Wagon Mound*).

- Apply the rules to conclude that Guranjit is probably liable in negligence.

- Are any defences available to Guranjit?
  Explain the doctrine of contributory negligence.
  Did David take reasonable care for his own safety or was he partly to blame – he was a former employee and possibly should have been aware of the rules?
  State the consequence that damages may be reduced by appropriate percentage to reflect David's share of responsibility.

- In respect of Etesham's claim, consider the special rules relating to nervous shock:
  Identify Etesham as a secondary victim (*Page v Smith*).
  The requirement of a close personal relationship with the primary victim – this will have to be proved as Etesham is neither a spouse nor a parent/child of the victim (*Alcock*).
  Proximity in time and space (not a problem as Etesham present at the scene).
  The need for identifiable psychiatric illness (*Hinz v Berry*).
  Requirement that Etesham be a person of reasonable fortitude – is psychiatric injury to such a person reasonably foreseeable (*Page v Smith*)?

(c) The question requires you to discuss the concept of vicarious liability and to apply the rules to the facts given. A good answer could:

- State the doctrine of vicarious liability.

- Explain the concept of the scope of employment (*Whatman v Pearson*).

- Discuss the effect of an express prohibition by the employer (*Twine v Bean's Express, Rose v Plenty*).

- Explain the effect of an unauthorised act (*Century Ins. v N. Ireland RTB*).

- Apply the rules to the facts given to conclude whether or not GGC Ltd has vicarious liability for Guranjit's acts.

The question is worded in such a way that you could also consider whether or not GGC Ltd may have primary liability for failure to supervise its employees properly. The tort of negligence is relevant as is the concept of duty set out in the Occupiers' Liability Act 1957. A good answer to this part of the question could:

- Refer back to the information given in answer to (b) to explain the tort of negligence.

- Explain the duty imposed by the Occupiers' Liability Act 1957 to lawful visitors (David is a customer and it is reasonable to assume that he is a lawful visitor).

- Apply the rules to decide if GGC Ltd have a primary duty to David and Etesham and resulting primary liability.

(d) This part of the question draws on general legal knowledge. A good answer could:

- Explain the concept of legal personality (*Saloman v Saloman Ltd*).

- Consider that GGC Ltd will be liable as regarded as legal personality in its own right.

(e) This question allows you to demonstrate your ability to discuss whether the legal rules achieve justice between the parties. A good answer could:

- Explain the concept of justice.

- Consider the issues of fault-based liability and liability without fault including who should be liable and who should pay.

- Discuss issues of access to the courts.

- In relation to the problem for local residents:
  Discuss whether courses of action other than legal action in the courts, e.g. the use of ADR (alternative dispute resolution) or conciliation services might be more effective in solving the problem
  Discuss the fairness of the fact that the residents come to the nuisance is no defence to GGC Ltd (*Sturges v Bridgman, Miller v Jackson*).

- In relation to possible vicarious liability for Guranjit's negligence:
  Consider whether the doctrine of vicarious liability is fair.
  Can the apparent unfairness of the doctrine be justified?
  Consider why the doctrine exists.
  Guranjit is probably uninsured and would be unable to pay damages.
  GGC Ltd gets profit and should bear loss.
  GGC Ltd probably insured.
  Costs can be shared among customers/clients.
  GGC Ltd should have been more careful in selecting, training and supervising employees.
  Discuss the reality that employer cannot have total control over what employee does and the problems created by the employment rights legislation.

Question 2

(a) The question requires you to discuss the issue of negligent misstatement. A good answer could:

- Define and briefly explain the principles of negligence.

- State that negligent misstatement is an exception to the rule that pure economic loss is not recoverable.

- Set out the requirements for liability:
  A special relationship between claimant and defendant (*Hedley Byrne v Heller*).
  Reasonable reliance by claimant (*Caparo v Dickman*).
  Knowledge by defendant of the purpose for which the advice/ information is required (*Caparo v Dickman*).
  Possible assumption of responsibility by defendant (*Henderson v Merrett*).

- Consider the effect of a disclaimer (*Hedley Byrne*, Unfair Contract Terms Act 1977).

(b) The question asks you to apply the information you have given in answer to (a). A good answer could:

- Discuss whether the target audience and the general nature of the programme mean that there is a likelihood of which the presenters should be aware of reliance by listeners.

- Is the disclaimer likely to be effective?

- In relation to Uma:
  Direct advice was given, apply the rules to reach a conclusion.

- In relation to Carol:
  She was a member of the audience.
  Should she be regarded as a person likely to act on the advice given?
  Is the disclaimer likely to be effective?

- In relation to Fred:
  Carol contacted him after the programme – does this show an assumption of responsibility?
  Are the other criteria satisfied?

(c) The question requires you to explain and apply the doctrine of vicarious liability. A good answer could:

- State the doctrine of vicarious liability.

- Explain the concept of the scope of employment (*Whatman v Pearson*).

- Consider the position of independent contractors – employer not generally liable.

- Explain the effect of an unauthorised act (*Century Ins. v N. Ireland RTB*).

- In relation to Walter:
  Consider that on the facts given he may well be an independent contractor.
  If this is so, Lifeline Radio Ltd have no vicarious liability for the loss suffered by Uma.

- In relation to Carol:

Explain that on the facts given she is probably an employee – Lifeline Radio Ltd have vicarious liability for acts committed by her in the course of her employment.

Discuss whether, given that she telephoned after the programme, she is acting in the course of her employment.

(d) The question draws on general legal knowledge which you may have acquired as part of your earlier study of AS law. A good answer could:

- Identify that the matter would be heard by the civil courts.

- Give the basis of jurisdiction of the County Court and the High Court.

- Consider the difficulty that you are not told the value of the claim.

- Is the matter likely to be legally complex even if the value is relatively low?

- State that small claims procedure is unlikely to be used in view of likely value and complexity.

(e) This question is very widely drafted and you could have a long argument as to what the most important development since *Donoghue v Stevenson* actually is:

As the rest of the question is about negligent misstatement, you could consider the development of the law in this area tracing the development from *Donoghue* through *Hedley Byrne, Caparo* and *Henderson v Merrett.* Appropriate comments could be made about the opening of the floodgates by *Donoghue* and the gradual imposition of restrictions to deal with this imposed by the later cases.

Other areas of law which could be used to answer this question include the development of the rules of nervous shock, particularly the recent decisions in *McLoughlin, Alcock* and *Page v Smith.*

The mark scheme provided by the examination board makes it clear that any development explained by the candidate where significance is shown will received credit.

Question 3

(a) The question requires you to consider the tort or private nuisance, public nuisance and possible remedies available to the residents. A good answer could:

- Define the tort of private nuisance.

- Distinguish between physical damage and personal discomfort (*St Helens Smelting v Tipping*).

- Explain the matters taken into account by the court to decide if an activity is reasonable:
  Location (*St Helens Smelting v Tipping*).

Abnormal sensitivity (*Robinson v Kilvert*) – not relevant on the facts given.

Duration (*Andreae v Selfridge*) – the time at which the work is done is very relevant.

Malice (*Christie v Davey*).

- Explain that only a person with an interest in land can sue (*Malone v Laskey*) – is the area in which cars are parked owned by the claimant?

- Consider the possibility that the problems with car parking and access could amount to a public nuisance:

  Define public nuisance.

  Explain that a class of persons in the locality need to be affected.

  State that victims who have suffered more damage than others may be able to claim even if they do not have an interest in land (*Halsey v Esso Petrol*).

  Consider the remedies which may be available and their effectiveness.

  Discuss whether other courses of action e.g. the use of ADR or conciliation services might be more effective in solving the problem.

(b) This question raises two issues – what duty did Nathan owe to a skilled visitor and was he negligent when he installed the wiring? A good answer could:

- Define negligence.

- Explain the elements of duty, breach and damage.

- Explain that a duty exists by virtue of Occupiers' Liability Act 1957 to ensure safety of visitors (s.2).

  Skilled visitors are expected to safeguard themselves in relation to the hazards of their profession (s.2(3)(b), *Roles v Nathan*).

  Occupier (Nathan) is liable for injury caused to skilled visitor by occupier's negligence (*Salmon v Seafarers Restaurant, Ogwo v Taylor*).

  The issue is whether or not Nathan has been negligent and caused Owen's injury.

- Explain that the second element of negligence is relevant – breach of duty.

  Nathan undertook a skilled task and is judged by the standard of those of average competence to undertake the task (*Nettleship v Weston, Bolam*).

  Even if the way in which the task was carried out was not negligent, would a reasonable man have informed Owen of the existence and whereabouts of the cable?

- Conclude that Nathan may well be liable for breach of duty under Occupiers Liability Act 1957.

(c) As you are told only that Richard has collapsed with shock, it is reasonable to assume that any injury he has suffered may amount to nervous shock.

- Consider the special rules relating to nervous shock:
  Identify Richard as a secondary victim (*Page v Smith*).
  The requirement of a close personal relationship with the primary
  victim – this will have to be proved as Richard is neither a spouse nor
  a parent/child of the victim (*Alcock*).
  Richard would appear to be in the position of a mere bystander –
  probably unable to claim (*McFarlane v EE Caledonia*).
  Proximity in time and space (not a problem as Richard close enough to
  see what happened).
  The need for identifiable psychiatric illness (*Hinz v Berry*).
  Requirement that be a person of reasonable fortitude – is psychiatric
  injury to such a person reasonably foreseeable (*Page v Smith*)?

(d) This question relates to matters which are within your general legal
knowledge and which you may have studied for the AS examination.
A good answer could:

- Refer to the new scheme introduced by the Access to Justice Act 1999.

- State that allegations of negligently caused injury are excluded from
Community Legal Services Fund – should be dealt with under
Conditional Fee Scheme.

- Owen may be able to get advice under a *qui bono* scheme operated by
local solicitors or from a firm of solicitors which has been franchised.

- Owen could also obtain advice from:
Citizen's Advice Bureau.
A local law centre.
The Community Legal Service website.
If he has legal liability insurance, the insurance company.

(e) The question requires you to consider the role played by policy in the
development of the rules relating to nervous shock. Points you could
make arise from the important recent cases such as *McLoughlin v
O'Brian* which can be said to have opened the floodgates, *Alcock* which
recognised that some limitation needed to be put on the categories of
claimants, *McFarlane v EE Caledonia* which effectively ruled out claims
by bystanders and *Page v Smith* which separated claimants into primary
and secondary victims and introduced a requirement that a secondary
victim be a person of reasonable fortitude and foreseeability that such
a person might suffer nervous shock.

Question 4

(a) The first part of the question is concerned with occupier's liability for
persons injured on premises. A good answer could:

- Identify Lucy as a trespasser and state that the 1984 Act applies.

- Explain occupier's duty to take reasonable precautions to protect trespasser from known dangers when it is likely that a trespasser may come into the vicinity of the danger.

- Explain that children are expected to be less careful than adults.

- Consider the concept of an allurement (*Glasgow Corp. v Taylor*) – a gap in the fence leading to someone else's garden could be such and so could a bowl of liquid which looks like cola.

- Discuss the issue of adult supervision (*Phipps v Rochester Corp*).

- Apply the rules to reach a conclusion.

The second part of the question is concerned with the potential liability for damage caused by a dangerous product. A good answer could:

- Identify that Lucy has no contractual relationship with Smershco.

- State that Lucy may have a claim under s.2(1) if a defect in a product has caused her injury.

- Define the term product under s.1(2) and identify the wood paint as a product.

- Consider the requirement that the product be defective under s.3 explaining the meaning of defective – in the light of the advertisement the product would not appear to be dangerous. Was the necessary warning given on the packaging and instructions for use?

- Explain the categories of damage covered by the Act.

- Discuss the appropriate defendant applying ss.2(2) and (3).

(b) This question requires you to discuss the issues of negligence and liability for nervous shock. A good answer could:

- Define negligence and explain the elements
  The requirement that the defendant owes the claimant a duty of care
    (*Donoghue v Stevenson*).
  The need for breach of duty setting out the test of the reasonable man
    (*Blyth v Birmingham Waterworks*).
  Matters taken into account is assessing standard of care relevant to the question, i.e. degree of seriousness of risk (*Paris v Stepney BC*), likelihood of it happening (*Bolton v Stone*).
  The need for consequential damage including the 'but for' test (*Barnett v Chelsea & Kensington HMC*) and the requirement that the damage is not too remote (*The Wagon Mound*).

- Apply the rules to reach a conclusion.

- Consider the special rules relating to nervous shock:
  Identify Nigel as a secondary victim (*Page v Smith*).

The requirement of a close personal relationship with the primary victim – this does not exist on the basis of the facts given

Proximity in time and space (not a problem as Nigel present at the scene).

The need for identifiable psychiatric illness (*Hinz v Berry*).

Requirement that Nigel be a person of reasonable fortitude – is psychiatric injury to such a person reasonably foreseeable? (*Page v Smith*).

- Can Nigel be considered to be a rescuer – if so he would not be regarded as a 'professional'?

- Rescuers regarded as primary victim if they suffer nervous shock as a result of what they have needed to do (*Chadwick v British Rail, White v Chief Constable S. Yorks*).

- In case of primary victim, foreseeability of injury all that is required (*Page v Smith*).

- Egg shell skull principle applies.

(c) The question requires you to discuss the way in which the law relating to nervous shock works and to evaluate it as to whether or not it is satisfactory. A good answer could:

- Refer back to the information given in answer to (b) for legal rules.

- Discuss points arising from the material including:

  That the law is satisfactory in the case of primary victims.

  Is it reasonable to require a secondary victim to be a person of reasonable fortitude?

  Do policy reasons (encouraging people to be helpful) justify the different treatment of rescuers?

  Is the requirement of close ties of love and affection reasonable – a bystander could suffer just as badly but would be unable to claim?

  Does the policy decision to restrict potential claims (the floodgates argument) justify the rules?

It would be appropriate to make suggestions for reform, perhaps by reference to the Law Commission's recommendations for the reform of the law relating to nervous shock.

Question 5

(a) The question requires explanation and application of the rules relating to pure economic loss and negligent misstatement. A good answer could:

- Explain the concept of pure economic loss.

- State that as a matter of principle pure economic loss is not recoverable (*Spartan Steel v Martin*).

- Consider that the rules relating to negligent misstatement are an exception to the general rule.

- In relation to negligent misstatement explain the relevant criteria:
  The existence of a special relationship between claimant and
    defendant (*Hedley Byrne v Heller*).
  Knowledge by the defendant of the purpose for which the information
    is required (*Caparo v Dickman*).
  The need for reliance on the information by the claimant – was such
    reliance reasonable? (*Caparo*).
  Did the defendant assume responsibility? (*Henderson v Merrett*).

- Apply the rules to the facts given:
  Is there a relationship between Simon and Prince and Company?
  Probably not unless the company was aware that Rupert intended to
    make the report available to someone buying the land from him.

(b) There are two parts to this question – the issue of the escape of the
   gravel onto Thomas's land and the issue of the noise and smells. The
   first part of the question requires you to consider the rules relating to
   Rylands v Fletcher. A good answer could:

- Define the tort and explain the various elements:
  Accumulation (*Rylands v Fletcher*).
  Foreseeability that the thing may cause damage if it escapes (*Cambridge
    Water v Eastern Counties Leather*).
  Escape (*Read v Lyons*).
  Non-natural use of land (*Read v Lyons, British Celanese v Hunt, Cambridge
    Water v Eastern Counties Leather*).

- State the defences:
  Consent (*Peters v Prince of Wales Theatre*).
  Fault of claimant.
  Act of God (*Nichols v Marsland, Greenock Corp. v Caledonia Rlwy*).
  Act of a stranger (*Perry v Kendricks Transport*).
  Statutory authority.
  Necessity.

The second part of the question requires you to discuss the possibility of an
action in nuisance, private and/or public, by the residents and the owner of
the fish and chip shop. A good answer could:

- Define the tort of private nuisance.

- Distinguish between physical damage and personal discomfort (*St
  Helens Smelting v Tipping*).

- Explain the matters taken into account by the court to decide if an
  activity is reasonable:
  Location (*St Helens Smelting v Tipping*).
  Abnormal sensitivity (*Robinson v Kilvert*) – not relevant on the facts
    given.

Duration (*Andreae v Selfridge*).

Malice (*Christie v Davey*) – on facts given does not appear to be relevant.

- Explain that only a person with an interest in land can sue (*Malone v Laskey*).

- Consider the possibility that the problems could amount to a public nuisance:

  Define public nuisance.

  Explain that a class of persons in the locality need to be affected. State that victims who have suffered more damage than others may be able to claim even if they do not have an interest in land (*Halsey v Esso Petrol*). Has the owner of the shop suffered over and above other members of the affected class in which case he can claim damages?

(c) The question requires you to evaluate both *Rylands v Fletcher* and nuisance as a means to protect the interests of a land owner. You will need to refer back to law explained in answer to (b). A good answer could:

- In relation to *Rylands v Fletcher*:

  Discuss the problems created by the concept of non-natural user.

  Read v Lyons and *British Celanese v Hunt* suggest that the local environment and public benefit are relevant.

  Cambridge Water suggests *obiter* storage of chemicals a classic case of non-natural user – by analogy could this include gravel?

  Consider the need for foreseeability.

  Has the introduction of the requirement in *Cambridge Water* lessened the effectiveness of the tort?

  Is there an element of fault required in the light of knowledge at the time of the accumulation?

- In relation to private nuisance:

  Discuss the apparent injustice of the need for an interest in land.

  Consider the uncertainty of establishing that the activity complained of is unreasonable.

- In relation to public nuisance:

  Discuss the need to establish exceptional damage in order to recover damages.

  Does the rule that there need be no interest in land mean that the claimant has a fairer chance?

- Discuss the delay, cost and uncertainty of bringing a court action – would other courses of action, e.g. the use of ADR (alternative dispute resolution) or conciliation services be more effective in solving the problem?

- Consider the remedies which may be available and their effectiveness.

- Discuss whether legislation, e.g. Environmental Protection Act and enforcement by Environmental Protection Agency and local authorities, is more effective.

Resources for further study

Books

Rogers, W.V.H., *Winfield & Jolowicz on Tort*, Sweet & Maxwell (an authoritative university text).

Brazier, M. and Murphy, J., *Street on Torts*, Butterworths (an authoritative university text).

Martin, J. and Gibbins, M., *The Complete A–Z Law Handbook*, Hodder & Stoughton (a law dictionary containing useful definitions and explanations).

Martin, J., *The English Legal System*, Hodder & Stoughton (useful for review of AS material).

Vanstone, B., Sherratt, L. and Charman, M., *AS Law*, 2nd edn, Willan Publishing (useful for review of AS material).

Charman, M., *Contract Law*, 2nd edn, Willan Publishing (useful for some areas where there is overlap with contract law, e.g. consumer law).

References to books cited

In addition to the above, the following books have been used and referred to in the text:

Howarth, D.R. and O'Sullivan, J.A., *Hepple, Howarth and Matthews' Tort: Cases and Materials*, Butterworths (5th edition, 2000).

Jones, Michael A., *Textbook on Torts*, Blackstone Press (8th edition, 2002).

Heuston, R.F.F. and Buckley, R.A., *Salmond and Heuston on the Law of Torts*, Sweet & Maxwell (21st edition, 1996).

Newspapers and journals

The Times (always good for current developments and articles, particularly in the supplement on Tuesdays, and a good source of current cases).

Student Law Review Cavendish Publishing (published three times each year – useful for recent developments – see below for on-line version).
The New Law Journal (the major journal for current developments and academic articles on civil law issues).
See below (the Internet) for journals available on-line.

The Internet

If you have access to the Internet a new world of legal information is available to you. I have collected here a selection of addresses of sites which may be of interest and which should be useful to you in your studies. They are arranged into categories, very broadly, according to content, although some sites will contain material which belongs to more than one category.

This is a fast developing and changing resource, so the content of a site may not be the same from one visit to another. These addresses were all accurate and operational at the point of publication.

Parliament and legislation

http://www.parliament.uk (for general information on Parliament)
http://www.legislation.hmso.gov.uk (for Acts of Parliament and other legislation)
http://www.swarb.co.uk (for Acts of Parliament and other resources)

Case law

http://www.parliament.the-stationery-office.co.uk/pa/ld199697/ldjudgmt/ldjudgmt.htm (for House of Lords judgments since November 1996)
http://www.the-times.co.uk (for articles and law reports from *The Times*)
http://www.casetrack.com/casebase (for selected Court of Appeal cases)
http://www.lawreports.co.uk (for sample reports of the Incorporated Council of Law Reporting for England and Wales)
http://www.curia.eu.int/en/index.htm (for recent cases and information on the European Court of Justice)
http://www.courtservice.gov.uk (for selected judgments and news items)
http://www.bailii.org (for reports of cases in High Court, Court of Appeal and House of Lords)

Articles and news

http://www.cavendishpublishing.com (for recent cases and articles and
back issues of *Student Law Review* useful to students – registration
required (currently free of charge)
http://www.lawzone.co.uk (for recent cases and articles)

General interest

http://www.venables.co.uk (for huge collection of legal resources)
http://www.the-lawyer.co.uk (for general legal news)
http://www.lawgazette.co.uk (for general legal issues)
http://www.lawcom.gov.uk/homepage/htm (for reports and
information on the Law Commission)
http://www.infolaw.co.uk (for general legal material)

Glossary

Absolute privilege a defence to defamation which allows a statement to be made freely without fear of court action

Act of God a natural phenomenon which cannot be anticipated nor guarded against; a defence only to *Rylands v Fletcher*

Actionable per se the tort does not require the claimant to prove that actual damage has been caused

Assault a threat to use immediate and unlawful force against a person

Autonomy an ethical principle which safeguards personal freedom to make choices

Battery unlawful use of force against a person

Beneficence an ethical theory which imposes an obligation to do good

Bolam principle the standard by which the actions of a professional person are judged

But for test a test for causation in negligence – would the injury have occurred had it not been for the breach of duty?

Causation the chain of events leading to the damage

Claimant formerly referred to as the plaintiff; the person who seeks a legal remedy from the court

Consequentialism an ethical theory also known as utilitarianism, the moral rightness of an action must be decided by its consequences

Contributory negligence the extent to which the victim of an accident is to blame for the injuries caused

Damages financial compensation for loss

Defamation	the tort which protects a person's reputation by preventing publication of something which is not true
Defendant	the person against whom a legal action is brought
Deontology	an ethical theory by which an action is right or wrong regardless of its consequences
Duty of common humanity	duty on occupier to take reasonable steps to protect trespasser from known dangers on premises
Economic loss	loss which arises from a defect in the property itself rather than damage to property or persons caused as a consequence of that defect; not generally recoverable
Ethics	a branch of philosophy which helps us to decide whether an action is right or wrong
Ex turpi causa non oritur	now known as 'participation in unlawful act'; a person injured as a result of their own unlawful act may not be able to claim compensation
Fair comment	an opinion based on true facts on a matter which relates to the public interest
False imprisonment	unlawful restraint of a person's freedom of movement
Fault	the concept of blameworthiness
Injunction	an equitable order to the defendant to do something lawful or to refrain from doing something unlawful
Justice	an ethical principle which means fairness
Justification	a defence to an action for defamation; the statement is true or substantially so
Libel	a part of defamation; generally relates to a statement in permanent form
Limitation period	the period of time within which a court action must be started

Literal rule	a rule of statutory interpretation whereby the judge uses the ordinary grammatical meaning of a word to decide the meaning of a statute
Mesne profits	a reasonable payment for wrongful occupation of land
Mischief rule	a rule of statutory interpretation whereby the judge ascertains the wrong which the statute is intended to correct and gives the words used a meaning which has the desired effect
Necessity	a general defence available to a person taking urgent action to deal with a reasonably perceived danger
Negligence	breach of a duty imposed by law causing damage to the victim or the victim's property
Negligent misstatement	an exception to the rules of economic loss; a person owes a duty to be careful in making a statement where there is a special relationship of reliance
Neighbour principle	Lord Atkin's definition of those to whom a duty of care is owed, i.e. those so closely connected to the act that damage ought reasonably to have been foreseen
Nervous shock	diagnosed psychiatric illness caused by trauma suffered directly or in some cases indirectly as a result of the negligence of the defendant
Non-maleficence	an ethical principle which imposes a duty to do no harm
Novus actus interveniens	something which breaks the chain of causation
Nuisance	a tort which protects a person's right not to have their land interfered with by activities on nearby land; may be private, public or statutory

Obiter dicta	things said by the way which may have influence as persuasive precedent
Occupier	the person in control of premises
Precedent	the principle of law settled by a past case
Prescription	the acquisition of a legal right after it has been exercised without objection by someone in a position to object for twenty years
Primary victim	a person who suffers injury as a direct result of the defendant's negligence
Purposive approach	a rule of statutory interpretation which enables a judge to give effect to the overall purpose of the statute
Qualified privilege	a defence to defamation which allows a statement which is believed to be true to be made, in limited circumstances, without fear of court action
Ratio decidendi	the part of precedent which is binding in future cases
Reasonable man	the fictional person whose behaviour sets the standard of care required in connection with negligence
Re-entry and ejectment	a self-help remedy which allows an owner to re-enter land using reasonable force
Remoteness of damage	was the damage which resulted from an act of the type or kind that was reasonably foreseeable
Rylands v Fletcher	a tort which gives protection from the escape of dangerous substances stored on land
Secondary victim	a person who suffers psychiatric injury as a result of injury caused to another by the defendant's negligence
Self-defence	the use of proportionate and reasonable force to defend oneself or another or to defend one's property

Slander	part of the tort of defamation; concerned with transitory statements
Stare decisis	stand by the decision – future similar cases should be decided in the same way as past cases involving a similar set of facts and subject to the same legal principle
Statutory authority	a defendant has no liability for a wrong committed as an inevitable consequence of complying with a statute
Strict liability	a defendant may be liable regardless of blame or fault
Tort	a wrong which may be remedied in the civil courts
Tortfeasor	a person who commits a tort
Trespass to land	unlawfully entering or placing something on land, in the subsoil or in the airspace above it
Trespass to the person	assault, battery and false imprisonment
Utilitarianism	an ethical theory also known as consequentialism, the rightness of an action is judged by its consequences
Vicarious liability	a situation where a person who is in fact blameless is held liable for the wrongful acts of another
Voluntary assumption of risk (volenti non fit injuria)	a person who is aware of a risk and voluntarily runs that risk cannot complain if they are injured as a result
Woolf reforms	the ongoing process of reforming the rules relating to bringing an action in the civil courts

Index